Resilient Therapy

Whilst much has been written about the identification of resilience in children and their families, comparatively little has been written about what practitioners can do to support those children and families who need the most pressing help.

Resilient Therapy explores a new therapeutic methodology designed to help children and young people find ways to keep positive when living amidst persistent disadvantage. Using detailed case material from a range of contexts, the authors illustrate how resilient mechanisms work in complex situations, and how Resilient Therapy works in real-life situations. In addition to work with families, helping welfare organisations achieve greater resilience is also tackled.

This book will be essential reading for practitioners working with children, adolescents and their families who wish to help their clients cope with adversity and promote resilience.

Angie Hart is Professor of Child, Family and Community Health at the University of Brighton and Academic Co-Director of its Community University Partnership Programme. She is also a Psychotherapeutic Counsellor and Research Practitioner at Brighton and Hove Specialist Child and Adolescent Mental Health Service (CAMHS). Alongside the other authors, she works in a specialist team supporting fostered and adopted children. Professor Hart also has many years experience of parenting children from care.

Derek Blincow studied Social Philosophy before taking up Medicine and Psychiatry. He holds an NHS Consultant post in Child and Adolescent Psychiatry practising in a deprived area of Brighton and has developed services across the local area. He has acted as an External Professional Advisor to the UK Health Ombudsman and an Expert Witness to the Family Courts.

Helen Thomas is Head of Systemic Psychotherapy at Brighton and Hove Specialist CAMHS. She read Psychology at University College London followed by Applied Social Sciences. She has practiced as a Psychiatric Social Worker in London and the South of England for 25 years with a special interest in child mental health and neglect.

Resilient Therapy

Working with Children and Families

Angie Hart & Derek Blincow with
Helen Thomas

Routledge
Taylor & Francis Group
LONDON AND NEW YORK

First published 2007 by Routledge
27 Church Road, Hove, East Sussex BN3 2FA

Simultaneously published in the USA and Canada
by Routledge
270 Madison Avenue, New York, NY 10016

Transferred to digital printing 2009

Routledge is an imprint of the Taylor & Francis Group, an Informa business

© 2007 Angie Hart & Derek Blincow with Helen Thomas

Typeset in Times by Garfield Morgan, Swansea, West Glamorgan
Printed and bound in Great Britain by TJI Digital, Padstow, Cornwall
Paperback cover design by Design Deluxe

This publication has been produced with paper manufactured to strict
environmental standards and with pulp derived from sustainable forests.

British Library Cataloguing in Publication Data
A catalogue record for this book is available from the British Library

Library of Congress Cataloging-in-Publication Data
Hart, Angie.
    Resilient therapy : working with children and families / Angie Hart & Derek
Blincow with Helen Thomas.
       p. ; cm.
    Includes bibliographical references and index.
    ISBN-13: 978-0-415-40384-9 (hbk.)
    ISBN-10: 0-415-40384-7 (hbk.)
    ISBN-13: 978-0-415-40385-6 (pbk.)
    ISBN-10: 0-415-40385-5 (pbk.)
    1. Resilient therapy. 2. Resilience (Personality trait) in children. 3.
Resilience (Personality trait) in adolescence. I. Blincow, Derek, 1952- II.
Thomas, Helen, 1956- III. Title.
    [DNLM: 1. Adaptation, Psychological. 2. Psychotherapy—methods. 3.
Adolescent Psychology—methods. 4. Child Psychology—methods. 5. Family
Health. 6. Self Care. WS 350.2 H325r 2007]
    RJ505.R43H37 2007
    618.92'89156—dc22

                                                                    2006039501

ISBN 978-0-415-40384-9 (hbk)
ISBN 978-0-415-40385-6 (pbk)

Contents

Boxes

Acknowledgements

We wish to thank the Community University Partnership Programme at the University of Brighton for funding the development of this work, the parents, carers, students and workers who participated in the workshops that have helped us shape Resilient Therapy and all the children and families we have worked with in this way.

We are indebted to the considerable research endeavour over many years that has kept resilience as a concept alive. We are also indebted to the Child and Adolescent Mental Health Service and to the National Health Service in the UK for providing us with the opportunities to practise in a resilient mode. Many individuals working in social services and education in Brighton and Hove have also contributed.

We must thank our colleagues for helping us to refine our arguments, especially Kim Aumann, Barry Luckock and David Secrett. We thank Chloe Gerhardt for her help in editing and preparing the text, Clara Heath for administrative support and Dr Lewis Derrick for creative and diligent copy-editing. Our University caretakers facilitated out of hours access to buildings and campus librarians helped us to source our large reference library. Lastly, and with gratitude, we wish to acknowledge the contribution of each of our families for making it possible for us to write this book.

Abbreviations

ACCE	Accepting, Conserving, Commitment, Enlisting
ADHD	Attention deficit hyperactivity disorder
BPD	Borderline personality disorder
CAMHS	Child and Adolescent Mental Health Service
CBT	Cognitive behaviour therapy
CPN	Community psychiatric nurse
DBT	Dialectical behaviour therapy
ERA	English Romanian adoptees
GCSE	General certificate of secondary education
GP	General practitioner
LAC	Looked-after children
MST	Multi-systemic therapy
NSF	National service framework
SW	Social worker
RSF	Reflective self-functioning
RT	Resilient Therapy
RTs	Resilient therapists
SENCO	Special educational needs coordinator(s)
TFC	Treatment Foster Care

Chapter 1

Conjuring up Resilient Therapy

> Every blade of grass has its Angel that bends over it and whispers, 'Grow, grow'.
>
> The Talmud

Why pick up this book, let alone buy it and then even read it? You might think that therapy has been done to death. And there are scores of tomes and hundreds of journal articles about resilience on the market. We have systematically searched the literature, including books, journal articles and web-based information. Our quest has led us to scour international publications over the past 30 or so years. It may come as no surprise, then, that the library we have amassed fills a filing cabinet and nearly an entire book stack. It numbers over 500 publications. Some names come up more than once, but that is still over 300 authors around the globe defining, exploring, measuring and critiquing 'resilience' and related concepts.

Many of their publications tell us how to *spot* resilient children and young people. They also give us a lot of information on what particularly fragile children look like. Yet, when it comes to getting down to the nitty gritty of *building* resilience, the library shelves look less crowded. Of those 500 odd publications we have in our own collection, approximately 35 concentrate on this issue in any depth. Proof enough to us of Pfeffer's point that, in tackling inequalities, we still have not yet accepted 'that the skills of getting things done are as important as the skills of figuring out what to do' (Pfeffer, 1992: 12) . Of course, the skills of getting things done with some children are quite different from getting things done with others.

Of these 35 publications, most offer ideas, programmes and activities that are designed for work with *all* children. Only a handful of publications concentrate on the most disadvantaged in our society. This book is for those children and their families.

Resilient Therapy (RT) presents a strategic methodology with its own frame of reference and practice philosophy. It is *strategic* because it harnesses a number of therapeutic interventions into a coherent programme. We refer to it as a *methodology* because it represents a particular approach to working with those interventions. RT draws on evidence from scholarship and from our own experiences with disadvantaged children and young people, their families and practitioners working alongside. The essence of RT is a relentless search for ways to help children and young people bounce up when life is particularly tough. We say bounce up, rather than bounce back, quite deliberately. Many of the children we know have rarely, if ever, been anywhere they can benefit from bouncing back to. Avoiding pathologising children, understanding how resilient mechanisms work in complex situations and building resilience (individual, family, organisational and community) are core to RT's strategic approach. We call this 'upbuilding'. Precisely what RT involves will unfold as the book progresses. However, this paragraph and the following two tell you what it comprises in a nutshell.

RT is delivered according to four key principles. These are RT's *Noble Truths*. They describe how we go about addressing the needs of the most disadvantaged children, their parents/carers and the practitioners and agencies who work with them. Working with these Noble Truths involves developing the skills of *Accepting* the precise starting point of children/families, *Conserving* any good that has occurred hitherto, *Commitment* to working with them over a sensible time period and thoughtfully *Enlisting* appropriate others to help. In Chapter 2, we go into some detail as to what these Noble Truths really mean.

RT also represents a range of interventions that are the constituents of five separate, but related, conceptual arenas that we term compartments or remedy racks. These form a systematic whole, which, for some audiences, we have summarised through the device of a Magic Box. Interventions within each of these conceptual arenas are designed to increase resilient responses to overwhelming adversity. This may seem complicated, but the rest of this book will go through these ideas systematically and in detail. Let us summarise them here.

The conceptual arenas are: *Basics, Belonging, Learning, Coping* and *Core Self*. There is a chapter on each of these in this book. The first three compartments *Basics, Belonging* and *Learning* include strategies and practices for working directly with children but also involve practitioners strategically linking with and reaching out to others. Most of the interventions in *Coping* and *Core Self* consist of a set of micro-therapeutic approaches designed for direct work with individuals. This is the major difference between the two. Core Self focuses on working at a deep intrapersonal level, whilst Coping provides children with strategies to manage better in the moment rather than waiting for some deeper personal transformation to occur. Of course there is some overlap between the two and like all the conceptual arenas, they are to some extent a pragmatic presentational device.

Masten, a developmental psychologist who has been working on resilience for many years, calls resilience 'ordinary magic' (Masten, 2001). She says, 'Resilience does not come from rare and special qualities, but from the everyday magic of ordinary, normative human resources in the minds, brains and bodies of children, in their families and relationships, and in their communities' (2001: 235). Her idea inspired our use of the magic metaphor to produce user-friendly materials with and for parents/carers and young people (see the diagram in the appendix).

We have drawn directly on the rich resilience research and practice base and added strategies and practices uniquely developed through RT. We have brought to this our own experiences, and some synergised research, policy and practice bases outside child and adolescent mental health. This has led to the development of new concepts, which, despite the wealth of research activity, have not, until now, been articulated within the research base.

Basics, for example, has an entire compartment of its own. As we shall see, our inclusion and articulation of this brings therapeutic approaches firmly into line with inequalities frameworks that have been developed quite separately. This represents something of a departure from traditional therapeutic concerns and introduces a clear politicisation of what we mean by 'therapy'. Within other compartments, we trial specific techniques conceptualised as core features of RT. With a view to the five compartments, some will seem immediately familiar to the resilience aficionado, and some quite new. Even where they may seem familiar, we have moulded them to our own design.

So how did we pull all this together? A modest grant through our Community University Partnership Programme (www.cupp.org.uk) made it possible for us to experiment with research and practice development. For some audiences we have used the device of the magic box to plan and execute work with families, with practitioners, and to challenge organisations and blocks to resilient therapeutic work. We did this through individual consultations, systems analyses, workshops, drama and mentorship. Our metaphors/graphics for presenting materials have varied depending on the audience. Of the people involved in the development work many responded enthusiastically to the magic metaphor and related artwork. The idea of magic gave them a creative metaphor to free up thoughts and feelings, and also to laugh a little as they learned. This was something of a relief in an area of work that seems often hard and depressing, and it is worth noticing that having a sense of humour is also associated with resilience. So the magic metaphor helped some parents, practitioners and young people to experiment with what makes children more resilient and how short- or longer-term specific outcomes can be achieved.

Others preferred the more neutral language of 'conceptual arena', 'mechanism' and 'intervention'. Still others using our methodology spoke of 'building blocks' or 'tool kits'. These different preferences reflect a wide variety of learning styles in the people who have engaged in development work to date. This has presented us with a linguistic dilemma. We reflected this dilemma by using the terms 'conceptual arena', 'compartment', and 'remedy rack' interchangeably. Likewise, when we talked about 'interventions', we employed the terms 'potions' or 'remedies' to refer to the same thing. So the way we have designed RT for particular audiences has taken their varied tastes into account.

Sociologist Furedi is right to critique the truism 'abused as a child, abusive as a parent'. However, to deny the 'toxic effects of psychological damage' seems somewhat cavalier (Furedi, 2004: 120). RT avoids pathologising children, but recognises that some children and their families need help. When viewed within an inequalities framework, we can also understand that this is their right.

RT facilitates productive engagement with children and families in the moment, rather than having to wait until their lives settle. For many, at least during childhood, it may never happen. RT gives practitioners explicit goals to work for in contexts that may seem futile and confusing. It can have the effect of advocating for children who may not have many other adults in their lives who do this as a priority. In the context of child disability and special needs, it can also help therapists ally with parents and carers worn down by the relentless demands of unsupported parenting. RT helps people understand that, however hopeless a situation might seem, there is *always something* that can be done to make things better for disadvantaged children.

In this book we will be demystifying 'therapy' and specific therapeutic techniques that are used in RT. This means unpacking concepts and using language to make interventions as accessible as possible. Language is important. When we talk of 'Resilient Therapy', some people hear the name differently. They hear 'resilien*ce* therapy'. This might seem a fine distinction but it is crucial. We are not simply instilling resilience in children and families. We are configuring therapy to be resilient through and through. Resilien*t* describes our experience of, and aspirations for the therapy we do. Resilien*t* too is the effect on children, families and the practitioners who promote RT.

Another aspect of being resilient is that we hold to the view that there is always *something* that can be done. Our work aims to be relentless in this respect. There are no exclusion criteria and we will try anything if it helps children to do better. We think our approach helps children beat the odds when they are stacked against them.

In sum, RT is a matrix of resilient mechanisms that works resiliently on those who use them. We think that the therapy we practice should role model the resilience-enhancing processes that we want children and their families to develop themselves.

Talking of role models, a key message throughout this book is that the people carrying out RT, and the approach they take, really matter. We use the term 'resilient therapist' or 'resilient therapy practitioner' to describe those who apply the methodology.

We are not only describing professional therapists here. There are perhaps a few elements of RT better left to them. But most of the techniques and certainly the principles and ideas can be drawn on by any competent, reflective, helping practitioner. This most definitely includes parents, carers and indeed children and young people themselves. So our approach aims to be as user friendly as we can make it. Other therapies are not so inclusive. Although there have been some moves to take therapeutic work in this direction, historically therapy has tended to have the opposite reputation. We consider this issue in our final chapter. For many, therapy still conjures up an image of an affluent elite lying on the couch in the thrall of a privileged expert. Even those therapies such as multi-systemic therapy that have been specifically designed to work in the context of constellated disadvantage are certainly not that easy to simply pick up and run with (Henggeler, Clingempeel, Brondino, & Pickrel, 2002).

RT does need to be resilient in this sense too. It starts in, and remains committed to, tackling those areas that therapies have found it so difficult to influence. These are situations where the odds are heavily weighted against us as practitioners, parents or children trying to achieve any change for the better. As we say, there are no exclusion criteria in RT, but that does not mean that it is vague and unfocused. Many findings of resilience research can be applied to *every* child. So too can RT. Yet the children for whom we are writing, the ones for whom we have most acceptance, energy and commitment, are the most disadvantaged children in our society. They have been termed deprived, distressed, delinquent, poor, at risk, unequal, abused, neglected, excluded, special needs, vulnerable and so on. In academia, there is a veritable debate about what language describes them best (Lubeck & Garrett, 1990). Earlier we introduced the term '*constellated* disadvantage' to think about their lives and identities. The concept is not meant to conjure up a starry bright night sky. Rather it brings home the fact that, for some children, disadvantage comes in many shapes and sizes, often *all at the same time*. Each individual disadvantage can, and probably does, interrelate with others to generate new patterns of disadvantage, each with varying consequences. These include the 'negative chain reactions' that Rutter has so clearly articulated (Rutter, 1999). Socioeconomic status, mental illness, ethnicity, disability, genetic inheritance, sexuality and geographical location may all feature. It is to the children in constellated disadvantage that we give most thought in this book. Our practice examples and illustrations are all geared towards working with and for them.

In constellated disadvantage, child protection dilemmas, treating severe mental distress and managing disability are deeply woven into the fabric of daily practice. We can add to this list working with people who are sceptical of professional involvement. They are likely to be in a permanent state of crisis and placement instability. How to make a difference to children's mental health and emotional wellbeing in such contexts is a persistent challenge that can drag us down. RT gives us a focus for our endeavours and keeps us energised.

This is very important because not all practitioners will have a working knowledge or personal experience of constellated disadvantage. Those of us who do, may all too easily forget what hardship actually feels like, or we can also too readily assume that our own experience is universal. Working with race, ethnicity and cultural difference in the context of constellated disadvantage can be particularly challenging; a very foreign land, if you like (West Stevens, 2005). Some practitioners will need to develop an 'inequalities imagination' (Hall & Hart, 2004; Hart, Hall, & Henwood, 2003; Hart, Lockey, Henwood, Pankhurst, Hall, & Sommerville, 2001). This involves a thorough understanding of the effects of health inequalities in its broadest sense and puts this awareness at the heart of practice. However, knowing that systems fail children and that they are the victims of poverty, disablism and other inequalities can engender confusion over what needs to happen therapeutically. In RT this context of inequality and social exclusion is worked through as a specific focus so that the practitioner's work is not overwhelmed and eventually undermined by it.

Introducing Janice, Louis, Sally and Jason: Constellated disadvantage in process

Time now to tell you about what constellated disadvantage looks like for some of the children we have met over the years. We will be drawing on their stories throughout the book. Of course we are not giving you any real names or actual circumstances. But the realities these stories are based on are all true.

> Janice, age 6, is of Anglo-Irish family background. She has already been excluded from school and sent on her way from five foster homes. Janice has a diagnosis of foetal alcohol syndrome, thought to bring with it global and specific learning difficulties. There is some potential for her to catch up once settled in a long-term placement, but she is unlikely to achieve functional literacy and numeracy. Janice is angry and violent towards her brothers, both of whom have been moved to separate new carers. She hits people or stares into space in her spare time. A succession of social workers, assistants, placement support workers, volunteer mentors and children's advocates have all tried to befriend her. Janice defecates in a corner whenever she sees her birth father. Her name comes to the top of the Child and Adolescent Mental Health Services (CAMHS) waiting list—she is a priority case. She is assessed at a joint

appointment by a psychiatrist and a psychologist. The letter back to her referrer describes her as 'too disturbed for therapy at the present time'. Her networks are described as 'not sufficiently stable to support Janice through the therapeutic process at the current time'. She is referred back to Social Services and her case is closed.

Seven-year-old Louis. White British. Louis is once again living at home with his birth mother and three much older siblings. Louis has only just moved back to live with them. Before that he was in and out of foster care. Louis has an ugly burn scar on his head where tea was tipped over him when he was two. His social worker visited the home one morning and cajoled his mother out of bed. The social worker went with Louis' mother to the GP to get some anti-depressants. The medication has at least helped her get dressed in the day and out in time to pick Louis up from school. But still Louis is sad, angry and failing at school. He spends at least six hours a day on the game boy a charity bought him. His mother thinks it keeps him calm alongside the medication he takes in the day. Louis plays football at lunchtime on Thursdays, when his learning support assistant misses his own lunch break to help Louis join in. Social services sent the family to CAMHS. Louis sees a psychiatrist every now and then for a Ritalin prescription. He has a diagnosis of Attention Deficit Hyper-activity Disorder (ADHD). The family were down for more intensive work, but Louis' mother felt humiliated by the two therapists she saw after not managing to get to her first three appointments. The clinic is two bus rides away, so the family would have had to be really motivated to get there in any case. Louis' mother will not bring him and the other children to family therapy again. She certainly would not come herself. And she misses the two further appointments they are offered. So his only contact with treating agencies is Louis' psychiatrist who is thinking whether she should move the Ritalin repeat prescribing over to the GP. This would mean closing his case.

Jason is nearly sixteen. He is of mixed parentage. His mother is White British, his father Nigerian living in Britain. Jason is allocated a bed on an intensive child and adolescent mental health unit, stays a day, then runs away. He is prescribed medication but will not take it, and his mother cannot seem to make him. Over the years, four psychiatrists and fifteen social workers have written reports detailing his pathology—potential schizophrenia—and his mother's deficits—a complex mixture of schizophrenia or personality disorder diagnoses have been suggested. Schools have not seen him much since he was seven. He has been arrested twice. Jason steals things from shopping centres and prostitutes himself outside toilets by day. He surfs pornography by night. His case swings open and closed.

Seventeen-year-old Sally. White British. Sexually abused by a paedophile ring between the ages of three and seven. She had involvement with so many different social workers that she hardly remembers any of their names. She has files in agencies all over town that are so thick that they cannot be processed as they should be into an integrated computer record. In and out of fifteen foster homes from eight to thirteen, Sally has been with her foster mother now for three years and wants her to be her proper mum. She had art therapy and play therapy in a specialist unit for children who had been abused when she was of primary-school age. Sally was driven to therapy by nineteen different taxi drivers. The best times she can remember were the twelve times that a student social worker took her to therapy and they went for a burger afterwards. Sally still gets a birthday card from her. Sally hardly ever went to school before the age of eleven. And she has been seeing another art therapist throughout her teenage years. At seventeen, we find her working at the counter of a newsagents. She goes out clubbing with her best friend every Saturday night and is planning a girls' trip to Ibiza. Sally cooks fabulous cakes.

Resilience

What is it that makes the lives of Janice, Louis and Jason so persistently miserable and Sally's later years at least so much more rewarding? Might Janice and Louis end up happy and successful enough at seventeen like Sally, or will they continue on their current paths, or even end up with even worse outcomes, as bad as Jason is doing at the moment perhaps? In the end if all these children live until old age, have legitimate occupations, stable partners, children and meaningful hobbies, or simply stay out of big trouble, how are the mechanisms that made that happen best understood? Are they external mechanisms—social, economic, political or educational— or internal mechanisms programmed into each child's genetic make up, or the end result of a deep therapeutic transformation? Or did they come about from really small shifts indiscernible to the naked eye? For each of the children the mechanisms at play are mostly likely to be a complex interweaving of all of these.

We should say up front that, while research findings can take us a long way, researchers are still far from being able to predict *for sure* what mechanisms and what chains of reactions will lead to what outcomes. When it comes down to predicting the lives of individuals, it is even more complicated. However, there is some research and practice wisdom that can set us in the right direction. Attending to this body of knowledge is important because it can help us think what parents, practitioners and the children themselves can do to help children from similar starting points turn out more like Sally than Jason in their later teenage years. The concept of resilience helps us to think this through.

Over the years resilience has been defined in a number of different ways, and there is a vast and complex literature on it, particularly in developmental psychology, and increasingly in social work and sociology. Two recent handbooks stand out as providing extremely helpful and comprehensive reviews of the debates to date (Goldstein & Brooks, 2005; Ungar, 2005a).

Some of those who write on resilience have questioned its analytic validity. Critics argue that because it is used in so many different ways, and to mean so many different things, it is tautological (Luthar, Cicchetti, & Becker, 2000). Others complain that its nonlinearity and failure to predict children's pathways through life makes it lack practical usefulness and renders it conceptually redundant (Tarter & Vanyukov, 1999). Still others settle for using resilience as a helpful impressionistic metaphor imported into psychology from the natural sciences (Boyden & Mann, 2005).

Despite these critiques, researchers since the 1980s have tenaciously held on to resilience as an organising concept. O'Dougherty Wright and Masten provide a helpful summary of the definition and illustration of key concepts in the debate where there is an emergent consensus (O'Dougherty Wright & Masten, 2005: 19).

We support resilience as a good idea with enormous pragmatic value. When we talk resilience with practitioners they are often buoyed up by the idea of helping children develop strength in the face of disadvantage and to protect them against the perils all too present in their lives. Developing more resilience in children, if it can be done, is something on which it seems most of us still agree. And doing this within the coherent framework provided by RT is, in our experience, the best way to do it.

We will not go into the vast debate on resilience and how it has been defined, but in Box 1.1 we summarise prominent definitions and descriptions. It suffices to say that there are three main trends in describing what resilience comprises. The first is what we call 'popular resilience', the second 'real resilience' and the third 'inoculated resilience'.

'*Popular resilience*' is resilience as used in everyday language to describe anybody who has overcome difficult times. Put this way, resilience is what almost all of us have. It appears to be programmed into the human race. Those of us who have had a good enough childhood get through the many challenges and difficulties we face, even though some of them may seem fairly monumental. There are always exceptions, people who will need guidance, coaching and explicit support, but most human beings have a fairly resilient mindset, understood in this popular sense. We love, we live, we work, we experience depths of sorrow and pain, and then we get over it.

Box 1.1 Ways of thinking of resilience

'A class of phenomena characterised by good outcomes in spite of serious threats to adaptation or development.' (Masten, 2001: 228)

'The indication of a process which characterizes a complex social system at a moment in time.' (Fonagy et al., 1994: 233)

'Adequate provision of health resources necessary to achieve good outcomes in spite of serious threats to adaptation or development.' (Ungar, 2005b: 429)

'Ordinary magic.' (Masten, 2001)

'Resilience does not constitute an individual trait or characteristic . . . Resilience involves a range of processes that bring together quite diverse mechanisms . . . .' (Rutter, 1999: 135)

'Resilience is an emergent property of a hierarchically organized set of protective systems that cumulatively buffer the effects of adversity and can therefore rarely, if ever, be regarded as an intrinsic property of individuals.' (Roisman, Padrón, Sroufe, & Egeland, 2002: 1216)

To us, popular resilience is a phrase that captures our awe at the human spirit but it seems conceptually redundant because, if it is used to describe and explain the reactions of most people in the world around us, it is too broad a concept to be of any specific benefit.

In what we call '*real resilience*' resides our major interest in writing this book. Real resilience is a comparative concept and helps us to understand what lies behind the differences between people and their respective journeys through life. It is what keeps us wondering, planning and ever hopeful for a better future for the children we know. Real resilience is evident where people with persistently few assets and resources, and major vulnerabilities—children like Janice, Louis, Jason and Sally—have better outcomes than we might expect given their circumstances, and in comparison to what we know happens with other children in their contexts. Rutter's description of resilience as 'relative resistance to psychosocial risk experiences' captures it well (Rutter, 1999: 120). In cases of real resilience we find ourselves trying to understand what it was that led to such surprisingly positive achievement, and to wonder how we can replicate it for others. Was it 'ordinary magic', some basic everyday practice, or was it a major structural change that occurred, which had an effect at grassroots level?

The concept of real resilience leads us to make informed hunches, working hypotheses if you prefer, about the protective mechanisms that have helped particular children get through and even do well. It also sets us thinking about those children who, from a really poor start, do not get any worse when we had expected them to sink further. So, real resilience does not simply alert us to improving things, it can also be about situations not getting any worse. Looking back at the children in our case studies when they are 30, we may decide that avoidance of major psychopathology and criminal convictions are evidence of positive outcomes, even if their lives are far from perfect. Resilience researchers are not united in agreeing with our interpretation here. Some insist that resilience is present only when children have especially good adaptation—not just the absence of evident maladaptation (Cowen, Work, & Wyman, 1997: 530). As part of our concept of real resilience, we prefer the more hopeful definition.

'*Inoculated resilience*' is the third category. This is complicated. Inoculated resilience can see us baffled, and our expectations confounded even more. It sees vulnerabilities as resources, or even protective mechanisms. Hence 'resilience', as a concept, represents the capacity to turn adversity into success or, at least, the ability to resist adversity's worst effects. Here, almost perversely, adversity realises optimal outcomes through resilience. Drawing analogies from immunology, Rutter's work and that of others has drawn attention to the steeling effects of what Rutter terms 'controlled *exposure*' (his italics) to the relevant pathogen and not its avoidance (Rutter, 1993: 627).

However, such controlled exposure rarely features in the lives of the young people we are writing about. An inoculation effect can still follow on from their experiences as long as they are not too overwhelming. Of course we need to understand that some environments are too much for anyone (Garbarino, 2005). You will hear more in Chapter 5 about how Sally's early school exclusions end up protecting her, relatively speaking, from the negative effects of her experience of further exclusions later. Being rejected from school abruptly and repeatedly could hardly count as *controlled* exposure and yet she has gained something from these experiences. In a psychological sense, she is to some extent inoculated. Some of the most influential thinkers in psychology have already beaten this path. We can think of Winnicott viewing lapses in good parenting leading to 'opportunities to contribute' for children, a vital experience if they are to develop a strong moral sense (Winnicott, 1965b). In another seminal work he inspires us to see 'delinquency as a sign of hope' (Winnicott, 1986).

Few researchers have yet studied these phenomena in detail, but such an intricate relationship of resilience to vulnerability and adversity has a definite reality. To just mention another example, we have seen how early neglect can serve to inoculate children from the most damaging effects of abuse. Children with a history of neglect have a pressing need for nurture. Abusive relationships may satisfy some of this need. In addition, neglected children may also lack a template for trusting relationships. The exploitative aspect of abuse is therefore both attenuated and may add something.

The overall impact of abuse on a child who has suffered early neglect is therefore rendered less traumatic than it might otherwise be.

This argument may seem perverse or difficult to contemplate: Abuse and neglect as containing positive elements? In the wrong hands it could be used to make a case against resource allocation and protection for our most disadvantaged children. This is not what we are saying or supporting; far from it. While acknowledging that politically this way of thinking can be dangerous, RT argues strongly and articulates in detail that we must address the problems of child neglect and abuse in the most effective way. As part of this we also need to face up to the reality of processes of inoculated resilience, conceptually and theoretically, so that we can better understand just how these resilient mechanisms operate and use them to even better effect. More of this later.

Resilience arenas in the research literature

With the exception of what is included in RT's '*Basics*' compartment, the broad areas involved in fostering resilience have been well rehearsed. In this introduction, we will present some examples to illustrate the formulation of the five main categories that are essential elements of RT. They include secure attachment relationships and *Belonging* (Cadell, Karabanow, & Sanchez, 2001; Fonagy, Steele, Steele, Higgitt, & Target, 1994; Hawley & DeHaan, 1996), *Learning*, including an adequate formal education (Doll, Zucker, & Brehm, 2004; Tiet et al., 1998). Work on what we term *Coping* (Buckner, Mezzacappa, & Beardslee, 2003; Cicchetti & Rogosh, 1997; Cowen, Work, & Wyman, 1997) and the client's *Core Self* (Lieberman, 2004; Marvin, Cooper, Hoffman, & Powell, 2002) are also key to the development of resilience.

Early accounts of resilience defined children as resilient or not. This was as a result of certain innate child characteristics such as intelligence, a cheerful temperament and conventional good looks (Patterson & Blum, 1996; Smith & Prior, 1995; Tschann, Kaiser, Chesney, & Alkon, 1996; Werner, 1986). Children were presented as either being born with them or not. According to these accounts, Sally would have got behind the till at the newsagents pretty well regardless of what anyone else did in her life. And by the same token, Jason would have ended up stealing things from that very same shop when Sally was busy serving someone else. In this sense, resilience is something you either have or you do not. If not, then it is very unlikely you will acquire it however hard you try. It is what we would call a *fixed* concept.

The next stage of the debate saw resilience researchers isolating vulner-abilities, resources, protective and risk factors (Rolf, Masten, Cicchetti, Nuechterlein, & Weintraub, 1990). This approach gave way to a vast body of literature amassing valuable information about patterns of resilience including innate characteristics and environmental factors. Researchers found that children they could describe as resilient tended to be bright, better looking, popular and with stable backgrounds. They are the children with secure attachments who have not suffered loss, disrupted care or exposure to parenting deficits. In this way of looking at things, girls showed up as more resilient than boys. Most of the attributes researchers focused on were also highly correlated with educational success. A great deal of research has been devoted to identifying these characteristics in detail. They are powerful predictors of later success and you will be constantly reminded of them throughout this book.

Stable backgrounds are important. And knowing, for example, that Jason would do well in life if he developed some realistic career goals and that Janice would stand a better chance of achieving happiness in adulthood if she managed to attach to a foster carer long term, gives us clear aims. However, our struggle is to identify whether we can turn the knowledge from resilience research to the advantage of children who do not have those favourable circumstances or characteristics. The findings on factors of resilience are very valuable in terms of guiding practitioners, parents and children in particular directions, but they do not say much about achieving *real resilience—how* to make resilient moves for children living in constellated disadvantage where the playing field will never be level. How we might go about achieving these goals within the context of day-to-day practice, and who might best be able to help, is a real challenge. The debate on resilient mechanisms that has gone on over the past three decades— helpfully summarised by O'Dougherty and Masten as the move from the first, through second, third to beyond the third wave—helps us to move in that direction (O'Dougherty Wright & Masten, 2005). We take a brief look at this now.

Resilient mechanisms

The heart of our struggle is how to harness the concept of resilience for the benefit of the most disadvantaged children and their families. How do we make resilience work for them? How do we make it work for them so it is not another resource they are deprived of and have no prospect of claiming?

The ten years since 1997 has seen a shift towards researchers looking at resilient processes, rather than innate individual traits, or even 'factors'. Box 1.2. summarises the different stages. For Rutter, 'Resilience does not constitute an individual trait or characteristic . . . Resilience involves a range of processes that bring together quite diverse mechanisms . . .' (Rutter, 1999: 135). He continues to stress the need to discover those mechanisms by which the best outcomes are achieved (Rutter, 1999: 135). Rutter suggests that practitioners should develop focused, briefer

---

Box 1.2 The three stages of focus for resilience research

- Individual attributes
- Factors
- Processes and mechanisms

---

interventions with clear goals and explicit hypotheses about why they might work (Rutter, 1999: 137).

Schofield and Beek also characterise resilience work as an active process, and part of a therapeutic agenda for social workers, foster carers and others. They suggest, 'this can include *increasing* felt security, *building* self-esteem, *promoting* competence and *working towards* a range of often modest developmental goals that nevertheless reduce risk and increase resilience' (Schofield & Beek, 2005: 2, their emphasis).

Wong and Lee are a bit more explicit about what this might mean. Drawing on the work of Gordon and Song (1994) they see resilience as not 'a single construct but a complex of related processes that need to be separately identified and studied as discreet aspects of health' (Wong & Lee, 2005: 316). Thus, for them, resilience as it relates to youth might best be understood as 'the combined preventive-promotive orientation of primary prevention efforts that have the potential to stop risk *factors* from affecting the behaviours of young people who are at risk' (Wong & Lee, 2005: 316, our emphasis).

We are broadly agreed with this, although we might substitute the concept of risk *processes* for risk *factors*. Factors are aggregates and do not tell us anything very much about specific situations, nor do they help explain how or why things happen the way they do. They are a research abstraction. Also, what might count as a risk factor in one context can be protective in another. Therefore even calling them risk processes can be misleading. Constellated disadvantage constitutes complexity, which means that things are not always what they seem. If we aggregate and abstract that far, we are too removed from what it is that we are trying to achieve in any specific context.

However, risk *processes* can be thought about and applied to specific contexts. They can be identified and hence can be drawn on, both conceptually and practically, to conceive of precisely how people can be diverted from particular pathways. For Rutter:

> Protection . . . lies in the ways in which people deal with life changes and in what they do about their stressful or disadvantaging circumstances. In that connection, particular attention needs to be paid to the mechanisms underlying developmental processes that enhance people's

ability to cope effectively with *future* stress and adversity and those that enable people to overcome the sequelae of *past* psychosocial hazards.

(Rutter, 1993: 630, original emphasis)

These mechanisms come in all shapes and sizes. As we have seen, Masten's view is that resilience comes from the everyday magic of ordinary, normative human resources (Masten, 2001: 235). The idea here is that the little things in life can have major consequences and that once resilient mechanisms are understood they no longer seem extraordinary.

This focus on social forces leaves the door firmly open for us all to become agents of therapeutic change if we take as our focus enhancing resilient processes. This is whether we are highly specialised or more generic mental health workers, teachers, paediatricians, social workers, parents, children or a range of other practitioners as we shall continuously notice in this book. As Rutter suggests: 'Therapeutic actions need to focus on steps that may be taken in order to reduce negative chain reactions . . . Protection may also lie in fostering positive chain reactions, and these, too, need attention in therapeutic planning' (Rutter, 1999: 136).

The idea of 'turning points', significant moments in a person's life that led them to follow one path over another, have also been singled out as conceptually and practically important (Quinton & Rutter, 1988). So, when Jason marries or registers a civil partnership with somebody who has maximum potential to be a lifelong friend and long-term good influence is a moment when those around him may truly celebrate. This example also demonstrates the importance of getting away from thinking of resilience as what Rutter calls 'the chemistry of the moment' (Rutter, 1993: 627).

In following these leads, we take resilience and turn it into a set of actions and working practices, mechanisms designed to generate better outcomes than would otherwise be expected. This is the core of real resilience. We make the interventions as comprehensive and effective as we can. They may be used in combination, they may be one single application of a key intervention or they may be sequential actions orchestrated over time. The overriding principle is, however, always to improve outcomes—short or long term—which we can demonstrate. We talk again here of resilient *practice* rather than of resilience, Resilien*t* therapy rather than resilien*ce* therapy.

There are further implications of making these distinctions. One of them is the transition from seeing families and children and the practitioners involved as *subject* to certain practices, e.g. they are in receipt of therapy, education, etc., to contemplating *them* as the co-driver of collaborative efforts within these contexts. 'Parent co-therapy' and developing 'attuned practice' are markers of such collaboration (Hart, Saunders, & Thomas, 2005; Hart & Thomas, 2000). This focus on the *active* individual derives from the need to view resilient practice as itself an outcome of individual–environment interactions. In a later chapter we widen our horizon to see how organisations and other collaborative forms can facilitate resilient practice.

Hence our application of the resiliency debate goes beyond a focus on the personality traits of individual children, and beyond isolating associated factors, towards demonstrating what can be done by practitioners to enhance resilience for children whatever their personal capacity to overcome adversity. This includes the practitioners too. We avoid what Masten, Neemann and Andenas (1994) lament is a potential blaming of individual children for not having what it takes to rise above a challenging situation. Nevertheless, the issue of individual or family traits cannot be ignored. Indeed, from a health equality perspective it can be argued that children with weak individual capacity for resilience should be prioritised for mental health services. There is also a tension here between on the one hand acknowledging the merit of structural explanations for children's adverse situations, and on the other helping them to develop the capacity to move towards better outcomes under their own steam. In practice, the debate can become polarised with one view leading us to see children as victims and another making them wholly responsible for their own destiny. Levelling this critique at the concept of family resilience, the same argument can be applied.

Applications of resilience research

We hope that by now we will have convinced you that there is a good argument for seeing what all the research on resilience might mean for practice—how mechanisms have been, or should be applied. However, as we said right at the beginning of this chapter, it is certainly the case that accounts of its application to the daily lives of practitioners constitute a far less weighty pile of paper than does the research base itself.

Social work is one of the main disciplines where a discussion of resilience-promotion in practice has emerged. Practice materials have been developed, although here conceptual issues are not always considered (Bostock, 2004; Daniel & Wassell, 2002a, 2002b; Gilligan, 1998, 2001). Seden demonstrates the contribution of ideas from the resilience evidence base to the formulation of the UK standardised assessment framework for exploring the needs of disadvantaged children (Seden, 2002). A research team at the Search Institute in the USA has developed a framework for assessing children's developmental assets (Sesma, Mannes, & Scales, 2005). And one at the University of Newcastle in Australia has put together a Resilience Identification Resource Kit, including a manual, checklist and materials for use with children (Clay & Silberberg, 2004).

In education too, resilience research has been applied to some effect, often through universal programmes that reach all children within a school, as you will see in Chapter 5.

Brooks and Goldstein apply the resilience research base to their self-help book for parents based on their own therapeutic practice with children and families (Brooks & Goldstein, 2001).

There are also some tailor-made direct therapeutic interventions conceived from the resilience research base (Cowen, Wyman, Work, Kim, Fagen, & Magnus, 1997; Egeland & Erikson, 1990; Luthar & Suchman, 2000). For example in North America, Gilgun and colleagues have developed the Clinical Assessment Package for Risks and Strengths, a collection of rating scales that incorporate research on resilience and a strengths perspective on clinical treatment (Gilgun, 2006; Gilgun, Keskinen, Marti, & Rice, 1999). Their work demonstrates how using the package can improve client outcomes.

A UK-based team has drawn on international resilience research and experiential knowledge of local parents and professionals to develop a multi-disciplinary practice framework (Croom & Procter, 2005). Their assessment tool helps to identify child and adolescent mental health problems and to build on community strengths in supporting them. Beyond these initiatives, there is ample room for expanding the application of resilience evidence bases to routine therapeutic practice with children. In Chapters 3 to 7 we will return to them, and to the research base itself, in detail.

Therapeutic work with young people like Janice, Louis, Jason and Sally can draw on interventions from each of our five compartments. However, RT is a pragmatic strategic methodology that involves explicitly prioritising areas on which to work. This approach does not appear at first sight to fit the resilience evidence base. This is because, as some have convincingly argued, resilience research lacks theoretical development in understanding which particular mechanisms should be prioritised for promotion (Fonagy, Steele, Steele, Higgitt, & Target, 1994). Finding the right remedy holds an element of trial and error, and matters of chemistry are relevant when we consider how different interventions might work together. But, as others have cogently argued, other processes beyond those laid down in the text are relevant, particularly how you enact them (White & Stancombe, 2003).

Let us unpack this. Researchers may emphasise that Louis is likely to become more resilient through his learning assistant helping him to join in with football every day. They have less to say about how to get that going in the first place, let alone maintain it. As you may recall, when we first told you of Louis, his learning support assistant is missing his own lunch break and going out of his way to help him. And once we delve into the world of statements of special educational need and Louis' school culture and organisation, there are even more processes we will have to engage with. And then we will seem further than ever from putting into practice what the researchers urge us to do.

This example reminds us that therapeutic practice with disadvantaged children fuses at least art, science, organisational culture, monetary resources, policy directive and psychodynamics. Complexity theorist Klein defines the art of being professional as one of managing complexity (Klein, 2004).Think about the different dynamics involved in the simple story of Louis getting to football and you will see what she means. Haynes, drawing on Cilliers (1998), argues that complex systems come to solutions via dynamic processes that are evolving and are not likely to result in a single, final conclusion (Haynes, 2003: 27). Fonagy et al. use the word complexity directly in relation to resilience. They see resilience as characterising 'a complex social system at a moment in time' (Fonagy, Steele, Steele, Higgitt, & Target, 1994: 233).

All the scholars mentioned above point to the difficulties in knowing precisely how mechanisms work. However, despite the conceptual difficulties in knowing what works for whom and in what context (Carter & New, 2004), we do know more or less what kind of interventions we need in RT. And we also know that some interventions come in handy for most situations. In lieu of definitive answers, which may yet be forthcoming from research, we have to fall back on personal judgement to connect to the available evidence base if we are to formulate an effective plan of action in the moment (White & Stancombe, 2003).

Making up Resilient Therapy

Before we spell out Noble Truths, compartments and interventions in the following chapters, a word about how RT has developed. It has arisen both from the research base, and also through embedded knowledge, tested in what Eraut describes as 'tacit' practice (Eraut, 1994). This 'tacit' practice is our work in areas of high socioeconomic deprivation, also with foster and adoptive families, and with families of children with special needs across the socioeconomic spectrum.

Between the authors there is in-depth knowledge derived from professional training and many years of experience in social work, psychiatry, family therapy, working with the legal system, psychotherapy and counselling. Two of us work in CAMHS and with the university in the capacity of research-practitioners. We have all been involved in developing innovative specialist services for fostered and adopted children. In addition, Angie's personal history of intensive and prolonged service engagement with health, education and social care as an adoptive parent has significantly informed the development of RT. However, there has been a much broader range of direct influences on the development of this book.

A considerable spur to the work came from 'developing a community of practice'; a group of practitioners informally bound together as a result of a shared passion and expertise for a joint enterprise. Knowledge and expertise is shared in ways that do not readily fit conventional organisational structures and processes. This frees people up to pool experiences, skills and problems in a way that allows new forms of knowledge and creativity to emerge (Wenger, McDermott, & Snyder, 2002: 5). We secured modest funding to develop the application of our RT methodology in this way.

The emphasis on 'practice' as a base for community allows worlds and discourses—for example professional organisations and user groups—that are usually quite separate, to be integrated (Hart & Luckock, 2004). The practice development work for this book has certainly taken place in this spirit. In developing RT we always aim for a genuine transfer of knowledge, experiences, resources and expertise across quite different constituencies. Our partnership is between CAMHS colleagues, academics, social workers, youth workers, nurses, teachers and learning support assistants, voluntary sector workers, lawyers, parents/carers of children with special needs, young people themselves and artists. This shared passion can compensate for the relatively low status and esteem afforded to anyone working in the context of social deprivation, disadvantage and special needs. In fact, it can positively energise us and helps us to feel a much stronger sense of self-efficacy about meeting the needs of disadvantaged children. This development work also informs the way we have written this book, the language we use, and for whom therefore it is intended.

Well, it certainly is for professionals, for example in CAMHS, social work practice, psychiatry, paediatrics, general practice, special education and across teaching more generally. However, the term 'professional' presents a number of issues here. RT has implications for occupational authority, power relationships and status that will keep on emerging throughout this book. As background to this, there is a lively debate in sociology on the subject of professionalism that is worth examining. Evidence from our daily practice continues to confirm the published research evidence base that it is not always professionals who do the most effective work. This is one reason why we have been very careful to include a range of practitioners, including parents and young people, in our RT development work.

We have therefore added a sociological interpretation of *'practice'* and *'practitioner'* to our understanding of who is best involved in RT. While these terms may be quite unfamiliar to you, they do offer some advantages. For sociologists, practice implies an analytic focus on *everyday business* and the *detail of life*; for example, getting up, going out or staying in, eating, drinking, work or leisure and then finding somewhere to sleep at night (Bourdieu, 1996). Østerlund and Carlile provide a useful explanation of this sociological way of thinking. They are hopeful that practice theory sidesteps a substantialist view and bridges the subjectivism–objectivism dichotomy because, as they see it, in practice the subject and the world combine and recursively interact (Østerlund & Carlile, 2005).They suggest that a focus on social practice emphasises the relational interdependencies between subject and object, person and world, individual and community, or community and network (2005: 92). Hence for them, 'A practice theory assumes that categories are forged out of blurred-edged social phenomena constantly produced and reproduced through everyday practices' (2005: 95).

Thinking 'practice' makes us put ordinary events and the little things that go on in life into the spotlight. In fact, we have used this idea to introduce you upfront to Sally and the other children. As you saw, the practice perspective makes us as interested in Louis' burn as we are in the systematised organisation of children's services or in the relative effectiveness of different therapeutic methods. Later in the book we will discuss the need for the 'management of effective detail' (Elisabeth Henderson, 2005, personal communication) to help practitioners focus on the everyday practices of life and to understand as clearly as possible what it is they need to do to make things better.

We can usefully extend the notion of practice to include, for example, an emphasis on psycho-dynamic processes. In our fictionalised case studies, the feelings of humiliation of Louis' mother when she went to therapy, are then also put into the frame. Psycho-dynamic processes and internal worlds are areas of human activity that sociologists have not always been as mindful of as they might be. On the other hand, some children's workers concentrate on psycho-dynamics to the exclusion of other important dimensions. A sociological understanding of practice can include, but also take us beyond, the language of internal worlds and intersubjectivity. We see Louis' carpet, his mother's bus fare and Sally's burger as real and important things that contribute to their lives as they are lived, and not simply symbols and metaphors in their internal worlds. Whilst psycho-dynamics can help us to understand the rich contribution of the internal world, sociology can help us grasp just what a practical matter it is being poor and disadvantaged.

Using the term practitioner in its sociological guise helps us identify the human agents involved in all these activities. Put into the language of RT, we can make or break specific outcomes for children through what we do in our ordinary daily routines, and regularities of work and home life. In the literature, the term practitioner is conventionally used to describe paid workers in health and social care. But for us, parents and young people also come together in the joint practice of RT. They too are practitioners in our use of the term. And our employment of the term practitioner in this inclusive way, while creating another layer of complexity, helps elevate parents and carers to a position of genuine partnership.

The linguistic challenges presented to us in writing this book mirror the challenges we all have in working across conventional boundaries. Resilient Therapy workshops involving parents of children with special needs and a range of practitioners working in the context of social complexity have greatly enriched the ideas we have developed in this book. We have tried to bring their tacit practices alive by offering the information and encouragement to enable them to experiment with RT in their daily lives. We have offered a loose but affirming structure within which those individual experiments can be reflected upon. This book should be seen as an extension of that developmental work and we invite all practitioners, in the sense we have used the term here, to take their part.

Structure of the book

In this introductory chapter we have given a rationale for writing this book, an introduction to its contents and have explained something of the process through which we have developed RT to date. Our brief review of the resilience literature demonstrates that we now know quite a lot about what might be helpful for children living in constellated disadvantage. Throughout this book we return to this evidence base in some detail, spelling out its components in order to guide our focus. As we have seen, the resilience evidence base in child and adolescent mental health and related services is still emergent rather than definitive and, as needs must, practice and ingenuity has to fill in the gaps.

We now want to revisit these same debates but in more detail. Chapters 3 to 7 will do this in relationship to each compartment and its individual interventions. Chapter 8 will look at how we can work organisationally with RT. The last chapter will examine the current context of therapy to see what we can build on that is already working along the lines of RT. In our next chapter we focus on therapeutics to highlight the fundamental part played in RT by 'Noble Truths'. This is in order to specify as precisely as we can which therapeutic principles and philosophies are prioritised. It also helps us to justify our decision to put the two concepts, 'resilience' and 'therapy', together to create the new methodology that we call RT.

Chapter 2

Four Noble Truths for resilient therapists: Accepting, Conserving, Commitment and Enlisting

Let other pens dwell on guilt and misery.

Jane Austen

Setting the scene

Let us pick up on what we hope to be the emerging fortunes of Louis, the seven-year-old with a diagnosis of ADHD that we introduced in Chapter 1. His family was offered various children's services. Louis' GP is now monitoring repeat prescriptions of Ritalin. There is some talk from his current social worker of a doctor once saying that he might need to be operated on when he reached the age of seven. This would help disguise the ugly burn scar on his head from the injury he sustained when he was two.

We would like you to imagine that Louis' fortunes take a slightly different turn. He is still living with his mother after going in and out of foster care. The professional system around him is moving in another direction. Imagine that his social worker has just completed two days basic training in Resilient Therapy (RT). Even though she is a senior social worker she works within a strong managerial culture and she has little autonomy. Just as well, then, that her manager went on the training course too. Box 2.1 sets out the story of how the social worker, we have called her Melanie, begins to work with RT.

We have articulated this story to demonstrate precisely the kind of thought processes that a novice RT practitioner might go through. Experienced RT practitioners will know already what is still only just dawning on Melanie; being Accepting of constellated disadvantage and complexity is where we start.

However, for those of you reading this book who are new to this way of thinking, we also need to demonstrate how an RT practitioner brings novices like Melanie along. What might Melanie expect from RT in taking a therapeutically resilient approach to her work with Louis and his family? As we saw in Chapter 1 there are many ideas about how to achieve resilience for

Box 2.1 Becoming a Resilient Therapist

Melanie is an excellent social worker. She has done a lot of work to get Jane, Louis' very depressed mother, out of bed and on the road to recovery, and she has helped access material support for the family. Melanie has also thoroughly read through Louis' file and has noted the suggestions from a doctor some years ago about operating on his scalp once he got to the age of seven. Changes of social worker can mean that details like this get lost in files, but Melanie has noticed what needs to happen. She helped Jane to get Louis along to see his GP and now an appointment with a specialist has been made.

Melanie has always been a critic of rational-techno-bureaucratic social work. However, doing the RT training has really moved her to think more strategically about how to work in the complicated world of constellated disadvantage. She especially liked the session on 'managing effective detail'. This helped her to think about her work differently and to appreciate some of the basic, everyday grounded work she did, work in which her manager's manager never seems very interested. It helped Melanie follow through the consequences of some of her own actions and she has now got a growing awareness of how little things can make a big difference. The course has also helped her to notice where her energy and commitment lies. Melanie gets enthused about doing all she can to help build Louis' life up, and makes a conscious decision to experiment with her personal power. Instead of making a blanket referral to the child and adolescent mental health services (CAMHS) she contacts somebody directly, who she knows will help her think about Louis through the techniques and processes of RT. Her manager, too, is enthusiastic for her to experiment with this approach.

Melanie understands better than anyone else that Louis and his family need something different from what is usually offered, or what sometimes can feel like force-fed to them, through the children's services network. It has taken her a while to realise this consciously, although her feeling about Louis and his family puts her in touch with it anyway. The daily tension in her neck embodies it. The trouble is, even though she feels committed to this family, the structure within which she works almost seems to set her up to pass Louis' case onto somebody else, or to case manage it according to a techno-bureaucratic imperative.

Melanie finds herself fretting that the old systems and processes just do not work. She is no economist, but she understands from the waste that has occurred in other cases—letters and assessments from different workers piling up in files with hardly a tangible outcome in sight—that it would not be cost effective to bother with them. Even though her local CAMHS is unusual for the UK—only a month's waiting list—there's no point in CAMHS sending Jane an appointment to come along with the children for family therapy. It will waste everybody's time and do nothing to build Louis' life up, nor that of his siblings. Neither would the decision to put Louis forward for individual child psychotherapy serve any use. It might even end up being counterproductive. Jane is not going to get Louis there—so the interventions will not fit the family. Melanie's practice manager could be persuaded to foot the bill for a costly taxi ride for them to go to family therapy sessions. However, sustaining that would need such close management and liaison that Melanie might as well think how she could use that very same energy to better effect. If Melanie had not attended the RT workshop she would simply have referred the family through the routine channels. Now she knows that a lot of files and paper-work would be shifted around the system, but Louis, his mum and the CAMHS therapist would hardly ever meet. However, Melanie wants to stay involved and she wants to take a more strategic approach. To do this, she enlists the help of resilient therapist Gill. The family is referred to CAMHS, but as a consulting case. So, Melanie gets supervision from Gill and takes the direct work forward herself.

children. So, why do we bother framing our approach within a therapeutic context at all?

We have already explained that in our work with constellated disadvantage we have found other approaches limited in dealing with the dynamics of disadvantage. In our final chapter, we will take you through how RT differs from other therapies, particularly how it meets the technical, emotional, political and practical challenges that constellated disadvantage presents. What we can say now is that despite these limitations we continue to see hope in therapy. Simply put, we see therapy as offering us something helpful in our resolve to improve disadvantaged children's lives. We have scanned the textbooks for definitions of 'therapy', but surprisingly have not come across any. So, we will make our own. At least in theory, therapy can be understood as a change management method—we are in the job of helping our clients bring about some kind of change to make their lives more fulfilling. For some people therapy concerns changing the way people think, feel or talk. For others it involves changing their actions too.

Of course, in some of the work we do, particularly in the context of constellated disadvantage, simply halting decline and maintaining the status quo is a goal worthy of achievement. Helping Jane to continue to steer clear of deep depression, rather than go for a life that she adores, is a big enough challenge for any therapist. Achieving this though could set up a whole chain of positive reactions. Less depressed, Jane will be able to drag herself out of bed in the morning and get those of her children who are not already in foster care off to school more or less on time. Even if Jane plateaus here for the next 10 years, the priceless work done by Melanie to help Jane control her depression carries on. It will mean that Jane's four children will go on living with her, and that the local authority will not take her to court for failing to get them to school. It also means that the children get an education and can stay where they want to be—at home. It will save the tax payer in foster care and court fees. Acknowledging these chains of reaction is important. Valuable status quo maintenance work is often a feature of working in the context of constellated disadvantage. Unless we acknowledge it, the work can go unnoticed and this, in turn, can contribute to feelings of hopelessness and ineffectual practice.

Whether you are just maintaining a situation so it does not get any worse, or generating positive chain reactions, underpinning effective work, the application of individual interventions, and just engaging with families to make RT possible all need thoughtful preparatory work.

Before we can intervene, we need to prepare ourselves to do so. Reflecting on what we call the 'Noble Truths' and instilling them into the souls of practitioners (well, metaphorically speaking at least) is the key task here. The Noble Truths are Accepting, Conserving, Commitment and Enlisting. ACCE is the acronym. We have borrowed the idea of Noble Truths from Buddhism; the four Noble Truths in Buddhism are the most basic expression of Buddhist teaching and the foundation of ethical living. We too have four Noble Truths in our methodology and they capture the basic principles on which RT is founded. We return to them when the complexity of practising in constellated disadvantage threatens to overwhelm us. In many ways they can be understood as a therapeutic intervention in their own right, working on and with all of us; workers, children and families at many levels. The rest of this chapter goes through each of the Noble Truths, explains why we have selected them as resilient principles, and spells out our interpretation of each concept. We also show the connection of each concept to therapeutic approaches. They are derived from, or can be linked to, specific therapeutic schools—Accepting (Rogerian), Conserving and Commitment (psychodynamic), Enlisting (family therapy and cognitive behavioural therapy), for example.

Accepting: 'Ordinary magic works best when we start where people are at'

Let's go back to Louis' mother Jane. Most of us will recognise her as a typical parent living in a complicated world of constellated disadvantage with family practices that will seem familiar. No surprise that she did not go back for another CAMHS appointment. No surprise, too, that she finds it very hard to get Louis to school. No surprise, too, that she does not choose to take the good things that children's services think they have to offer her. You could say that the scenario runs like a Greek tragedy—the chorus pretty well sets her up. The grand statistics on levels of child poverty, parental substance misuse and child protection are part of that chorus. They taunt us with the knowledge that all too often change comes slowly, if it comes at all. But the idea of resilience offers us a place where we can locate hope. Resilience reminds us that there are always exceptions to statistics and trends. Melanie and Gill, the resilient therapist, hold in mind that Louis' life could always take a turn for the better. Understanding precisely where Louis and his family are, and Accepting the need to begin alongside them, will give Melanie and Gill a head start in their efforts to apply resilient practices to this family context.

Of course, a big part of the challenge is actually understanding where we are starting from in people's lives. This can seem particularly difficult when working with children as the pace of their developmental processes can mean that goal posts change even more frequently than with adults. And there are many other issues to hold in mind. Part of understanding where we start from is the historical dimension; knowing how things have come to be the way they are. Yet when staff changes are frequent, and attention spans short, histories all too often get lost or ignored. Memories and legacies that could give us vital clues as to how to proceed in specific situations are often to be found somewhere in the files, but how many of us read them? And of those of us that do, how much of what actually happened can we apply in the present context? Much of our practice experience could illustrate this point, but in Box 2.2 we weave the moral of just one tale into our narrative about Louis and his family.

Melanie's work, described above, is an integral part of the 'management of effective detail' (Elisabeth Henderson, 1995, personal communication). Knowing when to find out the 'nitty gritty', how to go about it, and knowing what to do with that knowledge once you have it, are the steps involved. Taking time and care to understand the implications for current decision making of histories and legacies is part of our Accepting agenda. It sounds elementary and it is. It is fundamental to beginning to harness resilient mechanisms; i.e. working out the most helpful interventions to try to put together in this particular situation. And, although it is elementary, undertaking the task well demonstrates the resilient therapist's ability to work with complexity that should be highly prized. Indeed, a basic law of RT is that the more complexity a practitioner can deal with, the more effective they are likely to be.

So let us ask ourselves honestly: How often is this task done with sufficient application? Knowing why we don't do it is also important for resilient working, as we shall see.

First, the team around Louis' brother Craig managed a difficult task and did not alienate him in the attempt, but they could easily have done so.

Box 2.2 Accepting Craig's history

Louis has two older brothers. One of them, Craig (14), is back in foster care, this time with an expensive private agency because the local authority has no vacancies with its own foster carers. Craig is not in school at the moment. He boasts to his friends about being excluded four times for behavioural problems, and has had to move on for other reasons on a further three occasions. This time he is out because a teacher hit him. The school is being investigated as other young people have made similar allegations. Craig will not be going back and has spent five days of each week in the past month in day care. Day care in this case actually means young people watching television or playing on a play station all day in the homes of foster carers. Craig's current foster carer and social worker are looking for another school for him. His social worker, his advocate and his foster carer seek Craig's opinion. He tells them all that he wants to go back to his original comprehensive school. He was removed from there two years previously because his mental health deteriorated there. For the last three weeks at that school he had spent much of the day cowering under a table in the inclusion unit. Everyone working with him at the time agreed that Craig needed a much smaller school environment and specialist support. Now all those people have moved on. None of the new people involved know the history. So, in accordance with his wishes, Craig could have ended up back at the school.

   The current team around this child are all sensible and diligent. They are all aware that he needs extra support and nobody questions the details of his statement that includes a one-to-one support worker all week. But only one of them, social worker Melanie, reads the paperwork in his file, rings up the school and develops a historical understanding of Craig's needs. This awareness, coupled with a developmental perspective (Craig is adolescent now, and needs even closer supervision and input) leads the team to persuade Craig that his needs are best met elsewhere. They move him to a much smaller school where, with the help of his one-to-one support, he manages to remain until school leaving age and move on to college having achieved some basic educational qualifications.

While the intentions may be good, our attempts to find out what we need to know about people can have the effect of further alienating them from us. Some practitioners find it too hard to hear the depths of difficulty that people experience, and are quick to move away from the story being told. Others can be experienced as gratuitously interested. So they come across as intrusive, rather than 'alongside'. And people can get very frustrated when all that practitioners seem to do is find out about them, rather than getting on and doing something. Writing in the context of child protection, Reder and Duncan call this 'assessment paralysis' (1999). We avoid the term assessment in this section on 'Accepting' as this formal process has such an ideological ring to it now, saturated for so many recipients with negative, bureaucratic and formulaic meaning. However, you may still find it helpful to think of assessment as part of Accepting.

Quite often the way we approach constellated disadvantage makes Accepting the starting point of the children and families we work with impossible. Whilst we reach out with good things to offer, they are 'not ready to engage', 'difficult to help', 'hard to reach', 'impossible to work with', 'mad', 'uncooperative' and 'bloody minded'. Rare are accounts of workers describing the dynamics at work in any other way (Grant, Mills, Mulhern, & Short, 2004). This is a shame. Another reading could acknowledge those same workers as unfocused and dejected, and both clients and the children's services employees as defensively alienated from each other (Cooper & Lousada, 2005). On a bad day, even those of us who really take care not to do this can still find ourselves slipping into these dynamics. The ethnographic studies of social anthropologists and sociologists have illuminated this pejorative 'offstage' chatter (Goffman, 1968; Strong, 1979).

And whilst Melanie and her RT mentor may find it just too difficult to have what Rogers calls 'unconditional positive regard', according to Rogers' formulation of the concept (Rogers, 1951), for Louis and his family, a resilient approach encourages them to be adaptive. They are prepared to join the family precisely where they are at right now. So, the RT mentor's first piece of advice to Melanie is that if she accepts that she needs to start where Jane is at, the dynamics of dejection and alienation will work themselves out more positively.

This adaptive stance on 'Accepting' is a therapeutic one, and has its roots in Rogerian ideas. Rogers advocated the somewhat inelegant concept mentioned above of 'unconditional positive regard'. Despite some cogent critiques of the Rogerian school of thought (Clarke, 1999; Kensit, 2000), many of the millions of children's services professionals in the UK, including Melanie, will have been trained in accordance with his principles.

Before we proceed, let us take a reality check. Most of us know that Rogerian rhetoric is difficult for us to live up to. For those of us working in the world of complicated, constellated disadvantage it can be particularly frustrating that other people do not think, feel or behave in the ways that we would like them to. We can feel many complex and conflicting emotions towards them; some of these are our own feelings that get triggered off by the stress of the work, some dynamics are the result of powerful projections from others.

Projection, a psychoanalytic term (Freud, 1966), refers to a process in which a person who finds their own feelings too intense, overwhelming or painful unconsciously shifts them onto someone else, most often someone with whom they have a close relationship. This is an important aspect of the transference and countertransference of emotions that occur in these situations. An awareness of projections can help RT practitioners preserve a sense of self within the situation. When intense emotions and feelings are being projected into us from others it is important for the success of our work to name them and to understand what is happening. In the most extreme scenarios, if we do not we cannot distinguish what is theirs and what is ours, and we cease to be effective.

Projection is definitely worth understanding for RT and key to helping us accept the depths of what is going on for children and families. The concept has been critiqued by many learned scholars, as well as by disgruntled former therapists (Masson, 2003; Newman, Duff, & Baumeister, 1997). Despite these criticisms, we still think the concept is useful, and it is particularly helpful when thinking over the extremes of emotions that we are likely to encounter in constellated disadvantage.

The idea of projection points out the potential danger of burnout from the unhelpful over-involvement of practitioners. It also alerts us to what has been characterised 'system abuse', where the responding agencies play out, and thereby amplify, the abusive dynamics already operating in the situation. On the other hand, the idea of projection can be misused to such an extent that it leads to simply blaming other people for extreme or unwelcome feelings of our own and as an excuse for our own work failings. The use of particular defences, rationalisations and projections can leave workers themselves feeling overwhelmed, acting defensively and counter-projecting. As a result, defensive avoidance is another response. Avoidance and over-involvement are two sides of what is a traumatised reaction. Both can get in the way of Accepting where we start from.

In our world of complicated, constellated disadvantage, Accepting that we need to start where people are at can feel daunting in the extreme. It may also be uncharted territory because, for many of you reading this book, their worlds are so far removed from your own (West Stevens, 2005). Developing an inequalities imagination will help here (Hall & Hart, 2004). Rogers' work has been critiqued very wisely (Clarke, 1999; Kensit, 2000), but we still suggest starting with an appreciation of it. We hold to this because the evidence base confirms that *behaving as though* we had unconditional positive regard represents attuned and helpful practice (Hart, Saunders, & Thomas, 2005). This helps us to remain courteous, warm, helpful, empathic and engaged. It is also the foundation for being effective.

Accepting grounds resilience building mechanisms in the right place. Let us go back to the example of Louis' brother Craig and his school placement. If Melanie and the others had not known his history, and only thought about it in terms of Craig's current circumstances, their resilience-building efforts would have set him on a path back to his old school. This would, in all probability, not work out. Accepting is the art of maximising what you know, and then applying it to the situation at hand to achieve a better than expected outcome.

Conserving

Conserving is a new term we bring to the therapeutic literature. It is connected to one of the most important concepts in therapy, and an organising principle for psychotherapy certainly—containment. We will go on to explain why we bring in this new concept, rather than simply applying the word containment to our work. But first we begin this section by explaining the notion of 'containment'.

Of jam and jam jars

If we think of something as basic as jam in a jar, we can see that the jar *contains* the jam. There are two different meanings to the word containment here. First, the interpretation that the jam *is in* the jar. Second, the use of contains here means that the jar is *keeping the jam inside it*. You could say that the jar is looking after the jam, although admittedly this sounds a little fanciful when we are talking about jam and jam jars. The idea works better when applied to people. In the classic psychotherapy literature, containment refers to the idea of a therapist making a 'safe space' for the client (Brown, Pedder, & Bateman, 2000). In this interpretation, containment is a kind of looking after.

The idea of containment belongs to the famous attachment psychotherapist working in the mid 20th century, Winnicott (2005). Winnicott was never interested in metaphors of jam and jam jars. His ideas about containment actually have their origins in Freud's theories of regression, although scholars have only recently connected the two (Fonagy, 2001).

The aim of a psychotherapist working in the Winnicottian tradition would be to create a feeling of emotional containment. This involves establishing consistent boundaries with clear conditions of time and place, and with a great deal of attention paid to the need for the therapist's consistency, reliability, and capacity to contain complex emotional expression. This illusion of a protective parental relationship is seen as setting up the conditions for deep intrapsychic exploration (Modell, 1976).

For containment to occur it is important to maintain a consistent physical environment, with minimal disruption and change of furniture, etc. Furthermore, it is argued that once boundaries are established what a client does with those boundaries becomes an essential part of the material worked on in therapy (Brown, Pedder, & Bateman, 2000). This idea of containment as a curative regressive safety zone is the one that receives most attention in the literature. However, there is also another story, less often told.

A third interpretation of containment is that the jar is stopping the jam from spilling out. This use of the word implies restriction, a form of confinement even. Used this way the metaphor takes us away from responsive mothers soothing their children to the metaphor of adults pinning children down. Unequal, gratuitous power relations between therapists and clients, and the potential tyranny of the therapeutic 'holding' environment are put into the frame. The idea of containment then becomes one of an exploitative, regressive danger zone. Some therapeutic techniques, for example forms of holding therapy, have been criticised for just this (O'Connor & Zeanah, 2003). However, less extreme forms of such exploitation occur in more conventional therapies.

The idea of Conserving encompasses the concept of Containment, and yet de-emphasises the propensity in therapy of focusing on regression and children's negative, painful experiences. This is a resilient move, as we shall see in more detail when we consider issues of Coping and the development of a Core Self in Chapters 5 and 6. Focusing repeatedly on the negative leaves us with no feeling for resilience in mind. Seeing this negative focus as part of the culture of psychotherapeutic engagement helps us get at just how embedded and taken for granted this approach can be.

Thinking 'Conserving' gives us a different feel for therapy. One connotation takes us into the language of ecology, into ideas about preserving our natural environment for future enjoyment. Another towards elegant old buildings in need of care and attention. A further connotation takes us back to jam jars. Conserves are good things 'bottled up' for the future. And even things that seem bad at first sight may be worth Conserving if we think carefully about what we are doing. For example, Craig's history of school exclusion and removal does not make for easy reading. However, when properly conserved (implying care and attention), it helped the team around him make a resilient choice about his schooling. And it could have formed part of his own inoculated resilience in the new school environment—Craig may have learnt enough from earlier bad experiences to cope better in the present. Whatever the precise mechanisms at play, graduating from a nurturing school environment with some examinations achieved and a warm feeling inside him as to his place in the world is demonstration enough of a bad story turned good.

Another reason we use the term Conserving reflects our disquiet with the idea that therapeutic support must occur within an environment of regressive safety where stranger therapists create intense relationships with children for 50 minutes each week. We particularly take issue with the idea that these relationships were, traditionally at least, completely estranged from children's existences beyond the therapy room. Child psychotherapists claim that children transfer what they get from such therapeutic relationships into their everyday lives. No doubt this does occur. However, we do not see it as the organising principle for therapeutic engagement. The evidence base is alongside us here, whatever therapeutic method we choose. It continues to affirm parent-focused therapy or child–parent work as much more effective than simply working with children alone (van de Weil, Matthys, Cohen-Kettenis, & van Engeland, 2002; Weiss, Catron, & Harris, 1999, 2000). The evidence base should not be taken as gospel, as there are all kinds of methodological complexities that mean we will always have to make a professional judgement as to how the evidence can be applied in specific circumstances. Nevertheless, setting up estranged therapeutic support for Louis may simply increase his alienation from his mother Jane, rather than do anything to conserve any good that exists between them and build up their relationship. Of course this is even assuming that he actually gets to therapy each week. This is an entire issue in itself that is too easily treated as immaterial. As you will understand by now, these kinds of real, everyday details must be taken seriously in RT.

To sum up our argument so far in this section, as well as containing jam, jars conserve it. Conserving then gives us the idea both of keeping something within boundaries and preserving the good things that are in it. The potential for containment to be used in negative ways, even very subtle ones, and for Conserving to have such positive connotations is one of the reasons why we employ this term.

Conserving also relates to practitioners. First, it helps when RT practitioners can stomach the work: looking after, growth, preservation, and engagement with emotions are all aspects of the task that we must keep alive. The ability to rise above the difficulties of your situation is key to resilience. The more that Jane, Louis and family sense that Melanie can cope with their difficulties, and that she can hear them and understand them, the more likely they will be to respond positively.

Second, it helps practitioners to sustain their engagement by helping to create sensible boundaries in our relationships with families. Melanie will need to put in some structure, focus and realistic expectations, if she is to work effectively with Jane, Louis and family. Doing this will act as a basis for her to commit to working with the family.

Commitment

The 21st century could be described as an antivocational age. Applications to enter the priesthood are down, and professional practice has become increasingly regulated and restricted. There is widespread talk of 'positions', 'posts', 'jobs', 'glass ceilings', 'careers' and the 'career ladder', but the idea of vocation rings rather old fashioned.

In our experience, talk of making commitments often unsettles people. It can unleash emotions that take us in directions we had not intended.

Box 2.3 Melanie's approach to Commitment

Melanie's tendency is to care for Louis in such a way that her body becomes affected by what is happening. This for her is clearly a current occupational hazard. The daily tension in her neck soon gives way to persistent stomach-aches. She lies awake at night worrying that he has no friends at school and that his mother is not feeding him properly. She is worried too that Louis might fall victim to one of the many different boyfriends his mother brings home at night. Of course some of her worry is over being blamed for major mistakes. She frets about the media attention given to blaming social workers in high-profile cases. So, it is actually quite hard for Melanie to distinguish which of her fears are for herself and which ones are for Louis. While each of these pushes her further in the direction of her falling victim to burnout, they are also not helping her RT techniques. She gets muddled in her head about what should happen with Louis and finds herself lurching from one strategy to another without thinking anything through properly.

Indeed, one thing stands out from the workshops with parents and workers that we have undertaken to develop our ideas for this book. Achieving a balanced approach to Commitment was the most difficult of the Noble Truths for people to establish as part of their identity as RT practitioners. Whether parents or workers, the core issue of concern fell on either side of the same coin, dependence.

For some the difficulty lay in a fear of, or a reluctance to tolerate or encourage, dependence. For others over-involvement was at the heart of the matter. Here, difficulty with gaining enough perspective on a child and their situation to be useful was the problem. It was far more likely to be parents or carers who were over-involved than it was colleagues. These different sides of the same coin—over- or under-involvement—are both issues of occupational safety and therapeutic technique. Sorting them out frees up RT practitioners to commit to their clients in a way that is helpful.

Melanie needs to find a way of thinking and feeling about Louis that is safer for her emotionally, and more therapeutically effective than what is currently occurring, as illustrated in Box 2.3.

Melanie is able to think these issues through in supervision. Her first task to achieve this will be to observe herself in her relationship to Louis and his family. Psychoanalysis, in particular, has found itself very preoccupied with the dangers of becoming too close to clients. Kristeva's theory of abjection (1982) and Mary Douglas' work on the body as a symbol of coherence (1980) are relevant here. According to their ideas, all of us (whether client or therapist) are terrified of losing our precarious grasp on our sense of wholeness and as such find the dissolution of boundaries, of whatever sort, destabilising. This subconscious terror (on the part of the therapist) is hard wired into our constitutions and is a key factor driving the construction of boundaries within therapeutic relationships.

Other commentators have come up with rather less dramatic reasons for stressing the importance of treatment boundaries. Lomas suggests that there is a limit to the degree of emotional commitment of which we are capable: 'In therapy if the practitioner is to survive, the appropriate limits must not be exceeded' (Lomas, 1981: 148). Many practitioners would undoubtedly recognise the validity of this. And it is important for Melanie and Gill to understand how this can happen.

Menzies-Lyth's research with nurses who were exposed to very high levels of emotional need in clients, over long periods of time, identified the role of unconscious processes in undermining the conditions of social care (Menzies-Lyth, 1960). She found that nurses could not cope with the intensity of contact, would switch off from their clients and/or develop serious stress-related problems. Menzies-Lyth advocated the need for adequate supervision and training for nurses involved in such emotional labour. An important implication of her work for RT is that adhering to work boundaries is one way for us to preserve ourselves, particularly with clients with very complex mental health problems, and those with whom we spend long periods of time.

For many workers in the fragmented world of modern children's services, spending long periods of time with clients is an occupational hazard all too easily avoided. Contemporary children's services are littered with structures and processes compelling practitioners to engage in short-term interventions. We have some sympathy for this and the introduction of these ideas may in some cases come about as a backlash to the excessive time and resources that went into long-term unfocused work. Furthermore, for some specific difficulties, there is evidence for the effectiveness of short-term interventions over longer-term ones, particularly those that have a very clear intervention framework (Van IJzendoorn, Juffer, & Duyvesteyn, 1995).

However, we do not know of any studies of short-term interventions that have been able to demonstrate long-term positive outcomes for families living in constellated disadvantage. Most of these studies do not consider a holistic and systemic approach to children and families, hence therapeutic interventions such as Basics (see Chapter 3) are ignored. And a further trouble with many short-term interventions is that they take too narrow a view of a child's situation or difficulty. It seems almost trite to say, but a validated four-session, clinic-based intervention to increase the sensitivity of Louis' mother as a parent certainly will not work if she does not turn up, or if she is not in when the practitioner calls. We know from the work on multi-systemic practice, assertive outreach and other therapy outcome studies, that making and sustaining a good therapeutic alliance is key to success (Hart, Saunders, & Thomas, 2005). If we are to support short-term interventions in these situations, then it has to be done with care and sensitivity to the whole and is probably best delivered in the context of other long-term therapeutic commitments.

Our approach to Commitment is rooted in psychodynamic approaches to therapeutic engagement. This is because psychodynamic therapists were the first to take the issue of Commitment very seriously. They spell out to clients precisely how long they will spend with them and avoid going back on what they have agreed to. Reliability and predictability are key features in this work. Their approach is underpinned by acknowledging the importance of attachment relationships. RT takes up these psychodynamic insights and applies them to all practitioners.

The consequences of this for Gill is that she starts her consultation with Melanie by finding out how long Melanie is able to commit to being involved with the family. We have to recognise that other factors cut across this. High staff turnover, fragmented models of care and highly depart-mentalised social services will mean that Louis and his family find them-selves allocated to a succession of teams and individual workers, at the cost of long-term relationships. It is vital, if RT is to work, that the limitations that these organisational structures and processes put in place are in the frame from the start. If we can gain Commitment from Melanie to stay long-term involved, this will give us the possibility of much better outcomes.

Let us assume Melanie is able to give that commitment. Then she could be encouraged by Gill to reflect that in a commitment to regular meetings with Jane and other family members, and Gill suggests that she puts that in writing. The family should know how long Melanie plans to work with them. Ideally, a model of long-term (but not necessarily intensive) involve-ment, with the potential to move on to a health-promotion approach should be held in mind. What we know of Commitment is that when practitioners embrace it they can modulate the level of their involvement over time and in response to the outcomes achieved. There may have to be periods of time when it is more intensive, but our experience is that it is not the rule.

We also realise that the culture of Melanie's working environment may incline more to prioritising crisis work so that other planned work gets demoted. In our experience we have found that court work, for example, is frequently privileged to such an extent that field workers often seem to find it impossible to make any regular Commitments to clients in the course of their other work. In fact they often report that they avoid making a regular commitment just in case they end up having to disappoint children by cancelling appointments. Given what resilience researchers have discovered about the value of Commitment in relationships for disadvantaged chil-dren, this practice needs addressing. To work within a resilient frame argues for a shift in organisational culture, as we shall see in Chapter 8.

To sum up our discussion in this section, making an explicit Commitment to clients forms part of RT. Thinking about Commitment explicitly helps us to check that we are taking a balanced approach. It encourages us to consider our own fears of dependency and enmeshment. Adopting a Commitment agenda also guards against defensive practice in which we distance ourselves so far from clients that we are not sufficiently emotionally engaged to be of use to them. Thus committed, workers are more likely to be able to set in motion, and to sustain, resilient mechanisms. In the world of constellated disadvantage there are few quick fixes. Having practitioners who know children's histories because they have been involved with them over time, helps us better understand what might be helpful to try. This gives us the chance of making resilient mechanisms work to best effect.

Enlisting

Should Melanie and her RT mentor Gill go it alone or should they get other people involved to help out? If they do engage others, who should they be and how best do Melanie and Gill work with them in this particular context of constellated disadvantage? Finally, how do they persuade others that their approach is the most appropriate course of action? These are some of the questions that the Noble Truth 'Enlisting' helps us to focus on.

In contemporary British children's services the idea of 'joined-up' working between the different service traditions of health, education and social services has a long history. Policy documents continue to emphasise its importance (Department for Education and Skills, 2003), and the notion of the 'team around the child' is now commonplace in practice. On the ground, whatever the precise organisational arrangements, we can see that different agencies are now aware of the need to work more closely together.

Enlisting dovetails the right resources, through the appreciation of exactly what different people need to do. This is one aspect of the management of effective detail. It ensures that people are working in synergy and with an appreciation of how what might seem like a resilient move can turn out differently when looked at in the bigger picture. This is a systemic resilient point. Strategically thinking about what needs to happen, when, and by whom, fits with Rutter's ideas about resilient mechanisms (Rutter, 1999). As we saw in Chapter 1, resilience is a conceptual extraction to which we can put a name—an identifiable result of an ordinary magical process or of a set of ordinary magical processes observable at a given point in time. Carter and New see these kinds of extractions as 'recognisable points at which structure mediates agency by constraining, enabling and generally motivating people's actions in ways that give rise to certain tendencies' (Carter & New, 2004: 23). Enlisting is the process of orchestrating the right people and organisations into the right place to make resilient moves when and where they need to be made.

We emphasise the need to be strategic here since Enlisting, when not undertaken in a careful and considered way, can actually result in negative chain reactions rather than positive ones. We have a number of further thoughts to add here. First, we should remember that the people we enlist do not necessarily have to do anything, although of course they have to be prepared to do something. Having them standing by as a result of pro-actively planning for different eventualities, rather than simply reacting in a crisis, is part of resilient practice. A simple analysis of Louis' family context would tell us that Jane's mental health is essential to family health and stability. Therefore Melanie would be well advised to pay close attention to how she might enable Jane to receive speedy help should she need it through adult services via community mental health teams. This may involve enlisting new recruits, but attention should first be paid to old acquaintances. Keeping alive what we have learnt through Accepting, Conserving and Commitment is crucial as potential RT practitioners may already be involved, or waiting in the wings, in any given context. For people living in constellated disadvantage this is not all good news. Coercion into dependency with professionals and their agencies is part of the fabric of their lives. Sometimes this gets forgotten, and they can be pilloried for being over-dependent when they have been compelled into it. More advantaged people are spared these humiliating dynamics.

Second, we want to overcome unnecessary intra-agency divisions. In England and Wales, within social services, for example, there are many different teams through which a child and their family can pass. Louis would have started by being referred to the Duty and Assessment Team. The case would then have been passed on to a long-term field work team. When Louis reaches 15, if he ends up in foster care, his case will be transferred to the 'Leaving Care Team'. And in health services children can get batted back and forth between different specialist teams. The divisions between children's and adult services may also need addressing. For Louis' sake, getting to grips with Jane's mental health difficulties is key.

Third, we need to be mindful of our earlier argument—the modern tendency to (re)produce chaos in the context of constellated disadvantage. Too much Enlisting and the child and family disappear. They may disappear behind a flurry of redundant, badly planned and ineffective meetings, letters and phone calls. Earlier in the chapter we noted how practitioners risk becoming too emotionally detached to be effective. However, there has been very little research conducted on how practitioners actually act in relation to taking initiative and responsibility when they are part of a network or team around a child. The findings from experimental psychological studies may suggest that being part of a network or a team can increase emotional detachment. Latane and Darley's research, for example, studied how many people came to the rescue of people needing emergency help. Their findings suggested that the more people available to help, the less likely they were actually to help (Latane & Darley, 1968, 1970; Nelkin, 2005). Of course, caution is in order when simply taking the findings of these experimental studies and applying them to the work of health and social care practitioners. Nevertheless, we see the relevance of such studies to the contexts within which we work.

Some teams around children look well resourced. However, when there are too many people involved in this complex, hard work what we term 'collaborative inertia' can set in, with nobody doing anything much to move things on. Poorly defined job descriptions and a lack of understanding of the necessary roles and tasks contribute, but lack of motivation is sometimes a feature too. Advantage can be taken when there seems to be more than enough hands to the pump. Some therapeutic approaches, such as Treatment Foster Care (Chamberlain, 1998), seem to go the other way with myriad roles rigorously defined such that flexibility and responsiveness to context are thwarted. Finally, professional involvement can all too quickly fade when people get new jobs, move on, become overwhelmed and defensive or lose interest in the case when change does not come quickly enough. Sometimes this fragmented Enlisting can become a hazard enshrined in organisations too, as we will see in Chapter 8.

Fourth, in the light of ideas from schools of therapy, we also want to include the notion that as RT practitioners we need to enlist the most appropriate parts of ourselves. This is not just about other people and other agencies. Family therapists, particularly those working in the multi-systemic tradition (Henggeler, Schoenwald, Rowland, & Cunningham, 2002), will have experience of Enlisting. We can use ideas from psychoanalysis to understand Enlisting as a way of putting us in touch with, and then drawing on, different parts of ourselves. Here we are talking both professional and personal selves. Melanie Klein, child psychoanalyst, was the originator of the concept of 'splitting'. Bits of ourselves that seem unbearable become separated (Klein, 1975). We can use her ideas to help us to work effectively with the emotional aspects of Enlisting, guarding against flitting from one extreme position to another, and reflecting the all too frequent dynamics operating in constellated disadvantage. As we have seen with projection, there is a real tendency for us all to be overwhelmed by the power of disadvantaged circumstances. This can be reflected in how we enlist too.

Of course the story we sign up to is that we enlist others to help a child or family. However, sometimes we will enlist others because the burden is too great to go it alone. At other times it is because we cannot cope with the frustrations that the child and family bring us and so we want to push them on to someone else at least for a bit of a rest. In every case it is best to recognise our motivations for what they are. Some of them are legitimate. Recognition of the limitations of our ability to work independently can of course be put to the service of the family in RT. There is no point in going it alone if we are not up to the job. Conversely, if RT is to be effective, we also need to guard against fragmenting the dynamics even further.

Finally, the Noble Truth of Enlisting is there to remind us that we need to educate others in our approach and in the keys to resilience for children. Enlisting, for example to the army, connotes a top-down activity. However, we can reframe the concept as RT Enlisting other people to give them the opportunity to learn how to work with its principles and techniques. And our experience of developing RT tells us that we learn as much from others as we can teach them. So, reframing the concept of Enlisting in this way draws our attention to the limits of our own knowledge and experience. It is not just a matter Enlisting *people*. Enlisting the *evidence base* in the context of constellated disadvantage is part of the RT approach. Melanie's understanding of Jane's depression and how it affects her life, as well as an awareness of validated treatments for adult depression, could certainly help keep life sufficiently stable for Louis.

'All for one and one for all'

We want to end this section by reflecting on what might seem to some readers to be the evangelical zeal with which we have set up our Noble Truths. We are unapologetic about this. Alongside recognising the dangers of dogmatism and professional closure, we draw attention to the cynicism, defeatism and lack of focused discipline in modern public services. Sometimes it seems that the fact that we are paid public servants with a public service ethos is, like vocation, a lost relic of an antique world. RT is our attempt to make explicit the ways in which we aspire to practice our own public service. And this is not unbridled martyrdom or self-sacrifice. Research evidence increasingly confirms Aristotle's principles of the good life. We know that helping other people, and engaging in community service, is a key contributor to an individual's happiness. In fact, once needs for food, shelter and clothing are fulfilled, it is more important in predicting happiness than anything else including wealth (Layard, 2005).

Of course, although this work might serve to make us happier and more fulfilled, we are not claiming that RT and its Noble Truths will solve children's problems overnight. For us this book is just a beginning. There is a great deal in our methodology that is still at the level of tacit daily practice. There is much in the resilience research that has yet to be connected to therapeutic practice. So, while there is mileage still in developing RT we frame our own Commitment to the methodology and its further development as a resilient move.

In this chapter we introduced the four Noble Truths—Accepting, Conserving, Commitment and Enlisting. Our hope is that other practitioners will take these Noble Truths and consider them in relation to their own practice. The first two Noble Truths—Accepting and Conserving—drew on

Rogerian and psychoanalytic ideas. Accepting refers to the need for RT practitioners to engage precisely where people are at, including an awareness of their legacies and history. Conserving is a more complex concept. It incorporates principles of containment. However, the symbolism and metaphor through which we explain the concept relate as much to ecology and growth as it does to babies and mothers in the Winnicottian tradition.

Commitment, too, emerges from the psychoanalytic tradition, and also has vocational origins. Enlisting refers to two processes within the practitioner self, and two outside. Mobilising different aspects of the practitioner self, and enlisting the evidence base are the two that focus on working within the practitioner. The process of drawing up a sophisticated team around a child, as well as educating others about the RT approach are processes that will involve the resilient therapist with others.

We think that we have now sufficiently spelt out what preparation RT practitioners need and from where they should start. So, we now move on to exploring the detailed practice of RT. The first compartment we take out for examination is Basics.

Chapter 3

Basics as a fundamental part of Resilient Therapy

What do we live for, if it is not to make life less difficult for each other?

George Eliot

Introduction

This is the first of five chapters exploring the components of what resilient therapists can call upon to make effective interventions. Basics introduces a critical dimension to therapeutic working and is central to a resilient approach. It encompasses fundamental needs and is designed specifically to tackle deprivation and the health inequalities associated with it. Getting to grips with Basics is crucial for therapeutic engagement and efficacy and can work synergistically with other components of RT. Our case example featuring Jason's family and the workers involved details how this work can be taken forward in practice.

We know that some of the most fundamental aspects of human existence will have a big effect on the kind of life that young people such as Jason will lead—a decent roof over his head in a decent neighbourhood, enough money coming in to pay the rent, to buy nutritious food and to keep him and his family warm and safe. The foreword to the National Service Framework in England and Wales warns:

> . . . [I]nequalities still impact on children and young people. Some find it difficult to access the services they need, simply because of where they live or because of their circumstances. Child poverty, though greatly reduced, still means that children and young people from disadvantaged backgrounds risk not realizing their full potential. Life expectancy and infant mortality is greater in disadvantaged areas and among disadvantaged groups.
>
> (Department for Education and Skills & Department of Health, 2004: 2)

Evidence shows that reductions in child poverty are linked with reductions in premature deaths (DeNavas-Walt, Proctor, & Lee, 2005; Mitchell,

Dorling, & Shaw, 2000). We have known for some years now that it is the relativity of inequality—i.e. being worse off than others in the same society—which is particularly damaging (Wilkinson, 1997). Having these basic inequalities addressed makes the biggest difference to happiness and good mental health (Layard, 2005). Furthermore, prejudice and discrimination in relation to race, gender, sexuality, age and disability negatively affect many people's quality of life, including their mental health (Melzer, Jenkins, & Fryers, 2003; Tew, 2005).

It is fairly easy to see why. The mechanisms involved in meeting basic needs have been considered at some length. Decreasing stressors, so that people are freed up to manage their lives, and securing a safe environment, so that risks are reduced, are part of what needs to occur. Improving self-esteem and self-efficacy also feature. As Sennett and others have argued, inequality can breed a lack of respect from those who have, and deep feelings of inadequacy from those who have not (Sennett, 2003). No wonder, then, that the links between being poor and being depressed are so clear (Murali & Oyebode, 2004). And the relationship between poor mental health and poor physical health is well established (Mitchell, Dorling, & Shaw, 2000).

The members of Jason's family form part of these statistics. We begin this chapter by emphasising the following: attending to the compartment and its component interventions in Basics (summarised in Box 3.1) is fundamental. They should not be treated as afterthoughts, nor should they be simply taken into consideration as contextual variables.

Box 3.1 The Basics

- Good-enough housing
- Enough money to live
- Being safe
- Access and transport
- Healthy diet
- Exercise and fresh air
- Play and leisure opportunities
- Being free from prejudice and discrimination

Basics and Resilient Therapy

Basics comes first in our elaboration of RT. You might read this as an intervention according to Maslow's hierarchy of needs—ensuring that the people you work with have their basic needs met before we move on to matters of a higher order (Maslow, 1943). We do not see it like that. For us, there is no reason why Basics cannot be worked on at the same time as Coping, say, or Learning. We have put them first because we want to emphasise Basics. So their inclusion as the first compartment is as much a political act as it is anything else—it is to remind us that this is a fundamental area of work for resilient therapists. For some, this may seem obvious, and you might be used to directing your attention towards them to good effect. But others may need convincing. As we explore in Chapter 9, the case for attending to the basics as central to a therapeutic agenda is not integral to many therapeutic approaches.

We want to explain how connected 'Basics' is with resilience. Few make a theoretical case for this, although we can easily see how some of the definitions of resilience included in Box 1.1. in Chapter 1 (p. 10) would readily encompass this perspective. Ungar's definition of resilience as 'adequate provision of health resources necessary to achieve good outcomes in spite of serious threats to adaptation or development' (Ungar, 2005b: 6) is one clear example.

Prilleltensky and Prilleltensky make the boldest statement that we have seen on the interrelationship between Basics and resilience. They suggest that resilience as a concept needs to be redefined:

> Resilience must go beyond a phrase limited to understanding how individuals cope with adversity. It must entail a challenge to the very structures that create disadvantage, discrimination and oppression. This is not to pile more responsibilities on people who already experience challenges in their lives . . . Professionals cannot stand back and hope that personal resilience will emerge from their therapeutic interventions alone.
>
> (Prilleltensky & Prilleltensky, 2005: 101)

For the Prilleltenskys, 'Resilience stems in part from the capacity and opportunity to understand the role of adversity to one's life and the role of individuals and groups to challenge systems of inequity and discrimination' (Prilleltensky & Prilleltensky, 2005: 93). We go further still, and insist that in RT practitioners challenge and address social and other inequalities in their practice as part of a resilience agenda.

However, even the Prilleltenskys' somewhat less ambitious project has not as yet been firmly embedded in the practice-based resilience literature up until now. Pick up any texts that are practice applications of the resilience research base and you would certainly have been led to ideas and strategies that relate to some elements of those represented through RT. Yet when it comes to finding texts on the practice application of resilience concepts for tackling poverty, prejudice and other basic issues, we find that they are thin on the ground.

Most books offering advice to practitioners on helping young people develop resilience seem to take a context of social and economic deprivation as a constant, a 'factor' or 'variable' to be taken into account, rather than itself a potential focus for resilient interventions. Just therapy, which we consider more in Chapter 9, is the main exception (Waldegrave, Tamasese, Tuhaka, & Campbell, 2003).

If we want to find ideas on how to apply Basics as part of a resilient approach, we must turn to a different literature base; one developed largely through applying ideas from sociology, public health and social policy, rather than psychology and social work. Elsewhere, one of us has drawn on this interdisciplinary resource to develop a model for helping practitioners to think about practice in relation to tackling inequalities. As we explained in Chapter 1, this is known as the development of an 'inequalities imagination' and the model gives examples of how this is actually achieved in practice (Hall & Hart, 2004; Hart, Hall, & Henwood, 2003).

As we have already suggested, many practitioners working in constellated disadvantage do not have personal experience of growing up in such surroundings. A focus on 'imagination' takes us in the direction of people really understanding what it might be like for other people whose lives are very different from their own. In teaching professional courses, the concept can be used to good effect to help students put themselves in the shoes of those they work with and to develop empathy and understanding. Holding in mind the concept of imagination sensitises us to practice that is responsive, creative and mindful of the need to manage detail effectively, rather than bureaucratically and defensively. Practitioners who have developed an inequalities imagination may better develop the capacity to work in a way that systematically addresses inequalities. However, for some, imagination is still no substitute for actual experience. The journalist Polly Toynbee's book *Hard Work* neatly explores these issues (Toynbee, 2003). The book is an account of her sabbatical, as an undercover participant observer, working in low-pay jobs in contemporary inner-city London. Throughout it she constantly reflects on the difference between her own privileged life and that of her new colleagues.

Most would accept that some practitioners should have a role in addressing inequalities. Social workers, certainly, we might think. But if we were to be speaking of, say, a psychologist working in a child and adolescent mental health service or a school counsellor, many would argue that addressing Basics should be beyond their scope. Indeed, inequalities have been far from a central concern in the way therapeutic disciplines have evolved. Lack of time to work in this way is sometimes given as a reason. The absence of transparent casework audit trails enables this to be a coup de grâce that is hard to tackle head on.

Spoiling the purity of the therapeutic relationship is yet another reason given. This is a point of some moment. We have observed that novice resilient therapists trained psychodynamically often become preoccupied with, and anxious about, these matters. They are used to concentrating on the inner worlds of their clients, on matters such as transference and countertransference. In such a professional culture, external issues are raised purely to demonstrate the context within which the client–therapist relationship is developing. This selective attention, marginalising the ontological dimension, has been the hallmark of therapeutic scholarship in the 20th century. As we have seen earlier, RT directly challenges this idea. RT sees such work as the future and compelling business of all of us in the helping professions. Its importance compels us to give it the priority *within* the therapeutic endeavour that it deserves. Macrostatistics on increased inequalities in infant mortality, persistent child poverty and the many miseries of living on benefits or low pay should move us all into taking on our share of this work.

But how to tackle these difficulties? Many argue that a whole-systems approach is the only effective way forward. The need for wealth redistribution and a reduction in the tax burden for lower earners is a popular concept to which the analysts of health and social inequalities and campaigning groups continually return (Fimister, 2001; Kleinman, 2000).

We need no convincing that whole-population work is what will be most effective and that political will and a long attention span should be found to tackle inequalities. However, this knowledge does little to help resilient therapists do their job. As practitioners working in contexts of disadvantage week in, week out, our own view is that much can be done through RT to combat health inequalities of individuals, families and organisations. At the heart of RT there is a necessity to raise the status of direct work. Remember Pfeffer's point, 'Unless and until we are willing to come to terms with organisational power and influence, and admit that the skills of getting things done are as important as the skills of figuring out what to do, our organisations will fall further and further behind' (Pfeffer, 1992: 12). Changing the language we use to describe the relative contributions of workers may help. For example, we should stop describing front-line work as low-status training posts. Rather, front-line workers are at the 'sharp end'. Using this image, it follows that managerial functions are performed at the 'blunt end'.

In our context, getting things done means being imaginative and managing effective detail in order to improve outcomes for individual children. As we shall see in Chapter 8, taking an organisational approach to RT helps us see what can be done at that level to achieve more widespread change. While we are in agreement with leading policy analysts Hunter and Killoran (2004: 6) that holism is desirable in principle, but difficult to achieve in practice, we know that the energy and Commitment that is central to the RT approach produces results. It is our experience that using individual cases as illustrations makes it much more likely that we can achieve those wider organisational and societal shifts. Where broader changes need to be made, bringing in the detail and life of these cases animates the reality behind policy rhetoric and generalisations.

Jason, his family and Basics

Jason, you may recall, is a 15-year-old young man facing many challenges. One of five children, he is hardly ever at home. Jason spends his days stealing from shops and prostituting himself. Being arrested and beaten up by clients feature a lot. Identity issues are rarely in his consciousness, but one of the reasons that Jason truanted from school was because he was bullied for being gay and taunted by the other children for being 'half caste'. The following few paragraphs fill you in a bit more on Jason's world, and that of his sister Lucy.

Jason's youngest sister Lucy (8) is the other sibling who has a particularly hard time of it. She has muscular dystrophy and asthma. Lucy frets that her 'poorly body' as she calls it, has made Alice, her mum, go mental. Alice devours family packs of crisps, guzzles enormous bottles of fizzy pop, and chain smokes. She adds packets and bottles to the pile next to the sofa every day as she sits and watches television. One day, Lucy overheard her mother's doctor getting very cross. He said to Alice that she was getting so fat that she might have to go hospital to be wired up or something, and they would have to take the kids away. A few other people came round to tell off Alice. But those chats did not stop her sitting indoors every day bingeing and smoking. It did not get her to sort out all the stinking washing, which Lucy tried once to do herself. And it did not make her take a walk down to the shops.

Not that Lucy wants to go out much herself. She gets bullied by other children. There is something good on the horizon for her though. When she goes to bed at night Lucy does not count sheep—she counts bully busters in the playground. Soon she will get to be one and then maybe she will stop feeling like she might die soon. Who knows, thinks Lucy, her mum might even get to be less mental.

This all sounds very bleak, we know, but Lucy does have an adult in her life who has begun to make a real difference since she started working with the family six months ago. Social worker Julie plans to stay in this job for at least five years and her Commitment has a monetary incentive as well. She is on a scheme that rewards social workers for working in areas of constellated disadvantage. This is something that RT would support, but at the moment is more fantasy than reality. Lucy talks to Julie about all her problems, something which Julie saw recorded as Lucy's 'multiple comorbidity'.

Lucy's favourite time of the week is when Julie comes round for about an hour, always at four o'clock on a Friday afternoon. The best time, Lucy thinks, is the fifteen-minute chat that the two of them always have. They sit in the kitchen away from the television and the smoke. Lucy saves up all her worries in a special part of her head and spills a lot of them out to Julie. She has told Julie about being called nasty names at school, and that Jason is never at home. She has even said how lonely she gets with nobody much to play with and nowhere to go and that she would like to go to a holiday club for children with disabilities. Lucy would have liked to have told Julie about how worried she is that her mother might die, and that she keeps overhearing people say to Alice that she needs to stop smoking and lose weight. But she is afraid that if she does that, Julie will be the one to take her and the others away from Alice. Although it is not that good at home, it is the home she knows with her mother in it who likes watching the Simpsons with her.

Lucy is vaguely aware that it was Julie who arranged for them to have their first-ever holiday—two weeks in a holiday camp coming up next month. Thinking about the holiday makes Lucy really wish that Julie were a second mother to her or, at the very least, that she would come away with them. The thought of going on holiday without Julie takes up a very big space in her little head. Her biggest fears are that they will get lost on the train on the way there and that they won't have enough money to get home again. But she doesn't feel quite brave enough to tell Julie all that.

No wonder Lucy is worried. Poverty is very much part of the constellation of inequality in this family. On paper, it looks like they access health and social care services. But, there is little food in the fridge and the three-bedroomed house is far too small for them all—Alice, Lucy's stepfather Carl and Jason, when they are both around, Mat (13), Melanie (10), Lucy (8) and Brian (6). Lucy is still sleeping on a bed in the corner of the sitting room because she can no longer manage the stairs.

Gendered oppression features too. Money is particularly tight when stepfather Carl is around. Carl is a physically violent bully to an easily bullied Alice, but luckily he ignores the children most of the time rather than taking his own distress out directly on them. Of course, they suffer from being exposed to what he does to Alice and from his neglect of them. He cashes all the family's benefits and spends most of them on alcohol and gambling. When he is not there the fridge has more in it. This is because Alice has to ask her friend to go to the post office to cash the benefits cheques instead of him. Anyway, Alice hardly ever leaves the house so she can't do it herself. She used to work in a shop before the children were born. For the past seventeen years she has suffered with agoraphobia.

Preparing to tackle the Basics: Spotlight on the Noble Truths

Taking an upbuilding approach to the interventions in Box 3.1 shows that, although things look very bleak, there is a lot we can do. Julie understands the need to think about the family's difficulties strategically. Also, she needs to strike the right balance between avoiding focusing solely on Lucy and becoming overwhelmed by everybody else's needs. She bears in mind that little things she might do, could have big consequences. She cannot see how it will work, but Julie has a very imaginative concept of what might count as doing something therapeutic.

In planning her work with the family, Julie thinks precisely about who she needs to enlist to help her. Her first potential ally is, of course, Alice. So, Julie talks to her to find out how she sees her own role in relation to all the workers already involved in this family. Alice complains that there are so many people that she can not remember all their names, or what they do. Julie works with Alice to clarify this and to reposition Alice in the adult network, even just a little. Alice will need support in moving towards occupying a proactive, partnership status alongside practitioners working with the family. However, Julie structures her thinking resiliently, explicitly sharing with Alice the idea that the small moves she makes can set this in motion. She also understands that helping Alice to reposition herself as part of the solution, rather than the problem, will also probably improve her mental health.

A seemingly insignificant practical task is what actually sets them on this path. Julie gets on and helps Alice to sort out the mess of paperwork that she has discarded behind the sofa alongside the crisp packets and fizzy-pop bottles. Julie brought along new bright plastic folders to separate the letters and paperwork that had come over the past few years dealing with each of the different children. She paid for them from her own money and hopes that she will get it back from her organisation. A colleague told her off for this. Ideally, she said, Julie should have suggested that Alice went out and got them, but Julie's acceptance of precisely where Alice is attunes her to the fact that this would have been a step too far.

An entire positive chain of action could have become held up while Julie sourced the money for Alice to get them. Then Alice would have failed to go anyway because she is agoraphobic at present and would not see buying folders as a priority. This is not surprising since she has not even been to the school gates for two years. This example brings home the fact that small moves can have big consequences, and that positive chain reactions can result from them.

Once engaged in the process, Alice began to enjoy the sorting out. She tackled the job with someone else facilitating. It felt comfortable and collaborative and began to shift her away from being a passive recipient of service provision. In amongst the standard copies of medical assessments, social services review paperwork, warning letters from schools and social services, and educational statement reviews she found a few gems. Rereading the birthday card from her former psychiatric nurse, who had moved to another authority, switched Alice's internal rage at the professionals involved over the years to a softer feeling. She could then see the letter from Julie to her and Lucy saying exactly when she was coming round every week as a symbol of a promise kept rather than more interference and intrusion. Thinking how Julie had kept her promise, and working with her to sort out the paperwork, helped Alice experience someone who cared about her family. Despite all the help, she had rarely had that feeling in the past.

The best thing was the warm letter and photo of Alice, Lucy and the other children at the annual picnic run by a charity supporting parents of children with special needs. Even Jason turned up for it, and so did Carl—sober. Alice was proud that she had actually got out of the house that day so it was good to have the reminder. Julie, noticing Alice's mood lift when looking at the picture, suggests that she puts it on top of the television so that she can see it all the time.

For Alice, this simple sorting task rekindled memories of better times. It reminded her of the kind of thing she did when she worked in a shop years ago; a time when she had a reputation as being the one who could put her finger on important paperwork in an instant.

As they sort through the paperwork, Alice and Julie build up a picture of the roles and functions of each of the practitioners involved with different family members. Julie writes their names down on a sheet of paper and puts what their job is next to it and who in the family they are mainly working with. She also tries to put down what they are doing to help the family, but soon realises that for some of them she is not clear herself. This remains true even when she has looked at the relevant paperwork. Julie says to Alice that she will photocopy the sheet of paper and give her a copy. Even with the twenty-eight practitioners they have identified as currently being involved with the family, Julie can not see that any of them has tackled what Alice tells her is her main priority. This involves getting more space for the family to live in. The boys' bedroom is hardly bigger than a cupboard and Lucy has no privacy. And, most important, Alice thinks that if they sorted this out Jason would spend more time at home.

Julie has another Basics priority that she hopes someone might be able to help with. The household nutritional intake is very worrying. She does not burden Alice with her thoughts on this at the moment. Julie thinks that Alice probably knows she should not be eating all the junk food. She has enough imagination to realise that there have probably been at least twenty people telling Alice that over the past few years. Plus, Julie knows how much television Alice watches, and she is sure diet and exercise would have been mentioned on the chat shows she watches. So, Julie wants to wait to talk about it until she thinks she's found something that will move the family in a positive direction.

Julie arranges a meeting and invites everyone involved with the family to attend—the practitioners including the special educational needs coordinator from Lucy's school and Alice's friend Carol. Of course in this situation, arranging a meeting where people are actually likely to turn up, and then undertake some effective practice as a result of the meeting, is far easier said, or indeed written, than done. Despite policy exhortations to work together with other agencies and practitioners, and despite the obvious sense of more joined-up approaches, how actually to achieve success in this area is rarely something that we have seen tackled by professional courses in social work, psychiatry, psychology, nursing or therapy, beyond implicitly in practice placement. Once again, this comes down to the management of effective detail. Yet another reminder of Pfeffer's suggestion that the skills of doing really need to be taken more seriously (Pfeffer, 1992).

Exploring the Basics compartment

Our final task in this chapter is to take a direct look at Basics to show you what remedies are contained within it, and to illustrate our use of them through practice examples.

Good-enough housing

Housing inequality is often a key feature of the lives of children and families living in constellated disadvantage. We take our evidence from the UK, but the picture is similar, and often worse, for disadvantaged children elsewhere. In Britain, more than one million children live in poor housing, with black and ethnic minority children featuring more in the statistics than white children (Preston, 2005: 188). Disabled children are disproportionately represented too (Burchardt, 2006). More than half a million households are overcrowded, and record numbers of homeless families are in temporary accommodation (Thomas & Dorling, 2004). Furthermore, poor housing has a close association with health inequalities (Thomas & Dorling, 2004). Fuel poverty, damp houses, and housing situated on busy roads has been linked with lung disease, for example (National Energy Action, 2005). At their website, http://www.nea.org.uk/About_us, National Energy Action has collated valuable research resources on this topic, as well as training guides for front-line practitioners. And the disparity between people with collateral and those without, leads those who are unlucky enough to be born into housing poverty very likely to stay there. If current trends continue, in thirty years' time the 10% of children in the wealthiest areas will have access to more than 100 times the housing wealth than the 10% of children growing up in the poorest parts of the UK (Thomas & Dorling, 2004). All this should be proof enough that anything practitioners can do to help improve the housing situation for families living in constellated disadvantage should feature in a resilience-building approach.

Inheriting property or, indeed, owning a house that can be remortgaged to tide them through bad times has not figured in Jason's family. Julie is not thinking home ownership; the issues are far more basic than that. She knows that being offered a bigger house from the council would be Alice's preferred option, but her local knowledge of the housing situation and how houses are allocated makes her consider this to be completely unrealistic. She notes, however, that there is a large garden at the back of the house and that it may be possible to persuade the council (with the right lobbying) to build on a bedroom for Lucy and another bathroom. Julie prioritises this idea for action, and she seeks Alice's support in preparing this aspect of the meeting. She invites the assigned housing officer along to the meeting. And once the meeting is underway, they find out that Jason's social worker is ready to support them in this idea. They discover that the social worker has long thought that Jason would spend more time at home if there was actually room for him.

As well as the family needing more living space, there are, of course, other issues that Julie needs to consider in relation to securing an adequate living environment. At the moment the house is very dirty and in a complete mess. Julie has made a start by helping Alice to sort out her paperwork. However, the family need regular domestic support. In the old days Julie would have had to carry out an assessment of Lucy's needs, then request funding from her manager for a worker to come in and do the housework. We would like to think that she could have the authority to consider the family's needs holistically and to make some budgetary decisions herself. Then she would consider that rather than having a cleaner, the family could do with some help in learning how to manage the household. So, let us imagine she arranges for a Family Aid, who also will work on getting family members involved in the task, to come round at set times for a few months, with a yearly follow-up. Julie knows that the Family Aid will have her work cut out in engaging Alice and the children in cleaning up the house, but any small steps in this area may have big consequences later on. To prepare the family for this, Julie lends them recordings of a popular TV programme. She is surprised that they have not already seen it. In the programme two charismatic women help families to clean up their homes and Julie knows that this programme is presented in a way that Alice and her children will enjoy.

Enough money to live

Over the last six years 700,000 children have been officially lifted out of relative poverty in Britain. However, in 2006, the UK Labour administration missed its targets to reduce overall child poverty (Department for Work and Pensions, 2006). So, despite our benefits system, minimum wage and working family tax credits, in Britain figures collated by the Child

Poverty Action Group estimate that around 3,500,000 children continue to live in poverty (Child Poverty Action Group, 2006). As with housing inequalities, black, ethnic minority and disabled children are overrepresented in these figures (Burchardt, 2006). Enough justification now for this intervention to be included in Basics.

We know that all the children in Jason's family are part of this impoverished 3,500,000. But what can Julie do about it? First, she reviews that the family members are receiving all the benefits to which they are entitled, since she is aware that many people do not fully claim. To be sure that they are, she arranges for a welfare rights worker from the local charity for parents of children with disabilities to come along to the multi-disciplinary meeting that she has planned along with Alice. A further issue, which is most pressing, is for Julie to find a way to ensure that Carl no longer has direct access to the family's benefits. She will need advice from the welfare rights worker for this, as Julie has never met this specific difficulty until now.

Julie has another idea that relates to the family having enough money to live on. This concerns the links between unemployment and poverty. Both psychologically and practically, Alice seems a world away from being able to go to work herself at the moment. With two school-aged children and three others, even if she were not depressed, work might be far down on her list of priorities. However, Julie holds it in mind as a possibility for the future. Working family tax credit could be a resource that Alice might eventually use, even though Julie knows that accessing it is no guarantee that a family will be lifted out of poverty (Preston, 2005).

The poorest people in our society are those most often exposed to dangerous environments and, if employed, who often have stressful, unrewarding and depersonalising jobs. So, accessing work is not necessarily transformative. However, before she became ill, work was very important to Alice. Julie knows of the many schemes that successfully help people with mental illness to recover. Despite our caveat about the demeaning and underpaid work often done by people like Alice, we still acknowledge that achieving social inclusion, learning or demonstrating skills and increasing income by rejoining the workplace can contribute to mental health recovery (Crowther & Marshall, 2001). Julie understands these dilemmas and she holds in mind just how carefully thought through work options need to be in this family, if they are ever to be of benefit to Alice.

Any eventual decision by Alice to return to work will need to be considered alongside childcare issues too. For, although Alice does little to supervise her children at present, she is at least a predictable presence on the sofa in her living room most of the hours of the day, and she does ensure that there is some food for them when they are not at school. As Felner argues, it is important to ensure that work and childcare are considered together. 'Social programmes and policies that require parents to go to work or pursue training without providing for high-quality child-care are, in fact, asking parents to engage in what may well be chargeable neglect' (Felner, 2005: 144). Given Alice's current circumstances, for Julie these concerns are some way off. But if the time comes she will be able to address them. Let us imagine that Julie works in a local authority where back-to-work schemes and childcare schemes are well coordinated, and they all have integrated support for children with disabilities.

Being safe

With racially-motivated crime, bullying of disabled people, the dangers of muggings and other attacks concentrated in areas of high deprivation, it is often the most disadvantaged people who suffer (Ghate & Hazel, 2002). Living with the fear of attack is a cumulative stressor. It means that children have no secure base, and it also affects their sense of self-worth. Owing to the many environmental hazards parents find parenting more challenging in areas of low safety and high deprivation (Ghate & Hazel, 2002). Hence, strategies to improve physical safety should be fundamental to RT.

When thinking of safety issues for Jason's family, Julie has two main things in her mind. First, she wants to check how far family members feel safe in the neighbourhood and in school. She already knows from Lucy that bullying in school is one of the things that makes Lucy suffer. Hence she will be keen to hear from the school representative about how the bully-busting programme is working. She already knows that Lucy values this programme highly and it seems to be working in school. Bullying by other children is similarly an issue in the neighbourhood. So, Julie will want to ensure that school and the local neighbourhood regeneration scheme are coordinating their work.

Second, addressing safety issues would involve a much more delicate conversation with Alice. This means tackling Alice's current difficulties with being sufficiently emotionally available to her children to actually supervise them properly. Here, the main worry regarding safety in this family concerns Jason. Although the other children are poorly supervised by Alice, none is particularly inclined to venture far afield or to get into trouble with other children. However, Jason, as we know, is engaging in many unsafe practices. A way needs to be found to help Alice engage with the local Youth Offending Team social worker to begin to supervise his movements. The importance of regular and active supervision by parents of children and young people has a sound evidence base.

For example it is a cornerstone of the work of multi-systemic therapists whose model is firmly rooted in constellated disadvantage (Schoenwald, Brown, & Henggeler, 2000).

Julie notes that helping Alice improve her supervisory skills is likely to be slow work, and that first a rapport between Alice and the Youth Offending

Team social worker will need to be built up. At the moment, Alice seems hostile to the worker, but Julie has seen that she can be responsive to professional help. She suggests the worker undertakes some very practical, hands-on work with Alice. The aim of it would be to help Alice find ways of monitoring Jason's whereabouts and shifting their relationship in a way that moves Alice into a more authoritative parenting role. Julie knows that this work will be a very useful investment, if somewhat daunting. If Alice manages to improve her ability to do this with Jason, it will have a knock on effect with the other children and may avoid them following in their brother's footsteps.

Access and transport

Links between poor access, transport, health inequalities and social exclusion have begun to be highlighted and initiatives to address them are under way in various countries (Cass, Shove, & Urry, 2005; Clifton & Lucas, 2004). We know from a report by the Social Exclusion Unit on transport in the UK (Social Exclusion Unit, 2002) that too many people still encounter daily obstacles to the kind of mobility necessary in the 21st century to access services and to get to work. Examples of the difficulties that people face are numerous. Here are just a few. Food poverty affects people with poor access links and no transport as they are often unable to buy decent healthy food in their locality (Clifton, 2003a, 2003b). People with hip disease suffer more if they have no car for transport and children who live in areas with poor access links are less likely to be able to take part in social events and clubs (Eachus, Chan, Pearson, Propper, & Davey Smith, 1999).

How is this debate relevant to Julie's work with Jason's family? As Lucas (2004) points out, the convenience of car ownership is something that professionals like Julie are likely to enjoy. Julie is fit and active and chooses to ride her bike or walk around the town where she works but she has the imagination to hold in mind the fact that neither Alice nor Carl is a car owner, and neither is physically capable of walking very far at all. As is common in areas of high deprivation, the nearest bus stop can be a long way from the family home. A trip to some of the children's services in the local town is likely to take at least an hour and a half and involve several bus changes. In any case, in this family, Alice's agoraphobia precludes journeying out at the moment. However, Julie sees that if she is eventually to persuade Alice to go out, she will need to pick her up or ensure that taxis are provided for any suggested activities. Indeed, when Julie talks to Alice about what might help, she finds that an imaginative approach was taken the last time Alice went out to a picnic. The psychiatric nurse working with her at that time accompanied her and the family. They needed two taxis to get them all in. These were booked and paid for by social services, and the taxis turned up and ran on time.

Healthy diet

A reasonable diet is clearly associated with better health, and physical 'resilience', using the term in its most simplistic way. Positive mental health, too, is partly down to good diet (World Health Organization, 2003). Hence, successful attempts to improve children's diet will have a positive impact on their ability to withstand stresses and strains.

Julie is aware that much has been said by others about Alice's diet, and, indeed, that of the children, but always to little effect. Julie's conversations with Lucy have sometimes veered into food and cooking. Lucy is keen to garden. Imaginatively, Julie ties up Lucy's interest with the need to improve their diet. Her plan will mean that Lucy will learn some skills. Julie decides to ask the school to help her tackle this issue as she knows that they have an after-school allotment club.

Julie will also make sure that there will be some decent food available for Alice and for the workers when the multidisciplinary meeting is held. Her other plan is to over-cater so that the family can be left with some of the food. A problem like this one needs to be tackled on many different fronts. So, Julie also reverts to a successful strategy that she has used with the family in the past. She has a copy of a television programme in which a well-known celebrity chef helps a family to improve their eating habits. Given Alice's love of watching television, Julie imagines that she might well watch the programme, and, when the time is right, some of the messages she gets from it might sink in. Also, watching it with the children may stimulate them to lobby for better food. It is a long shot, Julie knows, but she has nothing to lose by trying it.

Exercise and fresh air

Successive policy makers have long pointed out the fundamental importance of exercise and fresh air. We know that they are correlated with achieving health equality (World Health Organization, 2003). But, once again, how can Julie use this common sense in her work? Julie knows that she already has a number of complex issues to attend to, and improving Alice's access to exercise and fresh air certainly seems far down the line. This distresses her, as Julie is very conscious of such matters, and she works hard to address the links between emotional and psychological wellbeing and physical fitness in her own life. For the moment though, in engaging Alice, her priorities are more to do with improving their housing and increasing the children's safety.

However, Julie is keen to consider whether the children are accessing as much exercise as they can. One issue she wants to raise is engaging them in sports clubs and after-school activities where they have such opportunities.

Access to the allotment club would be a good start. Lucy has already shared with Julie her loneliness and despair at not going to clubs and activities, so it's important for Julie to address this issue. Lucy's disabilities make the issue more complex to tackle when we think about exercise. The differences in the children's ages presents another challenge. Julie needs more local knowledge of special-needs clubs and inclusive after-school activities to make suggestions that will work. Julie is aware that, in the short term, Alice is unable to collect the children late from school and that she doesn't take any active part in helping them to access clubs and activities. This awareness helps Julie to be realistic, and to see that if the children are to take part in anything it will need to be coordinated and facilitated by workers involved with the family in order to get it going.

Play and leisure opportunities

Julie's strategic view on play and leisure for Lucy and her siblings ties in closely with her thoughts on their opportunities for fresh air and exercise. Yet this is no simple intellectual exercise. Her own feelings get muddled alongside and a slight labouring in her breathing signals to Julie that she needs to take some notice of them. Thinking about Lucy's play opportunities and what can be achieved by, with and for her makes Julie feel sad and anxious. These feelings come from the internal comparisons Julie is making between what Lucy has in her life and what Julie's own children experience. The gulf is so wide. Julie's anxiety reflects the enormity of her responsibility to help make things otherwise. It is also a respectful acknowledgement of just how bad things are for the children in this family at the moment and a reminder that it could, and should, be different.

Julie puts her own family to one side as she thinks about the specifics of Lucy's life. Having thought about her own girls for a minute was useful. First, because it helped her understand why she was affected. Second, because drawing the comparison made her aware that, although she is a mother, and already knows a lot about leisure activities for children, she does not have the local knowledge she needs to consider precisely what activities are available after school for Lucy and her siblings that are likely to work for the family. Julie wants to consider this issue at the multidisciplinary meeting alongside the SENCO from the school, and the special needs charity worker so they can match the children's interests and ages with what is available. Once they have a club in mind (and the allotment club may be the best bet), Julie will consider the logistics of how to ensure that Lucy can actually stay on after school at least for one session each week. And it is here that her breathing starts to labour again. Alice and her family have so little social capital to draw on. For the moment it seems like there are no friends or neighbours to step in and pick up the children when Alice is unable to make it to the school gate.

This may sound melodramatic. Families living in constellated disadvantage have few of the informal networks that provide the social support enjoyed by others (Parkes & Kearns, 2004). We know that this truth hurts those families, but it can also affect people who work with them. So, these are the kinds of emotions and experiences that practitioners may go through—resilient or otherwise. Best, then, to capture them so that we can explore and discover, through Julie and the others in the book, what can be done for effective practice. Having thought about the differences and similarities between her own family life and that of Alice enables Julie to draw on her private thoughts and feelings to serve Alice and her family rather than sabotaging her work with them. And in this ten-minute reflection she has processed her anxieties and can now hold them alongside other thoughts—moreover, it has made her aware of what can be done.

Julie knows that the town has opportunities for play and leisure for children with Lucy's disabilities, but for Lucy to access them much coordination is required. She has a number of children on her caseload who access the town's integrated clubs and activities with few problems, so she has not had to set her mind much to overcoming so many difficulties. Of course, when she analyses why this is so, she quickly realises that their parents or carers have been in a position to take the children to the clubs and play schemes. Lucy's situation is so much more complex. The family needs tailor-made help to get Lucy and her siblings to the activities.

Being free from prejudice and discrimination

There is no shortage of social-scientific literature detailing how prejudice and discrimination negatively affect a person's life experiences (Dominelli, 1997). They occur in all areas of life, and can mean unfair access to jobs, houses, schools, etc. They also impact on a person's self-identity, and can lead to an internalised sense of low self-worth. We know that health and social care workers, and the institutions within which they work, must guard against oppressing and discriminating against their clients (Hart & Freeman, 2005). So, any attempts to intervene in this way must start with workers thinking about what has been called an *inequalities imagination* (Hall & Hart, 2004). This describes their capacity to take themselves out of their familiar privileged position and envisage in detail what it would be like to live in persistent disadvantage.

In Jason's family prejudice and discrimination are part of the fabric of daily life. We have already seen how racist and homophobic taunts affect Jason's self-worth and how Lucy is the victim of prejudice from other children especially in relation to her disability. The stigma that Alice feels as a result of her mental-health difficulties and her obesity is not explicitly referred to by anybody, but Julie takes all this into account and she recognises its power. She knows that all the children are affected by it, as well as Alice. It is a part of the vicious circle that has maintained Alice's depression to date, and everything Julie does with Alice has this awareness at its heart. As well as the children, Alice's mental illness affects how neighbours, her friend and professionals see her. This can be termed 'devalued difference'. It gets internalised by Alice and she sees herself in an ever-increasing negative light.

One of Julie's goals in sorting out the folders with Alice and helping her to shift her subordinate position in the face of professional involvement, was to begin to disrupt the powerful external and internalised stigma that is woven into the fabric of this family's everyday life. Julie has developed her inequalities imagination to such a point that she can hold all these issues in mind. Then she acts on that awareness, filtering her own thoughts and suggestions for action through the lens of tackling prejudice and discrimination.

The most obvious example of this is Julie's commitment to improving Lucy's access to play and other leisure activities. Here we see an example of Julie putting the Noble Truth Commitment into practice. Reading about Julie may give the impression that she is an unrepresentative saint. She is good. However, the source of her effectiveness is RT. Seeing it work, and making it work are themselves resilient mechanisms that give a self-sustaining quality to Julie's relentless engagement.

Conclusion

Efforts to reduce health inequalities have received much attention since the mid-1990s in many Western countries. However, these debates, most often conducted in policy, public health and sociology circles, tend to be removed from the resilience literature, with its roots principally in developmental psychology and, more recently, social work. As we explained before, we have yet to come across another practice text that explicitly links resilience and Basics in the way we have outlined here.

This chapter has shown how important it is for resilient therapists to consider how to tackle Basics as core to their approach. Box 3.2 summarises key issues that you may find useful to consider when applying these ideas in practice. As we have demonstrated, Basics is not simply to be tackled as an add-on to other elements of RT. All resilient therapists will need to incorporate a consideration of Basics in their resilient work. Although we have used predominantly a social-work case scenario, all practitioners would need to think this way and ensure that Basics were addressed.

In relation to tackling inequalities, we now know what has to be done. To take Pfeffer further, it is the doing that now needs to be thought through carefully and given the *status* that it has not often enjoyed (Pfeffer,

Box 3.2 Developing Resilient Basics

- Think about the child and their family with an inequalities imagination. Tackling inequalities saves lives and improves quality of life.
- Learn how to set up an effective meeting, write persuasive letters and use secretarial and administrative staff to good effect.
- Don't just assume that someone else has checked that the child/family are getting their basic needs met. The mixed economy of care coupled with role fragmentation means that this family may not have been looked at in the way that you are looking at it.
- Have a working knowledge of the benefits system and understand precisely what it is that you can do to help the family get what they need.
- Understand your own personal process in relation to tackling the Basics. What similarities and differences are there between the families you work with and your own family circumstances and previous history? Explicitly consider how this helps or hinders the work you are doing.
- Know your networks and ensure that you facilitate contact between the family and other relevant agencies. Follow up any initial contact made.
- Find out what parents/carers do with all the paperwork they get through the letterbox. Make sure they get help in organising it if they need this help. This is often a big administrative task and demands skill and attention. Just getting on top of the paperwork can help people feel better.
- If you are working with an individual child, take the trouble to think about the child in their family and community context. There may be some help you can get that is intended for another family member, but which will also help the child you are working with.
- Consider how you can take what you're trying to achieve for an individual child up a further level—would other children in similar circumstances benefit from this support? Which strategic/political agendas do you need to influence?
- As a practitioner, you can do little about geographical inequalities. However, income inequalities and reduction in child poverty are issues you can tackle. Ensure that adults in the household you are working in have help to achieve employment if that is what they want.
- Press the agency you work for to develop explicit strategic partnerships with other agencies that have more experience in meeting basic needs. Check that the partnerships work by following through a selection of cases. The words 'referral' and 'liaison' are too vague and cover a multitude of sins.

1992). This chapter has made a start by drawing on what we know about effective inequalities work and integrating it into the RT approach.

Through giving voice to Julie's practice we have attempted to draw a picture to show how positive chain reactions can be set in motion and negative ones avoided. Part of this is understanding how Julie's own personal processes are part of the picture. Another part is to explain how seemingly insignificant things can potentially have major effects. Our focus now turns to a different family, different practitioners and a different compartment of RT—Belonging.

Chapter 4

Belonging

> One of the oldest human needs is having someone to wonder where you are when you don't come home at night.
>
> Margaret Mead

Introduction

Cast your mind back to that glimpse of 6-year-old Janice's story in Chapter 1. Imagine that the outcomes of love and care could be measured by the amount of public money that has been spent on adults trying to meet her needs during the past two years. The outcome of all this is far from something we might call well loved or well cared for. Nobody has stuck with Janice, and she has yet to find a safe place to call home.

As we will see later in this chapter, attachment theory can do much to explain Janice's current predicament. However, attachment theory only takes us so far (Hart & Luckock, 2004). Yet within the resilience-related developmental psychology literature, and indeed in social work, the concept of attachment holds a privileged position. In our day-to-day practice we notice time and time again that its explanatory value does not necessarily steer us towards resilient moves in contexts of constellated disadvantage.

Therefore our focus in this chapter is on the concept of Belonging and its practice application within RT. Belonging connects us to attachment theory and its valuable insights, but it also gives us freer rein to go out into the wider world and understand the role of other connections and affiliations.

As Sesma and colleagues point out, children develop in families, in schools, in neighbourhoods, and in the context of relationships. So any model attempting to enhance their resilience must attend to various settings (Sesma, Mannes, & Scales, 2005: 282). The legal status of children's relationships, where they live and under what conditions, is also intricately bound up with the issue of Belonging, and studies of fostering and adoption bring this home (Luckock & Hart, 2005).

It may not be stretching our argument too far to think of Belonging as a resilient concept. This is because Belonging can be understood as doing a lot more work than attachment theory. It gives us more possibilities of thinking how to effect change for children like Janice who have been failed by a focus on narrowly distilling attachment theory into practice applications.

The concept of Belonging has its home in sociology and anthropology, as well as in psychology and has not been refined through experimental studies in the way that attachment theory has (Bourdieu, 1996; Weston, 1991; Yngvesson & Mahoney, 2000). As a consequence, 'Belonging' has a broader, less analytically refined quality to it than 'attachment'. Belonging is a concept that can be very helpful in the practical task of strategically planning resilient actions for children and young people. In our RT community of practice, Belonging is an idea that most people—workers, parents and children—accept with enthusiasm as part of our RT framework.

But how far can we say that the concept has its home in resilience theory and research? Schofield and Beek argue that 'a sense of permanence, Belonging and being part of the family would not normally be considered as part of a resilience model' (2005: 5). We see this a little differently. Extracting from resilience research, where family and community resilience has been considered, we will show that the idea of Belonging does have a home there, although the concepts formulated are not always connected explicitly to the word 'belonging'. Also, as we explore below, researchers have found family cohesion and connectedness to be prominently associated with resilience.

This chapter takes out the interventions from our 'Belonging' compartment, broadening out our discussion to consider Belonging as widely as necessary for RT. We have summarised the interventions in Box 4.1. However, before we go through each of the compartments in detail, we first sketch out the relationship between the three different ideas that we are writing about in this chapter: attachment, Belonging and resilience. As part

---

Box 4.1 Belonging. We use these interventions to help a child make good relationships with family, friends and others

- Tap into good influences
- Find somewhere for the child to belong
- Belonging involves responsibilities and obligations too
- Help child make friends and mix with other children
- Focus on good times and places
- Make sense of where a child has come from
- Get together people the child can count on
- Predict a good experience of someone/something new
- Help child understand her/his place in the world
- Belonging is not just about people

of that discussion, we highlight those primary literature sources in which aspects of Belonging have been identified with resilience.

Attachment and Belonging

The idea that human beings need to feel that they belong, that they are part of something bigger than themselves, within groups of other human beings to whom they feel connected, is compelling. As a set of mechanisms, Belonging enables us to live our lives with at least some degree of predictability and facilitates survival (Baumeister & Leary, 1995). We need this because as babies all of us have started off our lives experiencing the world as a place of exploration, both stimulating and frightening. And throughout our lives this feeling probably never leaves us. Without a sense of where we fit into the world we become existentially anxious—lost and alone. The more anxious and disorganised a child is, the more they will need help in developing a positive sense of Belonging. If this is not achieved they may seek to belong in relationships or places that do not serve them well—gang culture is a powerful reminder of this (Pontell & Klein, 2006).

Children who miss out on positive belonging often can not relax into their lives in order to take up opportunities for developmental growth. This generally means that they find learning very difficult, and that they behave in such a way that people reject them. No wonder, then, that a vast body of research and practice experience concludes that secure attachments to a primary caregiver during the first two years of life are fundamental for optimal child development (Fonagy, Steele, Steele, Higgitt, & Target, 1994).

Belonging has been defined as 'the psychological need for people to form and maintain at least a minimum quantity of lasting, positive and significant interpersonal relationships' (Baumeister & Leary, 1995: 497). In this chapter we extend the concept to think about children's Belonging in a broader sense, beyond families even. And culture, heritage, ethnicity and geography are part of this picture. We know that these are all very important, although research has yet to determine precisely how they interact with other issues such as gender, socioeconomics, quality of attachment relationship, etc.

Howe and colleagues have lauded attachment theory as 'the theory that subsumes and integrates all others' (Howe & Fearnley, 1999: 10). Given this statement from leading scholars in the field, our decision to subsume attachment as a conceptual category within 'Belonging', rather than vice versa, needs clarification. Alongside this, the way in which the two concepts relate to resilience needs articulating. We shall tackle the first issue first.

Attachment theory is concerned with the consequences of individuals' early experience of relationships on their subsequent representations of relationships, and actual relationships in adult life. It grew out of empirical research on the affective relationships between parents and young children, first initiated by Bowlby (1969). The Strange Situation is the classic experimental test associated with attachment theory (Ainsworth, Blehar, Waters, & Wall, 1978).

There is much debate concerning how many potential patterns of attachment there are, with clinical and research categorisation not always in alignment (American Academy of Child and Adolescent Psychiatry, 2005). From scholarship and practice accounts since the mid-1980s, seven main patterns, or descriptors have emerged, some of which overlap—secure, insecure, avoidant, resistant, organised, disorganised and non-attached (American Academy of Child and Adolescent Psychiatry, 2005; Howe, 1995). On the whole, these patterns of attachment are considered to be relationship specific, rather than within-the-child traits, although there is continuing debate on this (Rutter, 1995a).

For our purposes here we will outline three main categories, which have been subdivided further: secure, insecure and disorganised. Broadly speaking, secure children are confident and can make use of adults and move happily within the wider world. Psychoanalytic thinkers believe that this is because they end up with a sort of blueprint of their primary carer inside them—what is known as an 'internal working model' (Howe, 2005: 28). Hence, a securely attached child will use her/his primary carer as a secure base from which to develop growing independence. Such children then find it relatively easy to broaden their attachments from primary care-givers to develop healthy and happy relationships.

Insecure children have an array of difficulties depending on the precise nature of their insecurity, with subdivisions of this category usually distinguishing between ambivalent and avoidant attachment patterns (Howe, 2005). Even more extreme, are children with disorganised attachment styles. This style involves a chaotic manner of relating to others characterised by extremities of behaviour, and a deep terror of relying on others because such children have so little straightforward experience of having their needs met. Not surprisingly, children with disorganised attachments can be extremely difficult to care for. However, researchers have shown that some develop what has been termed 'earned security' later in life (Pearson, Cohn, Cowan, & Cowan, 1994; Roisman, Padrón, Sroufe, & Egeland, 2002). And in research studies associations between insecure attachments and psychopathology have been found to be only moderate in strength (Belsky & Cassidy, 1994).

The main reason that children and young people with secure attachment styles are, on the whole, easier to care for is that they tend to trust other people. Here it is useful to see the child's 'internal working model', as a kind of built-in map, which they have followed many times before, and which, as a consequence, gives them a very good sense of where they are now going. Such children view the world as a benign place in which their needs are met. And, as a result, they feel good about themselves.

Attachment theory has given us the important insight that children's attachment patterns are largely determined by those of their primary caregivers. Most babies and young children who are continuously parented or cared for by sensitive, attuned adults develop secure attachment patterns. In addition to the Strange Situation, another classic test used by attachment researchers helps us understand adult attachment. This is the Adult Attachment Interview developed by Mary Main and colleagues (George, Kaplan, & Main, 1985; Hesse, 1999). Here, adults talk to an interviewer about their early life, prompted by questions from a highly structured interview format. The use of the Adult Attachment Interview can be helpful in assessing how competent an adult's parenting is likely to be.

Clearly, research shows that children's attachment patterns are intimately connected with those of their primary carers, although many questions remain. How this is culturally and historically mediated has been considered (Grossmann, Grossmann, & Keppler, 2003; Miyake, Chen, & Campos, 1985). In addition, other things seem to be going on. Studies show that temperament, and other genetic and/or biological components are highly relevant, although the precise contributions of 'nature' and/or 'nurture' to child development may never be known for sure (Farber & Egeland, 1987; Hetherington, 1989; Rutter, 1995a; Werner & Smith, 1992). It does seem that particularly fractious babies and children are harder for parents and carers to attune to (Rutter, 1990). Furthermore, although children may be categorised as secure in the Strange Situation, on other measures it has been shown that they can be classified as disorganised (Capps, Sigman, & Mundy, 1994). And, in the case of substitute care or parenting, the attachment style that the child brings with them into alternative care certainly affects subsequent parent/carer–child interaction (Dozier & Sepulveda, 2004). In some cases this can result in what has been termed 'secondary traumatic stress' in which carers are themselves damaged by the effects of the child's earlier traumatic experiences (Cornille & Woodard Meyers, 1999).

We know that for adults to establish relationships with children characterised as disorganised they will need to be secure in their own attachment styles. However, research has yet to show precisely which adults within the secure category are most likely to succeed with the most attachment-disorganised children. Furthermore, as we have seen, much more than the security of a parent's attachment pattern is relevant. A child's temperament and genetic factors, including intelligence, will all play a part in determining what actually transpires in any given context. Parenting support training, including the mastery of behavioural strategies, often helps. A deep sense of commitment from carers that systematically translates into action is a further factor to note. Those that achieve this are true RT practitioners and lead the way in realising the benefits of our Noble Truth, Commitment. Lavish helpings of patience, financial security and, as Bifulco (2002) has shown, the availability of wider support for carers and parents also seem to be key in any family context.

Rutter reminds us that, 'There is a need both to consider dyadic relationships in terms that go beyond attachment concepts, and to consider social systems that extend beyond dyads' (Rutter, 1995a: 556). And, indeed, these studies of attachment relationships beyond the laboratory have gone some way to achieving this, with researchers theorising attachment beyond primary carer–child dyads (Dunn, 1993). Two research-based models consider attachment in a systemic context—what Hill et al. describe as an ecology of attachment (Hill, Fonagy, Safier, & Sargent, 2003; Schofield & Beek, 2005). These researchers have made sense of their empirical data in a framework that sees wider affiliations as consequential to, and wholly reliant on, secure primary attachments.

Attachment theory understandings and models certainly have explanatory value, yet their relevance to making resilient moves for children in practice contexts can be enhanced if attachment is considered as part of a framework of Belonging (Schofield & Beek, 2005). This takes the language of the debate and the theoretical frameworks beyond the restrictive domain of attachment theory into a broader language of intervention.

Belonging: A resilient concept

As we have argued, the concept of Belonging subsumes that of attachment. However, at this point you may be wondering if it is worth considering wider affiliations and connections if we are led to believe that primary attachments within the first two years of life are really all that matter for *optimum* child development. Thinking back to Janice, this would just about write her off. Her first two years of life were spent in the neglectful care of her mother—a heavy drug user who, when she was not under the influence of drugs, was abusive to Janice and also herself a victim of brutal domestic violence, which Janice repeatedly witnessed. Nobody, not even Janice's mother, knows who Janice's father is. Clearly Janice missed out on any chance to develop a secure attachment during her first two years.

As we said in Chapter 1, a great deal of research has gone into isolating *factors* that, when present, are likely to be protective for children. We summarise these factors and the primary researchers whose work is to be associated with them in Box 4.2.

This list of factors can be used to help us understand where the children in our case studies have been let down, but it would not help us much in thinking *why* and *how* this occurred. For this we need to think about *mechanisms*. Without further analysis with regard to Janice and her specific circumstances, though, it does not help us to know what to do next. This is why we emphasise RT as an *active* process with its own coherent set of concepts and methods. We pursue how to enact processes that make a

Box 4.2 Protective factors distilled from the resilience primary
research base: Belonging

- Responsive care-giving from primary care giver during the first two years
  of life (Egeland, Carlson, & Sroufe, 1993; Egeland & Erikson, 1990; Fonagy,
  Steele, Moran, Steele, & Higgitt, 1991, 1993; Fonagy, Steele, & Steele,
  1991). These studies concentrated on attachment relationships between
  parents and children. Fonagy's cohort was 200 middle-class mothers and
  fathers, Egeland's 267 mothers were raising their children in poverty.
- Responsive care giving from a significant carer, such as a grandparent
  (Apfel & Seitz, 1997), older siblings (Werner, 1993), or babysitters
  (Werner, 1993) during the first two years of life.
- Sociable temperament (Luthar & Zigler, 1991; Werner, 1993: 504). A
  good relationship with a supportive or 'charismatic' adult such as a
  teacher, social worker or mentor (Freedman, 1993; Radke-Yarrow &
  Brown, 1993; Resnick, Bearman, Blum, Bauman, Harris, & Jones, 1997;
  Resnick, Harris, & Blum, 1993; Ressler, Boothby, & Steinbock, 1988)
- Staying married, or living with a supportive partner (Quinton & Rutter,
  1988; Werner, 1993)
- Ability to detach from negative family relationships and to find an appro-
  priate niche (Scarr & McCartney, 1983, cited in Werner, 1993; Werner,
  1993).
- Ability to detach when living in a hostile community environment
  (Brodsky, 1996).
- Experiences of being a family favourite (Radke-Yarrow & Brown, 1993).
- Families with core strengths in cohesion, traditions and celebrations,
  hardiness, versatility and stability (McCubbin & McCubbin, 2005).
- Smaller family size (Apfel & Seitz, 1997), and more spread out age span-
  ning between children (Apfel & Seitz, 1997); Werner's study suggested
  that four or fewer children in the family, plus age spacing of at least two
  years, increased resilience (Werner, 1993).
- An organised home environment (Egeland, Carlson, & Sroufe, 1993: 525).
- Safe and stable home environment, even within violent neighbourhoods
  (Richters & Martinez, 1993).
- Children's positive relationship with parents (Stouthamer-Loeber, Loeber,
  Farrington, Quanwu, van Kammen, & Mcguin, 1993).
- Close parental and/or carer supervision of children (Apfel & Seitz, 1997;
  Stouthamer-Loeber, Loeber, Farrington, Quanwu, van Kammen, &
  Mcguin, 1993), and teenagers (Baldwin, Baldwin, & Cole, 1990; Loeber
  & Stouthamer-Loeber, 1986; Werner, 1993; Taylor, 2006).

- Family construction of a joint meaning, which informs the family's understanding of itself (Bateson, 1978; McCubbin & McCubbin, 2005).
- Required helpfulness, mutuality: fulfilling obligations and responsibilities towards others (Jordan, 2005; Stevens, 2005: 51; Werner, 1993).
- Positive peer relationships (Conrad & Hammen, 1993; Radke-Yarrow & Brown, 1993; Werner, 1993).
- Membership of a community group, especially cooperative or highly structured ones such as a church (Apfel & Seitz, 1997; Baldwin, Baldwin, & Cole, 1990; Werner, 1993); YMCA or YWCA (Werner, 1993), scouts or guides, or indeed the army (Werner, 1993).
- Strong cultural and/or ethnic affiliation (McCubbin, 2003; McCubbin & McCubbin, 2005; Spencer, Dobbs, & Swanson, 1988). Studies indicate that own-group cultural identity processes support greater resilience of youth during periods of unusual stress. These identificatory processes have been described by Anthony (1987) as responsive coping mechanisms.
- Availability of formal community support such as homelink or other social service (Apfel & Seitz, 1997).

difference in specific contexts, rather than RT simply distilling findings from resilience research.

As our community of practice development work has shown, there is merit in spelling out what protective factors are in play. Parents, carers and workers find it instructive to have a template of what research tells us about where we might direct our efforts. The factors in Box 4.2 become more useful as tools with which to think in relation to *action*; to understand what might best be attempted with a specific child, in a specific context.

Opening up 'Belonging'

This section outlines what goes into our 'Belonging' compartment, and how we think the interventions can be used. Each section starts by explaining why we have included that particular intervention in our compartment, and demonstrates its link with resilience research.

Find somewhere for the child to belong

This intervention alerts us to how important attachment and belonging are. It encourages a relentless search on our part to find somewhere for the child to call home. Optimally, children will feel they belong within a family context in which, as the research tells us, they feel a sense of family cohesion. However, when this does not occur, other avenues can still be pursued.

These can include cultural or ethnic affiliations, clubs or activities outside the home, school, relationships with animals or even a favourite park, swimming pool or chip shop. As a resilient mechanism, two points are relevant. First, achieving a sense of belonging is protective; it gives children a secure base to return to, concretely or psychologically, when under threat. Second, we might think of this mechanism as immunising in accordance with the idea of inoculated resilience that we introduced in Chapter 1. With good experiences of belonging somewhere, children are better able to face rejection elsewhere.

Tap into good influences

As we saw earlier in this chapter, a secure attachment relationship during the first two years of life is optimal for child development and a strong sense of belonging. It almost goes without saying that setting up a relationship like this for a child would constitute tapping into a good influence *par excellence*. Luckily for Janice, and other children living in constellated disadvantage, other mechanisms of Belonging are still worth attending to. We know that good influences are important, but research has yet to demonstrate *precisely* how anything short of secure attachment during the first two years of life affects child development in any given case. As Rutter summarises, 'There is a sensitive period during which it is highly desirable that selective attachments develop but the time frame is probably somewhat broader than initially envisaged and the effects are not as fixed and irreversible as once thought' (Rutter, 1995a: 551). Studies reporting on 'earned security' offer further evidence in this direction (Pearson, Cohn, Cowan, & Cowan, 1994; Roisman, Padrón, Sroufe, & Egeland, 2002).

With this in mind, how is it best for us to work with Janice to tap into good influences for her throughout her childhood? First, we can hold in mind the fact that although we may not know exactly what damage the lack of a secure base has done to her, we do know that it is worth strategically focusing on other relationships. This may seem obvious, but we should not underestimate the degree to which practitioners working in constellated disadvantage can become disillusioned and overwhelmed by the seeming futility of the task in hand. Of course precision is not always possible—we do not know for sure how much interaction between adults with secure attachment styles children beyond the age of two might need, nor do we know what the duration should be. However, this can work to the advantage of the RT practitioner. If we do not know exactly what works to good effect, it is surely worth trying whatever might. Regarding the role of adults in children's lives, it has been repeatedly emphasised that a stable relationship with even one positive adult influence can enhance children's resilience (Dwyer, Osher, & Warger, 1998; Segal, 1988). They can act as a role model for the young person, give inspiration, and be a resource—a developmental tutor, if you like. For young people, knowing that somebody cares for them and is interested in their lives can improve their self-esteem. These relationships may not result in text-book security of attachment, but they may still enhance a child's capacity to escape serious pathology. In fact, the line we take in this book is that such relationships are a good example of what we call 'embedded therapy'. This is therapy that is fully integrated into the daily practice of children and families rather than being formally set up in a clinic environment. More of this below.

So, for Janice this would mean a relentless and creative search for any potentially good influences, someone who can stick with her. This person may be found in school, in a leisure club, or may be an overlooked member of her birth family.

Keep relationships going

We see time and time again in our practice that modern service systems are organised in such a way as to promote fragmentation and a series of short-term relationships. Much of this has come about through good intentions—increasing specialisation ensures expertise in a specific practice area—but the down side is that it sees children like Janice constantly having to connect with different workers at different life stages, or only when specific difficulties occur.

We should prioritise long-term relationships that see children through different stages of their development. In terms of resilient mechanisms, one of the reasons why long-term relationships are likely to be so helpful is that adults who have had involvement over time with children are more likely to understand their needs, are more likely to care about them, and more likely to put effort into doing things that, in their turn, enhance the children's resilience. Again thinking of mechanisms, knowing that they have long-term relationships with specific individuals helps children relax and gives them energy to focus on other things. Finally, long-term relationships can provide children with role models over time—'resilience coaches'.

In this way, we believe that our work must come to emulate as closely as possible the normative experiences of children. Imagine if parents were suddenly to move away when a child reached a particular age, and new parents with more experience of that particular life stage were to step in. This seems unthinkable and yet it is precisely what we do with our most disadvantaged children and young people. Time and time again principles of specialisation and role demarcation trump continuity of relationships in the modern service world.

If we are going to make a difference for children like Janice, service systems must change so that we can establish at least one enduring relationship for them that stays alongside them through and beyond different care arrangements. The case for this is overwhelming and needs to be made again and again.

So, it is time to establish which adult is going to make a long-term commitment to Janice. Of course, trying to make a foster carer stick would be our first port of call. If Janice had a distant family member, then this would be another possibility to consider. Social workers, teachers and learning mentors are others to consider. Janice might have a therapist, and if there was no one else available we would have to go to them. However, our view is that this really should be a point of last resort: therapeutic support, wherever possible, is best embedded in the daily life of children and families.

This last point needs some explanation. Although common in children's services, there is a question mark over the precise circumstances in which individual therapy for children with attachment difficulties forms the best way forward (Hart & Luckock, 2004). Given Janice's history the social worker is actually the obvious candidate for keeping a relationship going, and the research base is beginning to support this. At present in the UK, the reverse is likely to be the norm (Schofield, 2003). A study from the USA links poor child outcomes with discontinuity of social-work relationships (Flower, McDonald, & Sumski, 2005). Our personal and practice experience supports the emergent research base. It would certainly not be uncommon for children like Janice to have four different social workers in a calendar year.

The reasons for this lack of continuity are many, and they include recruitment and retention issues in social work, as well as the structural carving up of different social work and related professional roles and tasks. Practice where social workers are seen as 'case managers' also contributes to the problem. And it may not be too far-fetched to offer a cultural and psychodynamic interpretation of what is occurring. The fragmentation inherent in contemporary service systems can be read as a powerful cultural defence against the pain, frustration and, for some practitioners, boredom inherent in sticking very closely to children and young people with the level of difficulties that Janice has. In Chapter 2 we explored this idea more fully, and we will return to it in Chapter 8.

A resilient approach takes this issue on. This includes questioning changes of social worker and foster care as an acceptable norm. In the absence of robust systemic mechanisms to enable continuity of relationships to occur, all practitioners need to emphasise the importance of continuity and Commitment whenever and wherever they can. RT practitioners are role models for living this Noble Truth. In some situations, as we know from our own practice, this can involve challenging habitual behaviours, defensive practice and organisational promiscuity.

A final idea that can help us achieve at least a degree of continuity of relationships is the development of specific rituals. Social anthropologists have long recognised the importance of rituals for establishing and re-establishing ties and a sense of continuity (Hughes-Freeland & Crain, 1998). Appropriately stage-managed, they provide opportunities for children to feel good about themselves and their relationships through the message that they matter enough for others to celebrate and mark occasions for them. This comes back to the issue of enhancing self-esteem, a key resilience builder. As Bostock reminds us, sending children like Janice a birthday card each year, and continuing to do so even when she no longer has an official place on a practitioner's case load could be a simple, yet uniquely resilient, move (Bostock, 2004). Helping former foster carers to do this, even when a placement seems to have ended in tears is a further resilient move. We are not underestimating how hard this can be to facilitate in practice. We need to move beyond worries over dependency, worry over excessive demands and the slavish adherence to statutory responsibilities.

The more healthy relationships the better

Given that many disadvantaged children have numerous poor influences in their lives, it helps to increase the number of good influences they can have. Tapping into good influences can have an important 'compensatory' effect (O'Dougherty Wright & Masten, 2005: 19). These mechanisms can lead to a 'tipping point' being reached at which children's healthy relationships start to become more influential in their lives than the negative ones. This tipping point can, in the language of resilience theorists, lead to a 'turning point' at which children transit from one life course on to another (Quinton & Rutter, 1988). And here we are not just talking about children's relationships with people. Animals can be very helpful attachments for children, and promoting positive relationships with the children's immediate environment can also add to the effect.

Work by Fonagy and colleagues suggests that, to some degree, young children have the capacity to form a number of different kinds of attachments simultaneously (Fonagy, Steele, Moran, Steele, & Higgitt, 1991; Fonagy, Steele, & Steele, 1991; Fonagy, Steele, Steele, Higgitt, & Target, 1994). Hence they may form insecure or disorganised attachments with some carers, for example, alongside developing secure attachments with others. With the research knowledge currently available we can not precisely define the number of attachment relationships that a child might manage, nor do we know which relationship will triumph in influencing a child's enduring individual attachment style. However, as Rutter reminds us, this could be a professional caregiver, as well as a parent (Rutter, 1995a: 554). And, in the absence of definitive research evidence, we must adopt a commonsense approach; issues of manageability, sustainability and meaningfulness apply.

Once a child has a critical mass of healthy relationships, this boon can begin to affect the balance of their relationships. We say 'begin to affect', rather than 'transform', or even 'change', in recognition of the depth of the challenge. Many of the children and young people with whom we work have certainly tapped into continuous influences. They have long-term attachments and a sense of belonging with a number of different people. However, they also have attachments to adults and other children who have abused and neglected them. Resilience research suggests that children who can distance themselves from their abusive parents or carers have a better chance of positive outcomes (see Box 4.2). Beyond that literature base, in the social work and therapy textbooks and in textbooks on children's development, the importance of extracting children from their disorganised and dangerous attachment relationships is emphasised (Fletcher-Campbell & Archer, 2003; Howe, 1995, 2005).

This is an important point, because we know that for our most disadvantaged children continuing enmeshment in negative peer group and family relationships is more likely the norm than not. In our practice we have seen how relatively easy it may be to keep a 5-year-old child like Janice physically apart from an abusive birth parent, but in her mind she may still be at her mother's side. Of course, the older Janice gets the trickier the task of keeping her apart becomes.

The lack of a close supervisory presence will certainly not help keep Janice safe from the dangers of her milieu. Close supervision of a young person is considered by researchers to be protective (see Box 4.2). Although that supervision may not always result in preventing the young person from acting in a way that is damaging to themselves, giving clear messages and trying to stop them does seem to have a continuing effect. This becomes particularly crucial as children grow into teenagers. As workers, it is helpful for us to accept a seemingly contradictory fact: We cannot necessarily curb these attachments and the sense of belonging that a child has, and yet continuing to take supervisory measures that give a young person the message that we care is effective practice. Again, this helps with self-esteem. Taylor's qualitative research on criminal behaviour amongst teenagers in care in the UK demonstrated this (Taylor, 2006). Research in Sweden with a large data set concerning teenagers with very troublesome behaviour showed that parents/carers who *attempted* to supervise their young person, in a firm but warm manner, even though their efforts appeared to be in vain, were much more likely to be in a position to achieve change for the young person eventually (Kerr, Stattin, & Pakalniskienne, 2005).

Helping Janice to develop a number of continuous but lower-key relationships can have an effect that adds to the overall picture. Old-fashioned activities such as Brownies, Guides or Adventure Club, where staff are consistent and she can attend for many years to come, could be explored. However, a child like Janice will not manage to access these groups without scaffolded support. So a worker will need to commit to accompanying her, and to helping the group leader manage Janice's behaviour. Careful planning helps avoid failure.

The affiliations that she might develop with animals should not be overlooked. There is some discussion in the literature of the tendency for children who have been treated exceptionally harshly by primary carers to be very cruel to animals (Becker, Stuewig, Herrera, & McCloskey, 2004; Costello, Foley, & Angold, 2006; Mallon, 1992). We have certainly seen this occur in our own work. However, while mindful of these dangers, in our practice we have also seen how some children with neglectful and/or abusive care experiences attach to a pet far more easily than they do to human beings. Furthermore, some children develop a capacity to care about, as well as physically care for, these animals.

Hence, pets have an important role to play in the lives of children living in constellated disadvantage. Above all, we should encourage children's relationships with animals and affirm them. Indeed, the therapeutic use of dogs for helping traumatised children has been noted and instigated by some (Mallon, 1992). The idea of children in the care system having a therapeutic dog placed with them, who would move placement alongside them if this were to occur, and see them through their childhood years, is something worth pursuing, especially for hard-to-place children who endure so many breakdowns moving from home to home. Perhaps such organisations as Guide Dogs for the Blind (www.gdba.org.uk) and Dogs for the Disabled (www.dogsforthedisabled.org) could provide models that could be emulated in the foster-care context, and there are websites for a variety of other organisations that are closely involved in developing canine links (see, for example, the listing of links at www.ability.org.uk).

Take what you can from any relationships where there is some hope

This intervention is here to remind us that seemingly negative relationships may not always be so negative. We know from our own work that even the most abusive parent can have some capacity for positive change. Furthermore, in cases where young children are neglected, their parents' capacity to have more positive involvement with them later on, when they are not having to provide for their most basic needs, should not be overlooked. Potentially nurturing birth relatives can get buried at the bottom of children's files over the years. There might be a grandparent, aunt, uncle, cousin or someone else out there who has the capacity to become an important attachment figure in the child's life.

A key point is that this work takes effort and tenacity, it also takes a lot of skill. During our practice development workshops this was one of very few interventions for which we issued a health warning. Our advice is that if you are serious about trying to manipulate such complex family dynamics and you are not experienced at it, enlist someone who is.

RT has helped us facilitate relationships between children and their birth relatives that may seem untenable from the outside. The Noble Truths of Conserving, Accepting and Commitment enable us to pace ourselves. Supervising and facilitating face-to-face contact between birth relatives and children in care is a complex and stressful task that demands therapeutic and systemic skills, but much of worth can be achieved when we get it right. For Janice, five years down the line, this is likely to involve helping her and her mother develop a realistic idea of what they can offer one another.

Get together people the child can count on

If our strategies, outlined thus far in this chapter, have worked for Janice she will have a good number of continuous healthy relationships, and any positive harvest possible will have been reaped from her birth relatives. However, unless we pay close attention to the systemic dimension, these relationships will most likely be highly fragmented. We have already drawn attention to the plethora of people with a stake in caring for children in contexts of constellated disadvantage. Although we stick by our principle, the more healthy relationships the better, we emphasise that these relationships need a degree of coordination, and indeed leadership, to work.

In everyday parenting, research emphasises the importance of shared values and compatible parenting styles for children. Hence, we think it important to ensure that the multidisciplinary team around a child establishes a shared schema for caring for that child. And when it comes to formal roles, Ungar's principle of 'less is more' rings true (Ungar, 2005b: 12). With too many different workers involved collective inertia can set in and we have found that fundamental tasks get neglected. Psychological research on the behaviour of people in groups backs up our practice experience (Latane & Darley, 1968, 1970).

We know that it is a struggle for parents or carers to communicate sufficiently well to bring up a secure young person in a stable and settled family home, where everybody lives under the same roof and has daily contact. Imagine, then, what you need to have in place by way of sophisticated communication when a potentially large multidisciplinary team is caring for a disorganised child with so many fluctuating variables. To name a few: the members of that team are continually changing; are located in different agencies and/or hierarchies; have different care philosophies; managerial requirements; and, moreover, they may just not get along.

As we often experience, different agencies, and different workers, have differing ideas about who should have the ultimate say in what goes for any particular child. Janice's social worker, for example, may see herself as a case manager, but when another member of the multidisciplinary team takes on more of a parenting role, she may reassert herself and her agency as a corporate parent. At any one point a foster carer, therapist or teacher may see themselves as the person in the team who should be afforded most 'parental' authority, and act accordingly, against the principles and practices of other team members. In England and Wales, children's practitioners all working through a lead professional is coming on stream. However, difficulties are likely to remain unless the lead professional has strong personal and/or professional authority, comprehensive knowledge of what actually needs to happen, positive energy and a commitment to stay in the job long enough to see things through. We think it is worth considering the potential tensions explicitly within the team and putting maximum effort into appearing to the child with a relatively united front.

Service systems need to get behind the research and organise themselves for maximum continuity of relationships. As we have said, the ideas of keyworkers, lead professionals and relationship-based practice all involve some attempt to do this. However, none of these initiatives really gets to the heart of the matter. Janice's social worker may function well as her keyworker, and may have signed up to the idea of relationship-based practice. But how much does this help when she works within a service system that organises matters such that once Janice comes out of a child-protection remit into long-term foster care (let's say) the social worker is moved on to another case?

Belonging involves responsibilities and obligations too

Belonging is not just about giving or taking, it involves reciprocity. Bourdieu refers to the idea of family feeling that is created and maintained by 'the countless acts of reaffirmation and reinforcement that aim to produce, in a kind of continuous creation, the obliged affections and affective obligations of family feeling' (Bourdieu, 1996: 22). However, even a spotlight on Belonging in early attachment relationships shows that mutuality is key. Researchers have shown that babies who are fretful or who do not smile are harder for parents or carers to attune to (Dozier & Sepulveda, 2004). Mutuality may be hard won in such relationships, although, of course, with young children the primary responsibility for making relationships work must lie with the adults. This, of course, is not to deny the pleasure and self-esteem that young children can get from knowing that they are able to positively affect their parent or carer's mood, by a smile or an amusing turn of phrase.

However, as children grow older the balance of responsibility within relationships gradually shifts. There are other good reasons to start children off on a path that sees responsibility and obligation as a part of Belonging. We have known for a long time now that children and young people who have appropriate roles and responsibilities (including chores) have a good chance of developing positive self-esteem and a sense of self-efficacy. As we saw earlier, these have been highlighted as mechanisms associated with children's personal resilience. However, for many children and young people in care, or those living in disadvantaged home circumstances, developing a sense of belonging that is rooted in their own responsibilities and obligations is hard to achieve. Concerns about parentified children are one source of disquiet (Byng-Hall, 2002; Jurkovic, 1997). There is, however, a balance to be achieved here, and a contextual distinction to be made between adaptive and maladaptive parentification. Seemingly negative factors such as maternal employment or the need to take care of younger siblings features in studies of resilience in children, especially those relating to girls (Elder, 1974; Werner, 1993: 505). However, other studies have linked caring responsibilities for younger children to psychological damage (Elder, Liker, & Jaworski, 1984). Cultural and historical variations in expectations regarding children's responsibilities are also pertinent.

In England we currently see the following extreme dynamics at play. On the one hand the State over-provides for children. For example, the amount of money that children in care often receive as pocket money could be seen as guilt money from (corporate) parents who know at heart that they are neglectful in their basic duties. With no incentive to earn money or to take the initiative, children and young people can be rendered passive participants in their own lives with a host of professionals and carers organising them and providing for them, at least until they no longer qualify for Looked After status. And then they are out in the cold.

On the other hand, children can almost be set up to be masters of their own destiny far in advance of their developmental capability; chairing their own Looked After Children's review meetings, or being given major choices about where they want to live, for example.

Children's responsibilities and obligations should be developmentally appropriate. They should be geared towards underlining a child's reciprocity towards others, and to furthering their skills and experiences in taking responsibility. The balance is a fine one, and a word of caution is necessary. Elder and colleagues (1984) found that children with extreme levels of responsibility from a young age were damaged by them. Box 4.3 gives some ideas to help with developing children's responsibilities.

Focus on good times and places

With so much distress in children's lives it makes sense to highlight and bottle up good times. As far as mechanisms go, these can serve as helpful resilience reminders for children, and can quite literally cheer them up.

There is an important cultural component to this intervention, and the possibilities for this will depend on the background of the child. It reminds us to develop rituals that can be celebrated and then later remembered, and

---

Box 4.3 Helping children and young people develop responsibility

- Engage children and parents/carers in group activities that promote engaged citizenship—charitable projects, improving the school or home environment, for example.
- Having a pet and being its primary carer can be a useful way for children to start off on the road to developing responsibility. A first step would be to borrow one from somebody else to care for when they are away.
- Encourage children to remember birthdays and Christmas and make gifts or cards for people they care about, rather than buying them.
- Develop appropriate leadership roles for children at home and at school. These can act as helpful springboards for enhancing resilience in other ways. Home bulb-changing monitor, head bin emptier or school pet monitor are all examples of valuable leadership roles for children and young people.

---

to ensure that we have souvenirs. For Janice, for posterity, it will be very helpful to record trips to the animal farm park with a foster carer when everyone looked happy and smiling. In later years these can be revisited to help her understand that, although life has often been harrowing for her, she has many 'islands of enjoyment and fulfilment' that should not become buried beneath the misery. Furthermore, bottling up good experiences can help children reconnect to people in their lives who have had some degree of healthy relationship with them, and contribute to something of a positive autobiographical, or indeed family, narrative (McCubbin & McCubbin, 2005: 40).

Make sense of where a child has come from

Positive *shared* story making has been highlighted as a resilience factor in families, and as a useful way of connecting children and young people with parents and carers (Lacher, Nichols, & May, 2005). 'In the context of family life, resilience is enhanced through the family process of self-talk and story-telling, acts through which knowledge is transmitted about managing life events and managing change' (McCubbin & McCubbin, 2005: 40). In this way, family members, young and old alike, learn proven strategies for using resources and adapting to change; strategies that are resilience builders. Cross (1995) suggests that in story-telling families pass on stories of their lives, their skills, and that this is a way to parent for resilience.

But what if, as is the case for all the children and young people in our case scenarios, there is trauma and loss looming large in the stories to be told? For Janice, we hope that she may yet be able to undertake this work with a long-term foster carer and ideally even with her birth mother and other birth relatives too. However, in the meantime, with so many changes in her life, and seemingly no hope of alighting on a place that she will be able to call home for more than a few months, we are left with a conundrum. Do we get this work underway and use it as a potential mechanism for building empathy in her foster carer and to enhance their mutual connection (Hart, Luckock, & Gerhardt, 2002)? Or will this work be too short lived and ultimately add to her sense of abandonment and loss if the current placement does not work out? Research has yet to give us definitive guidance on this. Hence, our informed decision would be to attempt the work, proceeding with caution.

In our experience for this narrative work to avoid retraumatising children, it must go beyond simply excavating a 'trauma narrative'. With Janice, in the particular circumstances in which we find her right now, we would highlight the value of co-constructing a resilient tale as a starting point. Janice's self-efficacy and abilities to cope with the difficulties in her life would be the themes.

As Cohen shows, interventions for traumatic grief are best undertaken with clear resolution in mind, a tight therapeutic framework, and considerable technical competence (Cohen, Mannarino, & Knudsen, 2004). A focus on psychoeducation, cognitive behavioural approaches and the development of a trauma narrative followed by structured work to facilitate resolution has been shown to be effective (Cohen, Mannarino, & Knudsen, 2004). However, there is an important limitation. The research on treatment effectiveness for traumatic grief to date has to our knowledge been undertaken with children and young people who have positive attachment figures in their lives to support them. In our experience, undertaking such complex work with children who have no such attachment figures carries risk of retraumatisation. This is another reason why a focus on resilience is helpful.

Predict a good experience of someone/something new

This intervention complements that of maximising healthy relationships, and can be used as a mechanism for building up more. Hence, in the case of Janice, once one healthy relationship is established, and some trust has built up, say with a key worker, it can be brought in as a spring board to developing other positive relationships. A further way in which it may work is to act as a mechanism to help children learn that they can discard their defensive ways and put more trust in others.

The Noble Truth of Enlisting is what we hold in mind when we employ this particular intervention. The therapist can enlist others in the task of building resilience, and can use their own practice nous of what will work well to explicitly predict a good experience for Janice. This sets up the potential for a positive framing of the experience, even before it has happened, something that in our experience correlates with good outcomes. For example, the therapist could use this technique to persuade Janice to come along to the annual CAMHS picnic, telling her that she'll have good time, and that she will meet lots of people who will enjoy playing football with her. For the therapist to pull this off, she will need to have a good enough knowledge of what will occur at the picnic, and may need to brief others about their role in supporting Janice through it. So, predicting a good experience of it for Janice may well mean that the therapist puts more effort into making it work.

A further possibility is that once Janice's social worker has developed a good enough relationship with her, she could intervene to predict a good experience involving the football club that Janice had been vaguely interested in attending. And the worker can do a lot to make it a good experience. Accompanying Janice on the first visit is an appropriate start. She will need to prepare Janice by letting her know precisely what is involved. Helping to ensure that the club leader has the skills to work with Janice must also happen. In this example, too, predicting a good experience puts pressure on the worker to make sure that the experience works out. This is no bad thing as it enhances the efficacy of this intervention.

Help child make friends and mix with other children

The opportunity to develop positive peer relationships is clearly very important for children growing up in constellated disadvantage. As children develop what researchers have termed social capital, including those informal ties that help us get through life, this often provides them with a passport to success and happiness (Tayler, Farrell, & Tennent, 2003). Helping children access positive peer relationships provides them with others as role models, as well as providing them with safe and secure relationships within which to experiment and grow. However, providing these for children like Janice can be a real challenge.

Children's drive to find some sense of belonging can lead them to develop negative peer relationships and, as we saw above, gang membership is an example of this. Research shows how deleterious such peer relationships can be. For example, Luthar's work demonstrates that belonging to a peer group of other children who live in a context of constellated disadvantage is correlated with negative outcomes for those children (Luthar, 1995). However, rising above this is possible. Quinton and Rutter have shown that young people who manage to develop a loving partnership with someone who has more going for them than their partner, can be set on a path to highly adaptive outcomes (Quinton & Rutter, 1988). The message here is that forming one positive relationship can act as a turning point.

As with our discussion of children's unhealthy attachments to birth relatives, it is important to try to build up positive peer relationships with children and young people, even though they may have their own ready-made set of negative ones. We say 'their own', however this is not quite right. Modern service systems do much to create the conditions in which these negative relationships for children and young people are facilitated. They place disadvantaged young people together in foster care, or in special schools, with little recourse to more positive peer role models in their day-to-day life. Hence, with Janice it will be important to consider whom she is actually meeting in her daily life and to engineer opportunities for her to have contact with children who will be good for her. A study of children who were sent to different schools and who were given normative school experiences demonstrated better outcomes compared to other children living in the same residential home. Rutter reported that, although the precise mediating mechanisms at play are not known, 'it may be supposed that the experiences of pleasure, success, and accomplishment at school had helped the girls to acquire a sense of their own worth and their ability to control what happened to them' (Rutter, 1990: 197).

Help child understand her/his place in the world

This intervention reminds us of the need to consider affiliations of gender, ethnicity, disability, sexuality and race when attempting to enhance children's resilience. It helps us home in on the fact that for people with a minority identity, mobilising together and developing a sense of belonging and mutual respect can bolster against the demands and cruelties of the wider world (McCubbin, 2003). Janice is not yet in a position to consider defining herself as 'disabled', yet her degree of learning difficulty and her mild foetal alcohol syndrome will mean that others will do so for her.

Janice's identity will be structured according to the category 'disabled' by a whole range of workers, people in the community, the local educational authority and the benefits system. Precisely how she sees herself fitting into the world will need careful and sensitive discussion over time. Regarding the issue of belonging, it will be helpful for her to develop relationships with other disabled young people. This should decrease her sense of isolation and give her role models through whom she can develop her repertoire for managing the world.

Another issue to explore, regarding children's understandings of themselves, is that of spirituality and religion. In our increasingly secular society, and this may be particularly true of the UK, the role of these can seem an unfashionable topic to consider, and can even result in people feeling awkward in raising it. Two recent practice accounts provide a discussion of different ways of considering spiritual dimensions in practice (Hodge, 2005a, 2005b; Tanyi, 2006).

If we are serious about building up children's resilience we should tackle children's understanding of their place in the world. This is because studies of resilience repeatedly emphasise the role of faith and spirituality in developing resilience in children (Haight, 1998; Haight, Kagle, & Black, 2003; Jang, 2005; Poston & Turnbull, 2004; Werner, 1993). This has to some extent become popularised with programmes in which troubled young people are taken into the wilds for an outdoor activity programme. In a qualitative research study Ungar, Dumond, and McDonald (2005) consider the mechanisms involved in these kinds of activities.

Efforts to build up spiritual or religious affiliations for children, then, can be very helpful. It is likely that this is because having a positive sense of our place in relation to the wider world helps us feel safer, and gives us a sense of purpose, as well as specific rules to live by. Zohar and Marshall (2004) call this 'spiritual capital' and describe it as 'the wealth we can live by'. This intervention connects us to considering the roles and responsibilities we should have to take on in relation to others, and it fits well alongside a consideration of the earlier 'Belonging involves responsibilities and obligations too'.

The precise form that building up spiritual affiliations will take will depend on the child's cultural background, their experiences to date, availability of 'spiritual role models' and the child's predilections. In Janice's case, it will certainly be worth exploring whether her mother's Irish Catholic background has anything to offer. This may be at the level of kindling Janice's interest in her roots, and practitioners using their imagination to access anything that the Catholic church can offer her, for example a warm and nurturing Sunday School.

Conclusion

This chapter began with a discussion of the concept of attachment and showed why we prefer the broader concept of Belonging to help us with the task of planning resilient moves. Belonging builds on the valuable insights of attachment theory and includes the idea of human beings having a sense of where they fit in with others. However, this is not solely with primary carers. Belonging is more than that. While it concerns the fit between children and their immediate family or care circumstances (including siblings), it goes wider to their community, their school, and their past circumstances. And having a positive sense of belonging does not only come from feeling connected to other people—much wider considerations, for example those of culture and geography are at play here too. Thinking 'Belonging', rather than attachment, gives us wider purchase for intervening in the lives of children like Janice.

Following our discussion of attachment and belonging, we covered the ground of how research to date has conceptualised belonging as it relates to resilience factors, and attempted to draw these factors into our description of resilience-enhancing mechanisms. This chapter also highlighted the concept of 'embedded therapy'—the idea that, as a first principle, attempts should be made to embed therapeutic support for children in their daily life and relationships. We did not go as far as setting out a whole coordinated bespoke intervention for Janice, although there are some ideas suggestive of this. That is what we need to take further in the work we do with each particular child.

Chapter 5

Learning

One sacred memory from childhood is the best education.

Dostoyevsky

Introduction

Children can learn everywhere. Making the most of learning is crucial for those whose formal education has been jeopardised by the overwhelming adversities and uncertainties they have faced. A great deal will have already happened in these children's lives that has brought them to public notice and upset a smooth developmental progression into their first experience of school, and beyond.

This chapter explores approaches to deepening the learning process, through making the children's school work as well as possible for them. It also means making use of new types of practitioners—mentors, who work in schools. Crucial, too, is making use of what there is outside the school that will help children learn essential skills and plan for their future when their educational opportunities have been so compromised. All of these aims are directly related to what we know builds resilience.

In Chapter 4, we focused on 'Belonging' and how fundamental those interventions are for building resilience and children's long-term outcomes. Education can be seen as equally influential. Multiple initiatives have been aimed at enhancing resilience in children through school-based programmes. It does not take too great a stretch of the imagination to see why. The educational system is a universal provision founded on developing a sense of achievement, competence and step-by-step building of pathways to future success. It provides for socialisation into the prevailing culture. It furnishes young people with a safe and structured arena for normative peer-to-peer as well as adult-to-peer experiences. At its best, it nurtures and teaches life skills as well as academic knowledge that fuels self-development throughout an individual's life. Both through primary prevention programmes and secondary targeting of 'problem' groups, education provides a ready-made context of long-term access to help and support for many troubled young people.

Therefore we could say that, for many, education has been *the path* for resilience building. Rutter and Quinton (1984) discovered that a positive school experience, not necessarily related to academic achievement, was one of the main factors in helping vulnerable women break out of negative life trajectories. A stable school environment (Hetherington, 1989; Hetherington & Kelley, 2002) and the promotion of a sense of competence and positive self-esteem that goes with this (Werner & Smith, 2001) are highly starred when it comes to resilience. If we add to this the opportunities to learn problem-solving skills (Reivich, Gillham, & Chaplin, 2005) and to access programmes of social and emotional learning (Masten, Hubbard, Gest, Tellegen, Garmezy, & Ramirez, 1999), it is hard not to see the effective use of school as a must-do for RT.

Doing well at school has been viewed as one of the most protective factors in better than expected outcomes for vulnerable children (Rutter, Maugham, Mortimore, Aliston, & Smith, 1979). Long-term cohort studies have shown that resilience is highly correlated with academic achievement and educational success (Werner & Smith, 1992, 2001). Engaging in school and reaping its rewards both reflects and enhances a child's capacity to succeed over the whole lifespan. For these reasons, it might be argued that a good education *is* resilience. It provides the mechanism of choice for the long-term future proofing of children's development.

However, we also have to recognise that many of the children growing up in constellated disadvantage do not find school an easy, straightforward or rewarding environment to engage in. There will be many factors playing into the scenario of a child such as Sally, which will have profound significance for her ability to realise education's promise or even to access it at all. Sally, as we shall see, spent more time out of formal schooling than she did within it. Placement instability, low expectations of teachers, the low expectations of other practitioners and Sally herself, all worked to undermine her capacity to achieve (Fletcher-Campbell & Archer, 2003). Coupled with these were failures in corporate parenting so that practitioners did not work together and take joint responsibility for including those most at risk. There is little doubt that children like Sally would miss out even more if RT was to rely on her education taking place only through school-based programmes.

If we are to make the experience of learning positive for children like Sally it is vital that practitioners and organisations across the health, social care and education divides work closely together. This is important in every facet of working in constellated disadvantage, but it has particular importance here. Like Sally, many of the children that our book is based on come to be excluded from formal education (Department for Education and Skills, 2003; Fletcher-Campbell & Archer, 2003). They spend large amounts of time out of school disaffected with what mainstream education can offer. Many schools might be working hard to make the system responsive to these children's needs. However, the evidence continues to indicate that despite the move to greater inclusion and new initiatives, the children that this book is focused on still do not do well in the school stakes (Essen, Lambert, & Head, 1976; Harker, Dobel-Ober, Akhurst, Berridge, & Sinclair, 2004b).

Therefore, we have made a conceptual shift and called this chapter 'Learning' rather than education since the latter has so many connotations of consistent school engagement. As you will see elsewhere in our book, there are many interventions that schools might be seen as delivering best that we have placed elsewhere, for example in 'Coping' or 'Core Self'. 'Learning', while harnessing some of the functions that schools for the most part deliver, makes us think more broadly. We need to engage children like Sally into the learning process and concentrate on what it is that she will need most to learn and how best she can be helped to achieve it.

Contexts of learning

Studies repeatedly confirm the influence of low socioeconomic status on educational attainments (Forsyth & Furlong, 2000). Children in public care do even less well (Harker, Dobel-Ober, Berridge, & Sinclair, 2004a; Harker et al., 2004b; Heath, Colton, & Aldgate, 1994). Family background remains one of the strongest predictors of educational success (Buchmann, 2002). The socially most disadvantaged children, whose care is disrupted or sub-optimal, do worst in the educational stakes (Harker et al., 2004a, 2004b).

There are very obvious reasons why this occurs. Elias, Parker, and Rosenblatt (2005) discuss the three types of factor involved: student related factors; educator factors; and influences from outside the school that can disrupt school engagement. Children in constellated disadvantage experience difficulties across all three areas. Take, for instance, academic expectations.

Elias and colleagues (2005) note that, overall, disadvantaged children are subject to lower expectations; their own, those of their teachers and those from within their own families. They will be Coping with higher rates of stress outside school and may be called upon to take on responsibilities for themselves and their circumstances. This uses up any capacity that they might have to engage in schoolwork to the necessary degree. The culture in the family may be inimical to school norms. We could go on.

In the UK the children who are cared for by public authorities are at the bottom of the exam league tables and are often not accessing school at all during just those years when exams are taken and life chances are being forged (Fletcher-Campbell & Archer, 2003). The rates of school breakdown here are alarmingly high. Stirling (1992) found that half of the sixty children in residential care in one area of Britain were, or had recently been, excluded from school. These are children in the lowest socioeconomic groups. They have high rates of mental health problems approaching 70% in some studies (McCann, James, Wilson, & Dunn, 1996), and, as we have seen, these difficulties are further aggravated by very poor educational attainment.

Sally is a striking case in point. She was subject to so many early adversities. It takes some courage just to hear about them let alone to have to deal with them in life. Sally, we hear, had effectively no continuous education throughout her primary school career. Therefore she is considerably underachieving just from this fact alone, irrespective of any learning problems that she may have. What Sally needs, of course, is a school that she will remain at long enough to secure a robust pattern of educational progress. She will need some remedial help to catch up and, as she is helped to engage, she may also need dedicated extra help for any specific learning difficulties that she has to overcome.

Thus far, straightforward and simple solutions may suffice. However, and this is where the story takes a different turn, Sally has many other problems still going on in her life. She shows very poor concentration. She does not easily get along with her peers and they tend to close off into groups against her. She readily sees others as acting towards her in a more hostile manner than they intend. She takes up a defensive stance, which in turn invites aggressive interactions and thus her earlier prediction of hostility towards her becomes a self-fulfilling prophecy. Two terms into the academic year, her care situation changes and the new placement means a long travelling distance to the school. Sally's story exemplifies the exponential power that can sometimes work in negative chain reactions, and which characterises constellated disadvantage.

On the positive side, at the age of eleven, Sally wants to succeed in mainstream secondary school and this despite very few of her older siblings having profited from their school careers. Building on this flicker of hope, she has been enrolled in a school that is progressive in terms of supporting the most vulnerable children. Sited in a deprived neighbourhood, the school has received extra resources for special needs children. Her Head of Year is committed to making the school work for children such as Sally. Sally does have at least one friend in that school that she has known from her earliest years.

Which way will it go? Mainstream schools are struggling with many such pupils. For some there is engagement and success. The statistical likelihood for Sally, however, is school exclusion. In the UK children in alternative care are ten times more likely to be excluded than their home-based peers (Department of Health, 2004). So, it is overwhelmingly the case that at some stage she will be excluded and/or that she will be referred on for special educational provision.

Indeed, after two terms, Sally was excluded from mainstream secondary school and, because of this, she felt that she had failed. The school might have avoided going through the formal exclusion process but for the fact that Sally was in the midst of a change of social worker at the time, one of the many changes of practitioner she has been subject to. The school felt that they had to permanently exclude her in order to make the process of getting her an effective educational provision actually happen. Sally, you will also recall, has spent so long out of school already that you can see their point. Indeed, in this respect, one could view the school as acting resiliently in terms of obtaining the most desirable outcome for Sally under the circumstances. It appears to be a rule that, in constellated disadvantage, where systems are set up so that help is preferentially offered at points of crisis, then crises will happen more often.

Formal education for Sally has therefore been an arena of repeated failure and exclusion. Sally has been referred to the child and adolescent mental health service again as part of the cycle of re-establishing her in an educational environment. By the time she is seen, the placement is, after some early testing, going reasonably well. Sally has managed to keep some good peer relationships going. Sally is not as downhearted as we might have supposed. She had not allowed her expectations to get too high. This was, after all, the third time she had been excluded from a school. Also, relationships within the school were becoming so dire that it was something of a relief for her that she came out of the school when she did.

Sally's story illustrates a common scenario for disadvantaged children with respect to the promise formal education offers, and why we have turned from the potentially limiting concept of 'Education' to 'Learning'. We can not, certainly while dynamics are operating in the direction they have done in Sally's situation, be sure of the value of placing too great a hope on what education will achieve. Her needs remain considerable. Naturally, we would not wish to give up on what education can offer her. We will need to review and harness the manifold facets of Learning. Learning is certainly school learning, but should also include those mechanisms by which children develop capacities such as life skills, the ability to organise themselves and to know how, and also when, they have achieved something. For Sally, and others, such capacities are as much about enhancing out of school activities as utilising school capacity to the full.

Learning interventions

First, some technical considerations (see Box 5.1). As we have explained, RT is a strategic approach where efforts in any direction should be considered not only in their own right but also in combination and in terms of their effect on other resilient moves. We follow Rutter's lead in highlighting

---

Box 5.1 Learning interventions

- Make school life work as well as possible
- Engage mentors for children
- Map out career/life plan
- Help the child to organise her/himself
- Highlight achievements
- Develop life skills

---

how the interweaving of circumstances can create both amplified risk and amplified protection and how also one intervention might work against or negate the effect of another. There are both positive and negative synergies here. As Rutter (1990, 1995b) has so cogently articulated, protective factors can pose risks, and risk variables may confer protection. He therefore argues that we speak of processes rather than factors.

In Chapter 1 we reflected on these complicated processes, and introduced the idea of inoculated resilience and it could be argued, for example, that Sally's experience of previous school exclusion prepared her for a further experience of the same and mitigated what, for another child, could have had much more devastating consequences. Conversely, placing Sally in another school further away cuts out her, albeit limited, local relationships. While potentially offering some mechanisms to heighten her resilience, putting her in a school further away may, looking at it from the point of view of 'Belonging', cut across the good work going on elsewhere.

Another example illustrates a further complication. Take children who lack organisational skills. We might imagine that they would do well in schools with highly structured timetables. However, we find that they only do well when they have a great deal of carefully targeted support alongside (Shucksmith, Philip, Spratt, & Watson, 2005). So, there are potential risks and potential benefits interchanging wherever we look. And the nub of the matter is that RT works with them all in whichever direction they operate.

Life for Sally is complex in this way and the simple straightforward measures we might employ when we approach a child's situation as if it involves a single, readily definable problem may actually make the situation worse. Also, this takes us further along the path of recognising the complex relationship RT has to adversity. We can not decry adversity too vociferously given the advantage it sometimes confers. In this light the following description of Learning interventions comes with a strong health warning. They may be helpful but they need, just like all good medicines, to be taken judiciously, perhaps with other remedies or under certain circumstances not at all. We do need to act. But also in RT we must live with an awareness of uncertainty much of the time.

Make school life work as well as possible

There is no doubt that school, when it works well, is host to a wealth of resilient mechanisms. It can open up new opportunities (Rutter, 1987, 1995b), increase the range of available resources to a child (Masten, Neemann, & Andenas, 1994), increase access to challenge and stimulation (Swanson & Beale, 1991) and provide remedial help (Heath, Colton, & Aldgate, 1994). Better grades predict resilience (Gonzalez & Padilla, 1997). From an early age children's trajectories can already be set. Take a relatively straightforward example of this. Knowing that children at six years old who are doing well at school will be resilient as young adults (Werner & Smith, 2001), we might imagine that there is value in targeting extra school help at those before the age of ten who are struggling, say, with their reading, the hope being that some of the resilience-building effect experienced by their more successful peers will be transferred to them at this earlier age. This seems straightforward and encourages the school to do what schools do best.

On the other hand, including some children in such straightforward schemes might do more harm than good. We need to pay attention to a gallery of supporting processes to make them effective. What we know is that where inclusion works well it is due to schools collaborating to good effect internally and using support staff well (Giangreco, 1997) as well as possibly accessing outside consultation (Jordan, 1994). Then remediation is delivered through the child's mainstream classroom setting, something most children with learning difficulties appear consistently to prefer (Howlin, 2002). The mainstream classroom may also be best placed to deliver interventions additional to usual school provision, which are aimed at increasing children's social and emotional learning. This has been shown to reduce maladaptive behaviours, improve school performance and improve long-term academic outcomes (see, amongst others, Hawkins, Farrington, & Catalan, 1998; Masten et al., 1999). The link from such school-based initiatives to building resilience involves some twists and turns but it can be made. Additional collaborative mechanisms are necessary if we want to make it work.

This is particularly the case for disadvantaged children. It suffices to say that school matters a great deal. If you wish to make it work for disadvantaged children, every effort needs to go into ensuring that it does. There are multiple components to this. From maintaining good levels of school attendance to making sure that teachers' expectations of children once they are in school are commensurate with their abilities, school-based education needs to be deliberately and carefully configured into these children's lives and made to work.

Alongside, disadvantaged children's pattern of care outside school needs to be designed in ways that reduce the disruptive effect to their education. Placement instability is frequently a potent factor in generating school discontinuities (Fletcher-Campbell & Archer, 2003). Continuity is the watchword. The more we can reduce changes of care and associated geographical dislocations, the more focused on educational tasks disadvantaged children are likely to be. Then they are much more likely to reap the benefits of the additional activities and stable peer relationships that schools offer alongside curriculum-based teaching.

Therefore the effort to work with Sally's school was not misguided but we perhaps could have done more. Let us review how we approach this now and see if we could have done more. First, we need to think whether the school was the best one with at least some chance of success. Schools and their cultures are very variable places, both geographically and in time (Rutter, Maugham, Mortimore, Aliston, & Smith, 1979). We need to be able to work closely with them and to customise the educational programme Sally can manage as far as school flexibilities will allow. We need to know our patch, our local schools and who is currently best at managing these sorts of situations well. It is important to include school in all regular meetings and make sure they see Sally's progress reports. This is 'inclusion in the round'. The school needs to sign up to close supervision and a system of support for Sally within school that she can use, that is sufficient to head off crises and that can help to keep her attendance up and Sally roughly on task. There is extensive detailed planning required. In sum, we should assume little will go right and plan accordingly.

Let us fast forward to Sally's later adolescence. If we have managed to keep what works for her going, those peer relationships she has held on to during all the years of upheaval and disruption are still working for her. Indeed, the longest-term relationships have taken on an enhanced benefit as she moves into further education. We could have jeopardized such links by moving her to a distant setting and cutting off her ties. On purely educational grounds there was strong justification for this. Instead we took into account her needs for Belonging and we worked very hard to put that together with her educational provision. This is not to say that it was easy to accomplish. Compromises had to be made and a number of customary ways of working by agencies, for example sending her to out of area special school or expecting her to manage a rigid timetable, might have been challenged to near breaking point. However, the net effect of the consequent bespoke educational/care package could be seen as optimal in terms of all the resources available to her.

Engage mentors for children

Sally might also need someone in school who could be slightly more special for her than her teacher. A recent study of school-based mentorship concluded that this was an extremely helpful initiative and the more effective if the mentors were fully integrated into the structures of the school and aligned to its principal values (Harker et al., 2004b). The aims of the study were to increase school engagement, to reduce the impact of problem behaviours, raise academic attainments and reduce school exclusions. Mentorship was not the sole intervention, but it did appear to play a critical role in realising the benefits of the project aim as a whole. Mentors have also been rated highly in other resilience studies (Werner & Smith, 2001; Yates, Egeland, & Sroufe, 2003) and taken up by government initiatives (Department for Education and Employment, 1999).

Mentors can go under a variety of different names. For example, in the RALLY programme in Massachusetts, Noam, Warner, and Van Dyken (2001) talk of 'prevention practitioners' who focus in a combined way on the educational, mental health and health needs of vulnerable pupils. They work in the schools to raise educational attainments and to reduce problematic emotional and behavioural difficulties. This 'pull-in' model is aimed at greatly reducing the number of times that children have to be sent out of school for their difficulties. Others have focused more on mentors' home–school liaison roles and called them 'family learning coordinators' (Shucksmith, Philip, Spratt, & Watson, 2005).

Mentoring can also vary from counselling a child to working alongside them on purely academic tasks. For example, the Penn Resiliency Program (Reivich, Gillham, & Chaplin, 2005) focuses on problem-solving skills and the application of cognitive behavioural therapy (CBT) methods through school counsellors. Many mentors will move between a range of tasks as needs arise. The child has a regular and usually frequent (once or twice weekly) point of contact with their mentor and the mentor receives and reviews the teachers' reports of the child in question. Sometimes the mentor is involved over a set period of time, two terms say, and sometimes the arrangement is more open ended. The mentor becomes the child's key person in school for the time they are involved. Mentors need a good profile, to be integral to school structures and to be seen as important to its better functioning (Harker et al., 2004b). The child has to be in school for the mentor to work with them, although we are aware that some mentors also have an outreach function built into their role. There is an argument for mentoring to become integral to a teacher's roles. Benard (2002) talks of 'turnaround teachers' who model resilient behaviours, focusing on developing caring relationships, high expectations and maximising opportunities for children to contribute to classroom processes.

As with all such projects, there are some problems as well as benefits. Children with high levels of need can place too great an expectation on what a mentor can offer. Mentors can leave, with all the problems of further broken attachments. Set up insensitively, mentors can fail to engage children who do not wish to be conspicuously different. Some have argued for mentors to be available to all in order to reduce stigma (Noam, Warner, & Van Dyken, 2001).

However, despite these concerns, there seems little doubt that mentoring in schools is a valuable intervention for disadvantaged children and it can also help to support their out of school life. Mentors can often be tasked with linking school not only with family connections, but also with other professional involvement for a child and its family. They can become resources in themselves by knowing the local situation and finding useful activities the child can access out of school time. Furthermore, some of the beneficial effect of mentoring can be seen helping with other areas of resilience building. For example, mentors can use the 'Coping' interventions we are coming on to in our next chapter to help children best manage the daily vicissitudes of school life.

What does appear crucial is the integration of the mentor into educational structures and processes. Their primary aim is to enhance the child's school life and particularly their attainments. In this sense, mentorship may offer crucial advantages over other school-located modes of intervention such as counselling, which can have a different set of aims at some distance from those of the school. To our knowledge, no comparative trial of these interventions has yet been carried out.

As we mentioned before, schools are very different. Educational success varies greatly from school to school, from pupil to pupil and also with respect to time (see Rutter, Maugham, Mortimore, Aliston, & Smith, 1979). Rises and falls can occur over quite short time-spans. Mentors will inhabit this fluctuating context and will manage what they can within its confines. Whether a school employs mentors or not may reflect the school culture as much as the proven effectiveness of mentoring. Those that do may already have an inclusive, permissive approach to supporting disadvantaged children.

Undoubtedly, in the context of setting up what we call 'virtuous networks', mentors can also be seen as potential change agents. However, we may question whether they will have enough status, influence or authority to make substantial changes to school culture if they themselves are perceived as outsiders. Working with children who are viewed by the organisation as a problem can lead to exclusion and devaluation rather than inclusion for those that need it most. Mentors can be RT practitioners. Just as all other RT practitioners do they will need to assume status and take authority, as we will explore further when we look at the organisational context in Chapter 8.

Map out career/life plan

What is possible for you to do when you leave school, and what is impossible? Interestingly, there is little research on children's choices, at differing ages, and whether having certain ambitions promotes resilient outcomes, particularly in terms of children's school engagement. What work there is indicates that children and young people who do have a strong sense of purpose and of their future behave in ways that promote its realisation (Werner & Smith, 2001). In other words it has practical value for them in the present.

This is certainly our experience too. At crucial developmental stages and in the face of desperation at their past failures, mapping out career plans and life expectations can have a positive resilience-building effect, and is resilient in the moment. We argue that to actively engage with children at such points in their lives in this way holds a protective value and is enabling of a range of other positive steps that are in themselves also strongly linked with resilient practice. It can act as a powerful motivator to academic engagement and achievement, focused on obtaining results in the child's own terms. It also links in with other interventions, such as a view to the future and stressing areas of a child's life that they see themselves as having some control over. In Seligman's (1998) terms, we are encouraging the child to develop an internal locus of control. Both these points get picked up in some detail in the following chapter.

In RT we help children to formulate an idea of 'themselves in the future' characterised in terms of career preference or what kind of adult they see themselves wanting to be. Do they have a family and children, and, if so, how would they bring them up? It is an opportunity to explore with them hopeful visions of what might be and opens up the debate as to how they can achieve it. It has a reality in the here and now, giving the children a vantage point both outside and yet connected to their present plight. This has the effect of indicating to them, and to practitioners working with them, that the present situation and what has gone before could, in their predicted future, be otherwise. This is a strong aspect of RT's future-orientated approach.

At this point we should cast an eye sideways at the thorny issue of the 'tendency to repeat'. Undoubtedly there are mechanisms operating by which past patterns are highly likely to be reproduced in the present, no matter how alternative the child's view is of their potential future. We have seen it with Sally and her failures at school. These failures are fuelled by her persistent aggressive stance towards peers. This, in turn, is based on her reaction to the anticipation of them attacking her. Sally is likely to go on reacting in this fashion until this aspect of her cognitive stance is addressed. Work on that facet of her development is urgently needed and there are CBT methods that sound promising, for instance the problems solving skills training that CBT has to offer (Kazdin, 1996b). However, what we also know from such studies is that children with high comorbidity, school failure and histories of family disruption do not do well with such single-treatment approaches. Planning out what Sally wants to achieve in the long term, helps us to chain together sequences of discrete interventions that might help her to get there. This increases her motivation and possibly provides a degree of engagement and a sense of achievement if she does engage, which is also a Learning intervention as we shall see later in the chapter.

This future-orientated approach therefore opens up opportunities for the child *now*. Rutter has listed one of the main ways that resilience is promoted as widening opportunities for those with too narrow a life horizon (Rutter, 1990, 1995b). To actively engage with children and young people in this way is literally to widen their horizon in the here and now.

Help the child to organise her/himself

Brooks and Goldstein (2003) rate the capacity to self-manage as one of the key characteristics of building a resilient life style. More has been developed on this topic in the adult research literature. To develop this theme we might usefully borrow a distinction from the leadership debate in organisational theory. One strand of this discriminates spheres of control from spheres of influence (Senge, 1990). Underpinning this is need for the leaders to position themselves in situations as active participants in order to achieve desired outcomes.

On the one hand, in spheres of control we direct changes to fashion our lives to a preferred design. Of course this must lie within what is realistic but in spheres of control we have a direct say and it is important, if outcomes are to be achieved, that the necessary authority is taken. In spheres of influence, on the other hand, we are one amongst a number of players. Our task here is to communicate effectively, forging alliances and creating networks of advantage to further our aims.

These considerations may seem distant from the daily concerns of the children and families we work for. However, taking our cue from intervention programmes that promote emotional intelligence, we have conceptualised these children as leaders in their own lives (Fuller, Bellhouse, & Johnston, 2002). While this may have value for any child's development it is particularly important in situations of constellated disadvantage. This is because of the lack of opportunity for those caught up in constellated disadvantage to explore and exercise appropriate authority given their experiences, of abuse for example.

We can see that many disadvantaged children do exercise power and influence but it may not be to the benefit of either themselves or others. For those two terms that Sally attended mainstream secondary school her capacity to disrupt a classroom became something of a legend. There was a distinct air of relief in the staffroom when she left. Sally was notorious rather than influential. She could not help her reactions at the time. She played out an automatic script with little room for planning or choice.

Self-management indicates the power to choose. Even to see that she has a choice would be a considerable step forward for Sally at this age.

Winnicott (1965a, 1965b) talks of children's moral development as being rooted in opportunities to contribute. Small failures to plan for a child leave gaps they can fill in. Adversity can work for you if there is not too much or too little and it comes at roughly the right time. Sally has experienced such failures, but far too often and significantly too much. Her sense of contributing is either to look on passively while others might exploit her or, more likely now she is older, to go for absolute control of the situation and allow no one else to have the chance to influence her at all. Either way she is operating in a world of forced choices that are in neither her nor anyone else's best interests.

We have placed this intervention in the Learning compartment because self-management and self-organisation are so often developed by engaging with the educational process. As with many of the interventions included in this compartment, disadvantaged children will not often feel that they can make choices or do things differently and they may also lack a stable and predictable context such as school in which to try these capacities out. Schools do have some advantages in this respect. They are comprehensive, developmentally sensitive and they can act to coordinate a range of influences on the child. In short, they can provide children with a programme where they monitor how the children manage expectations of self-organisation. Beyond school, with children such as Sally, we may have to scaffold into her life a virtual school in order to provide the opportunities for self-development that for so many children are naturally occurring outcomes of a stable school placement.

Highlight achievements

This has a strong connection to social and emotional learning. Building children's self-esteem and confidence, and increasing their sense of competence, are all strongly linked to being able to overcome life challenges (Ciaprara, Barbaranelli, Pastorelli, Bandura, & Zimbardo, 2000; Haynes, 2003; Masten et al., 1999; Werner & Smith, 2001). Self-esteem and confidence are two of the most asymmetrical concepts in life. It takes so little time to undermine them, and so much longer to build them up. Integral to building them up is the need to deconstruct a whole range of counteracting influences that have come from the children's previous experiences. Let us take one of these—low expectations. Many studies have noted students' own low expectations of themselves and how these reflect family norms and also teachers' expectations (Elias, Parker, & Rosenblatt, 2005). You might imagine that low expectations would in some ways prevent harm to the child from not achieving. However, the opposite seems the case.

From an RT point of view, we view low expectations as a form of learning neglect. Let us explore two of the specific mechanisms involved in low self-esteem. The first is that the child is not encouraged to achieve and therefore this area of their life is undeveloped. Low expectations feed into children not seeing themselves as in any way determining or even influencing events around them, and certainly not achieving anything worthwhile in relationship to them.

Second, negative events can be presented to the child as their fault. Of course, for reasons we have rehearsed in earlier chapters, chains of negative reactions happen to them disproportionately. This is because they are told they are responsible for them and, as they try to make sense of this, the resulting effect is to drive down their self-esteem. Being identified with and feeling responsible for negative events are hallmarks of low self-esteem. That they may have achieved something, that they have overcome such difficulties, survived them, even made something positive out of them, are discourses unfamiliar to children such as Sally as they grow up.

Such pathways to persistent low self-esteem are invariable characteristics of the emotional development of the children for whom this book is being written. We should note, too, the infectious nature of this pattern of reaction, for it is so often part of the experience of their families of origin and sometimes, quite often in our experience, to be found in the practitioners who work in areas of constellated disadvantage. A little achievement talk in this situation can go a long way. Harker et al. (2004b) reported that young people, reflecting on their experience of care, voiced a regret that they received so little encouragement to achieve in education from their social workers and how much they would have liked it if they had.

Low self-esteem is woven into the fabric of the lives of children and families living in constellated disadvantage. Occasionally it can go the other way and unrealistic perceptions of one's worth create negative chain reactions of a different kind. While we need to be aware of this, when it comes to Sally, however, she needs building up in terms of her self-esteem. Self-esteem, as we know, is highly correlated with depression (Kendall, Stark, & Adam, 1990), as well as a number of self-defeating personal practices that we are all too familiar with in Sally's case. Highlighting what she has achieved will undoubtedly uncover the internal conversations that prevent positive messages being heard. Then it will reinforce strategies that have succeeded. As long as Sally can assimilate the positive message to some degree, it can work directly on her self-esteem and confidence with discernible effect. This process is a slow burner and will need to be reinforced time and again. Every opportunity will need to be seized upon and practitioners must be persistent and not easily put off in making sure that the message of achievement gets across.

Some of the criticism of a resilient approach has been directed at this tendency to paint a glossy picture of what, viewed more objectively, is abject disadvantage. There is a political point here, and a risk that, as part of wider debate, makes a great deal of sense. We could place even greater burdens on the disadvantaged by making them feel yet more responsible for their plight. This is not our intention and we argue that RT is explicit and thoroughgoing in working in the opposite direction. It does make us wonder how much it is the low self-esteem and poor internal locus of control of the practitioners that feeds into this criticism being made. Resilience has always meant challenging a deficit model. While accepting that there are risks to praising in dire situations, the experience of highlighting achievement is a positive one. As long as we are highlighting achievements that are clear, definable and have some resonance with the child's experience, the effect is to build self-esteem, confidence and resilient practice rather than the reverse.

Develop life skills

Sally loves cooking. Sally's talent was discovered at the age of thirteen and it quickly became of great value to her and to her foster carer at that time. She liked cooking; her foster carer did too. Noticing this talent in Sally they worked on it. The foster carer watched cooking programmes with Sally. Soon Sally was cooking meals and it was a sure way back into the foster carer's heart. Sally had found that royal road and the foster placement in question undoubtedly lasted longer than it should have, taking other factors into account.

Not all children have such a talent and there are some children who have precious little going for them. We mention Sally's gift because it opened out into a series of jobs during her teenage years that gave her a steady income and lots of positive feedback. This lasted long after Sally had moved on from the original foster home. It laid the foundations for Sally today as an up and coming employee with some prospect of success.

Sally had learnt a number of life skills as a result of her culinary interest. She learnt to shop with her foster carer and understood, through this, the value of money, sorting good food from the bad, and completing complicated tasks. She was drawn into making links with cooking classes and attended courses with her foster mother. This broadened her networks, especially of appreciative adults.

We are verging here on the contents of other chapters. Being able to derive solace from one's interests and hobbies is associated with resilience (Werner & Smith, 2001). Those interests also act as a portal into developing a range of valuable skills and virtuous networks, and into fostering positive relationships as widely as possible, all of which help to fit a child for potential adult success. It is a way in which beleaguered children just might become functioning adults with prospects.

Many life skills are learnt through family contacts and informal exposure to opportunities where children can take appropriate levels of responsibility. While schools can promote this, we have already seen that schools may not be best placed to meet children such as Sally's needs. Perhaps in another life Sally might have embedded in a school somewhere and they would have played to her strengths. For now all we can say is that if children such as Sally do not have the necessary opportunities then we must be alert and alive to providing them. The smallest flicker of interest may represent a lifeline for the future.

So, we come back again to how much of resilient work is attention to detail, the little things that we have described making all the difference. Once again we emphasise how crucial it is as resilient practitioners to be competent in the 'management of effective detail' (Elisabeth Henderson, 2005, personal communication). We need this as part of an RT strategic approach.

Conclusion

So much of resilient work is energy, commitment and perseverance; for example dealing with absence from school, trying to help the disaffected re-engage. Then there is supervising homework, making sure your child has everything they need and will remember the three things they have to do that day. We have to generate the right environment if children are going to learn and apply themselves to their schoolwork.

For children without the advantages of a stable, facilitating home environment where these tasks are carried out as part of the everyday fabric of life, emulating what works has be an articulated thought-through whole. We can not expect it to arise automatically. The fact is that children such as Sally will fail if we let events take their course. They may still fail but there is hope of achieving something and building upon this for the future if we pay attention to the detail.

There are some tricky issues here though. Do we, for example, place a high priority on providing Sally with a stable school but at some distance away and thereby jeopardise whatever social networks she has managed to preserve in her chaotic life? Alongside this practical question there are theoretical debates as to what has the greater influence on her life, say educational achievement or attachment, in RT terms 'Learning' or 'Belonging'. The relative value of these to her may change with her stage of development. At certain points in her life her more stable attachments may only be with peers.

There are no ready-made answers to these issues and, while we know that further large-scale research might shed more light, we can not be certain of this. The time-scale for our work with children like Sally is now. Of course, Sally's life course is a natural experiment in its own right and as RT practitioners, who learn as we go, we should treat it as such. In this sense our suggestions in this compartment represent early illustrative work. We are extrapolating from other more straightforward scenarios and even there the mechanisms by which they work may be somewhat obscure. However, it is by trying them out in real-life situations of constellated disadvantage that we can further refine the working models that will inform our practice to be more effective in the future.

In RT we try to make school work, and yet we recognise that we have to provide what it might offer in other ways if children such as Sally are going to reap the benefits of what Learning has to offer.

Chapter 6

Coping

Assume a virtue, if you have it not.

Shakespeare

Introduction

Building up a particular set of skills in children and young people to help them cope in everyday life is our task in this chapter. We start with the premise that acquiring these skills will not necessarily transform a child in any fundamental way although with a combination of luck, developmental growth, time and effort on the part of young people, carers, parents and workers this may well come eventually. We should also remind ourselves of the lesson from complexity theory. Small interventions can have big effects. And as others have shown, including Quinton and Rutter in their observations of disadvantaged children's positive experiences of school, this can be particularly the case in situations where children do not have much of a good thing going for them (1988: 98).

So, if transformation ends up being a by-product of some of the interventions in this chapter, all well and good, and we do not foreclose on the hope that it might. However, a proper consideration of how to work at a deeper level is left until Chapter 7.

Lazarus and Launier define coping as 'efforts, both action-orientated and intrapsychic to manage (i.e. master, tolerate, reduce, minimise) environmental and internal demands, and conflicts among them, which tax or exceed a person's resources' (Lazarus & Launier, 1978: 311). This sounds like a tall order for many of the children in our case studies, and we have a slightly less ambitious view of the concept. The metaphors we might use to convey our task in this Coping chapter are taken from the resilience literature and can be related to the idea of protective factors (Rolf, Masten, Cicchetti, Nuechterlein, & Weintraub, 1990). We are mostly concerned with helping children to insulate themselves against risks and adversities; helping them to withstand the storms that blow up around them.

Another way of thinking about this is to see the ideas in this chapter as ways of helping children develop a good enough fit between themselves and their immediate environment. In other words, optimal adaptation. In resilience research this is interfaced with the goal of developing 'social competence'. Crudely put, the following mechanisms are at play. Increasing a child's ability to cope with everyday life reduces the stress they are under. It can make them more amenable to others and thereby increase their self-esteem. Successfully managing the world around them gives children a sense of competence, and this also contributes to them feeling good about themselves. All of these will free them up for further, more productive, encounters. There is a direct line here into chains of positive reactions.

Of course, any individual child may be considered to some extent responsible for what happens to them as they make their way through everyday life. But, as Miles (2000) reminds us, young people's lives are an outward expression or negotiation of the relationship between structure and agency. So, most children living in constellated disadvantage will have more adversity than will most of us. For example, living in dangerous neighbourhoods, with family members who abuse, and attending schools for children with educational and behavioural difficulties, exposes these children to dangers, adversities and challenges that they have in no way precipitated. Hemmings talks of children's 'hidden corridor curriculum', the informal learning that goes on between peers to develop street-wise behaviour in response to environmental challenges (Hemmings, 2000). Indeed, the children and young people we work with will have developed ways of getting through adversities of which most of us have no actual experience. Looked at in this way, many of their reactions may actually be normative given the circumstances in which they find themselves. As Ungar points out, this is an argument often made by resilience investigators of marginalised populations where psychopathology can become exaggerated because of a lack of cultural understanding (Ungar, 2005b).There is also an irony here that should not escape us. Time and time again it is those children who have most difficulties in navigating a successful path through the world who inhabit its hostile terrains.

Social constructionist and cultural relativist accounts repeatedly stress the ways in which children's behaviour is constructed by the children themselves and that, within a particular cultural context, behaviour that can seem bizarre or downright pathological to an outsider can make good sense to those in the know (James, Jencks, & Prout, 1998). Still, however normative this behaviour might be within a given context, it is worth stressing what we call a therapeutic realist point: certain behaviours do not do young people any favours in the long run. Hence it is worth investing energy in helping them understand what they can do to make it through life in a different way.

So, there is something quite ordinary about this chapter. You might even say that it has a slightly superficial feel to it. Helping children and young people develop particular facades, helping them to *perform* in order to navigate the best way for their world is what we are talking about. 'Fake it until you make it' conveys this sense. The phrase neatly sums up the idea that there does not have to be a perfect 'fit' between what we do and what we feel deep down. And it is often the case that behaviour is more amenable to adaptation than are feelings. Of course, unconscious processes are at work in all our lives and we do not always understand why we do what we do, or feel the way we feel. However, even for the most troubled children, personal agency comes into the picture somewhere and children can choose to try and fake it, even if they haven't yet made it. So, we know that every child and young person we live and work with will have the capacity to be in charge of themselves to some degree.

This is beginning to sound like a major programme, particularly given what we said at the beginning of the chapter about disadvantaged children inhabiting more hostile environments. However, using the concept of 'Coping' somehow lowers the stakes. To us, Coping does not give the impression that big changes are expected, or indeed desired. For many children and parents this can be liberating. Thinking about Jason, one of the young people that we introduced earlier, we are not saying that he needs to completely change the way he is in order for things to be better. Nor does he need to have a psychological conversion of the kind that our next chapter on Core Self will be considering. This is just as well. Jason is in a particularly bad way at the moment and there is no sign that major personal enlightenment is around the corner. He is nearly 16, and has seen very little schooling over the years. Recently he's been in trouble with the police. He has been told that he has a serious mental health problem and psychiatrists have mooted the diagnosis of schizophrenia, although it is as yet still unconfirmed. Our task in relation to this chapter is to consider ways that children and young people like Jason can be helped to manage the world in a way that works for them rather than, as is presently the case, against them. The interventions we introduce in this chapter are summarised in Box 6.1. We will come on to exploring what they mean and how we might use them in detail later on in the chapter. Before that, we set out the links between coping and resilience.

Coping, self-control and resilience

There are many texts in circulation that advise on how to help young people modify their behaviour in order to exercise more adaptive control over their world. Fundamentally these processes are about self-regulation:

> Self-regulation refers to those processes, internal and/or transactional, that enable an individual to guide his/her goal directed activities over time and across changing circumstances (contexts). Regulation implies

---

Box 6.1 Coping (self-control and managing the world)

These interventions help a child to:
- Understand boundaries and keep within them
- Be brave
- Solve problems
- Put on rose-tinted glasses
- Foster their interests
- Calm down/self-soothe
- Remember that tomorrow is another day
- Lean on others when necessary

> modulation of thought, affect, behaviour, or attention via deliberate or automated use of specific mechanisms and supportive metaskills.
>
> (Karoly, 1993: 25)

Although this definition is comprehensive, it is a complicated way of defining what we are talking about. In more straightforward terms our task as resilient therapists is to help Jason and the others develop strategies to become better masters of their own destinies, with the proviso that we are aiming for them to develop mastery that will lead to more adaptive outcomes, to love well, work well and expect well, notwithstanding profound life adversity (Werner & Smith, 1982).

Few would deny that these are laudable goals, but what does self-regulation have to do with resilience? The answer is very much. Researchers have demonstrated that the ability to be in charge of your own actions, and indeed feelings, is a vital ingredient in resilience. The spin we put on this with children and young people is that they do better when they have learned how to manage the world around them. And a better fit is achieved all round. As Aspinwall and Taylor argue (1997), children with good self-regulatory capacities may be skilled at foreseeing potential stressors, analysing how to mitigate their impact and planning effective strategies to manage them. This has a knock-on effect, with such children both experiencing better mental health and also being faced with fewer stresses and strains to deal with. Children with these skills are also good at self-regulating after the event. When exposed to particular stressors, they have strategies available that stop them from escalating the situation and help them get through what has occurred in a productive rather than destructive way.

Within our overall emphasis on self-regulation, there are two concepts that are important to grasp in this chapter. These are 'internal' and 'external' locus of control. Broadly speaking, people with an internal locus of control tend to think that they are often responsible for their own destiny and life and they feel that they can make things happen. People with an external locus of control tend towards seeing themselves as victims of other people and of structures.

The resilience evidence base suggests that children and young people who have an internal locus of control are more likely to have positive outcomes in life (Hechtman, 1991; Luthar, 1991; Parker, Cowen, Work, & Wyman, 1990). However, some scholars have drawn attention to the difficulties of applying this to all contexts (Chen & Taylor, 2005). Excessively controlling and manipulative actions from individuals with a distorted sense of their own power and what they want to achieve with it, might well earn them a text-book classification of an internal locus of control. In these cases, resilient mechanisms are not at work. Parker et al. (1990) write of such children having an unrealistic sense of their own power.

Another group of children with an internal locus of control that is not ultimately very helpful to them are those who take undue responsibility for bad things that have occurred. Again, this is not what we are hoping for in children with a positive internal locus of control that will function as a resilient mechanism. Rather, these children will see themselves as agents of change, within structural constraints, who can negotiate and navigate through life for themselves. So, actually, what we are looking for is something of a balancing act.

In keeping with the modest aims of this chapter, our goal for children for whom it is suitable to use Coping interventions will be to shift them towards at least acting *as if* they have a greater positive internal locus of control than they actually do. Acting as if they have a greater internal locus of control will, in many situations, work as a resilient mechanism. Hence, the ideas here should help children and young people to develop strategies for dealing with situations that were previously beyond them.

Before we consider the interventions in detail, a word about our Noble Truths—Accepting and Conserving deserve a mention. The significance of Enlisting comes on board later in the chapter.

Accepting and Conserving

Knowing and understanding precisely where we start from with a child and family is for an RT practitioner an essential part of the Noble Truth 'Accepting'. In this chapter, the focus for Accepting is on understanding how much control a child or young person feels they have over their actions and what happens to them. These are important starting points for applying the Coping interventions.

In the case of some children, young people and families, we will know where they are starting from vis-à-vis their locus of control. However, in many cases this is 'internal world' information, and is not necessarily accessible to us in a straightforward way.

Take Jason. His workers may have only the vaguest understanding of his mental-health difficulties and they may think that he has taken some quite deliberate and purposeful choices not to be in school and to steal from shops. They may consider him to have an internal locus of control that is quite damaging. However, it may be the case that Jason has a quite different view of his recent life story that depicts himself further along the continuum towards external locus of control than people working with him might think. He may actually see himself as a manipulated victim, 'a feather for each wind that blows', as Shakespeare wrote in *The Winter's Tale*. It will be important to know where Jason is starting from. Only then can we think with him about how to apply each particular intervention and move him along the locus of control continuum in the direction he needs to take.

And of course there are more general question marks over the depth of his mental-health difficulties. At this stage in his life, whether they are anxiety related, trauma induced or symptomatic of a schizophrenic process is as yet unclear. It could be a combination of all three. Practitioners working with Jason will need the capacity to tolerate considerable uncertainty and be aware of, and manage, their own anxieties, some derived from transferences. And at some points of engagement with Jason his hold on reality may be so tenuous that it is difficult to understand him through everyday conversation. In such cases it is important to try and then try again in each period of engagement in the light of any change in context. There may only be transient windows of opportunity in which we can think with him how to apply each intervention and move him along the locus of control continuum in a positive direction. These must be seized.

In the case of some children and young people, it can be helpful to use tried and tested techniques to determine the current state of their locus of control status if it is not immediately obvious. There are various resources available that can be useful in teasing out precisely how children and young people see themselves in relation to their sense of personal efficacy and self-regulation. Plummer's resource book includes some helpful photocopiable sheets that in our experience children and adolescents will engage with (Plummer, 2001, 2005).

A simple checklist for ascertaining the degree to which a child or young person has an internal locus of control can be found in the third of Daniel and Wassell's volumes on *Assessing and Promoting Resilience in Vulnerable Children* (Daniel & Wassell, 2004: 98).

We have found the use of concrete resources helpful with many children and young people, even those who one might think would not cooperate with filling in worksheets. In our experience, it is worth trying to instigate an activity of this nature, as young people can find a focus and task in the moment, that goes beyond talking, very helpful.

In the absence of dedicated resource booklets, some simple therapeutic techniques can be very effective, and need little in the way of props. A technique that we use is to ask children and young people to give a percentage figure as to how in control of their own life they feel. The technique can also be used with parents and carers to eventually get at how much control they feel they have over their children. This is a method that is often used in cognitive behavioural therapy (CBT) and, although it can seem artificial and arbitrary to psychodynamically-trained practitioners, children, young people and parents/carers often take to it surprisingly easily. For children or young people who find numbers too complicated, a simple drawing exercise will suffice. In our experience, colouring in segments of a cake, to show the extent to which a person feels in control is rarely beyond the intellectual grasp of anybody.

Conserving also deserves a mention when we are thinking about Jason and Coping. Practitioners working with Jason may have to work hard to keep their own strong filters away from their framing of him and his situation. Negative cultural and moral discourses around prostitution are extremely provocative (Hart, 1998). Many of us will get caught up in them and will find it difficult to really focus on Jason. We will find ourselves drawn to his prostitute lifestyle as though it were him in his entirety. And we will be likely to feel that there is nothing good in it. We will urge Jason to get away from prostitution, but at the same time our message to him may be one of vicarious and gratuitous fascination. It is important, then, to think of some genuinely good things that he gets from what he does, or at least some of the ambiguities involved in prostitution, as many a novelist has portrayed (see, for example, the works of Jean Genet).

It will also be helpful to see Jason as more than a 'rent boy'. Once we start on this line it is not difficult to find an alternative perspective. Take the money. He has actually saved some of it. None is being spent on drugs. Friendship also features. He has a very good friend in Lee, a 22-year-old who works alongside Jason. In fact, Lee and Jason dream of moving to Thailand together and setting up a beach bar. These hopes and dreams all deserve to be bottled and conserved in the therapeutic practice and narrative.

We will shortly be moving on to think about the interventions in this chapter, and our exploration of how we see them working as resilient mechanisms. Before that, though, we present a summary, in Box 6.2, of research findings associating coping with resilience. As we have argued in previous chapters, these associations should not be taken and simplistically applied to individual situations. However, they do give us a general indication of what might be helpful.

Choosing your Coping interventions

As with each of our previous chapters, this section draws on the case study to show how each intervention might be applied in practice.

Box 6.2 Associations between Coping and resilience

- Children and young people who can be helped to understand their life story through a resilient framework, in order to see some meaning and significance in all their life events, can find strength and resilience (Ungar, 2004).
- The capacity to reframe negative life events in a positive light (Himelein & McElrath, 1996).
- The ability to problem solve. Although this may be considered to be a natural by-product of high intelligence, some researchers have demonstrated that it is a skill that can be learnt (Buckner, Mezzacappa, & Beardslee, 2003).
- An internal locus of control (Hechtman, 1991; Luthar, 1991; Parker, Cowen, Work, & Wyman, 1990).
- The development of specific talents and interests (Gilligan, 1999).

Understand boundaries and keep within them

In a previous chapter, Belonging, we talked about boundaries at some length. We revisit the subject now, slanting our discussion towards Coping strategies. Typically, as children grow up they begin to internalise the boundaries that their parents/carers have put in place for them over the years. While for some children adolescence can mark a period in which boundary keeping is tested afresh, for most the developmental process sees children and adults negotiating a coexistence that enables everyone to rub along reasonably well. For children growing up in especially challenging circumstances, for example within areas of high socioeconomic deprivation, as we saw in Chapter 4, resilience has been correlated with increased supervision from parents and carers. We are not exactly sure of the mechanisms involved here, but probably there are mainly two. Self-esteem—the self-worth that comes from others caring about us that we considered in Chapter 4—and the practical protection afforded. Put in very basic terms, children and young people need people who watch out for them. Those that have effective supervisors are less likely to get into risky situations that can harm them. And some children, like Jason, start off in risky situations in the first place, and so will need even more effective monitoring and supervision.

It is worth remembering that young people like Jason have not had the benefit of continuous consistent adults in their lives who have exercised a capacity to help them negotiate boundaries. Hence, the first message in this section takes us back to acceptance—attempts to help children like Jason understand boundaries will not be a simple task, yet it should be persisted with. The importance of enlisting others to the task, and to coordinate messages so that the young person receives a clear consensus from adults in the team around them, taking due consideration of their own wishes and needs, is fundamental. For young people with cognitive difficulties and for those with mental-health difficulties that distort their views on reality, the latter will be especially challenging. And when the going gets particularly tough, it is worth remembering the points we made in Chapter 4. Even though children and young people can seem to be rejecting the very people who put in place boundaries, they do need people in their lives who persist in trying to do this job alongside them.

Understanding boundaries and keeping within them so that children are not put under unwelcome stress is clearly an area of life that holds challenges for Jason and others like him. So, our first piece of advice is to keep any intervention on this level very simple, and as specific as possible. Using the idea of developing a bottom line, which children and young people might choose not to cross, is helpful in giving focus. Written contracts can also be helpful in practice with children who need something concrete to help remind them of what they agreed to.

In Jason's case, an important first goal will be, as we explained earlier in the chapter, to understand how he thinks about his own agency, and gain an awareness of his tendency to see the world through the lens of his external locus of control. Second, specific exercises can be attempted that help Jason shift his locus of control in favour of an internal one. In this case, in relation to understanding boundaries and keeping within them.

A third step would be to find out from Jason if there are any specific areas of his life in which he feels he would benefit from increasing his ability to stick within boundaries. Undertaking child-led therapy and social work tasks is, quite rightly, frequently emphasised in policy and practice these days. However, the communication challenges here are very real (Luckock, Lefevre, Orr, Jones, Marchant, & Tanner, 2006). Those of us working with children and young people in the context of constellated disadvantage know that they will not always provide ready answers to our questions. We will all have experienced interactions with children or young people in which they feel unable to articulate an opinion one way or another on a given topic, including their own state of mental health. 'Dunno', 'I'm not quite sure', or silence can greet even the most friendly and engaging Resilient Therapist. Asking children to give their 'best guess' is one technique that can be used. Another is to offer a potential framework, derived from a therapist's 'best hunch' that can be put to the young person as a possible starting point. In this case, to keep the therapeutic alliance intact, it is important to emphasise that the therapist's idea is only one possible way of framing the issue, and that it could be completely wrong.

In Jason's case his work as a rent boy would give a good opportunity for a starting point in relation to thinking about boundaries. Operating in the Coping domain, it will be important to avoid any hint of moralism or any attempt to explore deeper identity issues. A practical focus on personal safety can be introduced. Jason could usefully be helped to develop a few ground rules that help him avoid particularly stressful situations. Jason certainly has an external locus of control. He believes that the situations that arise in which men beat him up are completely beyond his control. However, giving him help to analyse his work patterns might lead him to understand that working in particular areas of the town, and with complete strangers, increases the likelihood that he will be attacked. As we know, Jason has a good friend in another rent boy Lee, but he does not use Lee to help him look after himself, even though Lee worries about Jason and wants to be a good friend. Working patiently, and in a very concrete and specific way with Jason to facilitate him understanding that his own behaviour has some relationship to the outcome of a given situation will be very beneficial.

This does not mean that we are trying to get Jason to take responsibility for himself in a moral sense. This debate risks complicating the issue too much and is better dealt with within the frame of Core Self, considered in the next chapter. Rather, our aim in helping Jason to cope will be to show him some quite simple laws of the world. Certain actions are likely to have undesirable consequences. Helping him to plan what he can do to avoid them will be key.

Once Jason and the team around him have a simple message about what the bottom line is for him in relation to keeping himself safe, a consolidation step can be taken. In order to consolidate this written prompts might be needed. Jason could write himself a card with his bottom line strategy on it. A worker could write him a letter spelling out what Jason had decided as his basic rules.

Other adults can be enlisted to help him keep within the boundary. A focus of parenting work with his mother, for example, could be this one issue—what she can do, in very specific, manageable terms, to help Jason to keep himself safe. We know that strong parental supervision constitutes a resilient move for children in the context of constellated disadvantage. Of course as we have seen from our discussion in Chapter 3, Jason's mother has so many problems that even thinking about helping Jason feels like an agenda for way down the line, and most of the professionals around have given up trying to get her to do this. However, workers should keep on trying to help her to take any very small steps that demonstrate her concern for him. Sitting down with Jason and his worker to have a conversation about safety, and to express the fact that she worries about him when he's not around would be a small start. Joining with the worker, and even possibly with Jason's friend Lee, in drawing up the bottom line that Jason agrees not to cross is a bigger step. Lee, the worker and Jason's mother could all be witness to his commitment not to get into cars with strangers. If Jason's worker pays attention to detail and understands the value of incremental steps, this should be achievable.

Be brave

We have little empirical evidence to directly substantiate this intervention, but in our experience, helping children to be brave appears to be correlated with developing resilience. Some of Brooks and Goldstein's practical ideas for helping children and parents acquire a resilient mindset are appropriate here (Brooks & Goldstein, 2001). Bravery implies working towards an internal locus of control, which as we said earlier, has been correlated with resilience. Of course any child taking on Coping interventions will be acting bravely just by that very act. Trying to be brave is a mechanism that encourages children and young people to expand their horizons, part of which gives them new possibilities for personal development and self-fulfilment.

This intervention is in keeping with our notion of the performative nature of some of the ideas in this chapter. In fact, some traces of the idea seem to be at the heart of popular conceptions of resilience. Resilient children are children who succeed against the odds. For some this connotes bravery and a determination to succeed. But what of children who seem excessively scared of everything, and have little internalised determination to do better? For these children we have found it helpful to take the principle of 'fake it until you make it' and apply it to the specific difficulty they face. Encouraging children to act as though they were confident and resilient, even if they feel that they are not, can be very effective. Brooks and Goldstein's (2001) work provides specific examples of how this can be achieved. One key approach that they advocate is for parents and carers to pay close attention to how they might be thwarting their children's emotional and social development. This may come about as a result of parents resorting to parenting techniques that their own parents used to use simply because they are familiar, rather than effective. Or it may be through the understandable goal of trying to spare one's children any pain or difficulty. The trick is for parents to avoid enmeshing themselves so much in their children's process that they end up trying to do everything for them.

For those of you reading this book who live or work with children where enmeshment is a reality, what is crucial is how to facilitate, rather than dictate, children's development. Brooks and Goldstein (2001) offer valuable practical advice on how to do this. In our practice, and in our Resilient Therapy workshops, we do come across parents who need help with disentangling from their children. However, it is our experience that the most disadvantaged children are rarely in this position. Sadly, it is very unlikely that the children in our case studies will experience many adults becoming enmeshed with them. Rather, most adults in constellated disadvantage are in danger of disengagement, including workers. With the exception of the complex birth family relations we considered in our chapter on Belonging, our task is always more about trying to get adults, including workers, to stick.

Some children may have little difficulty pinpointing their acts of bravery. However, it may be that 'bravery' is a concept that can be applied to one aspect of their life—a seemingly maladaptive one—and usefully transported to another. Most of us could point to acts that children and young people do that by most objective measures would seem foolhardy and the result of bravado. There is a gendered component to this behaviour, with boys more prone to it than girls (Pollack, 2004). However, with a little imagination some positives can be excavated from some seemingly desperate and destructive acts. Of course, this intervention needs to be used wisely especially with children experiencing abuse and violence. And, as researchers have shown, inculcating macho bravado into boys is a hazard of socialisation in school and family life that it is hard for boys to avoid (Keddie, 2003; Pollack, 2004).

However, for Jason, the reframing approach might work. For example, he could be helped to understand that there is a skill in being so street wise and also in stealing from shops with nerves of steel. These are both talents that can be usefully transported to another arena in his life, and a different twist on them could make them more adaptive skills. For example, for all his interaction with services, Jason has confided in very few people about his deep fear of talking to his mother about the whereabouts of his father, and his wish to trace him. Using Jason's obvious bravery in the context of stealing and prostitution and asking him if he could usefully transport that talent to help him with other things in his life could help begin that conversation.

Solve problems

'Cognitive intelligence' has been identified as a marker of resilience in children (Luthar, 1991). We cannot say definitively what mechanisms are at play. Amongst them are intelligent children's increased ability to generate different solutions to potential problems, and therefore more successfully negotiate adversity. The resulting feelings of self-efficacy can also be understood as enhancing resilience.

However, studies have shown that problem-solving abilities cannot simply be mapped on to cognitive intelligence, and that these are gendered to some extent too (Block and Kremen, 1996; Buckner, Mezzacappa, & Beardslee, 2003). Thus, despite the low attainment of the children in our case studies, there is great potential for them to develop their ability to solve problems. As we saw in Chapter 5, researchers have shown that the ability to be focused and organised, to generate alternative solutions to problems, and to be flexible in one's thinking are clearly skills that children can learn. And the clear message from the success of many intervention programmes to practitioners, parents and young people is that there are effective methods that demonstrate *how* they can be learnt. In Box 6.3 we draw on our own practice to suggest some techniques and advice for helping children and young people solve problems.

Put on rose-tinted glasses

Developing something of an illusory relationship with our own life experiences can sometimes be a good thing. Of course, matters of degree are of great importance here. And some argue quite the opposite. For example, the value of emotional catharsis and explicit emotional expression of negative experience has been a hallmark of psychoanalytic approaches.

Nevertheless, for some time now researchers and practitioners have demonstrated the worth of 'cognitive reappraisal'—i.e. helping people construct their past experiences in the best light possible. In one study researchers have, for example, shown that rape victims who are able to see their experiences as somehow meaningful in their lives, or who minimise the impact of the experience on their lives, do better long term (Dufour, Nadeau, & Bertrand, 2000; Himelein & McElrath, 1996).

Used wisely this is possibly the most important intervention in this chapter for Jason. Picture his social services, education, youth offending and child and adolescent mental health services files. They are all bulging. Jason has been assessed more times than he can remember, and he needs nobody else to tell him that much of what he is doing in his life is not helpful for his long-term outcomes. Jason's experiences of workers have included many different meetings highlighting his problems, diagnoses and formulations being explored and consequences spelt out.

There is now a growing recognition that young people like Jason can be better helped by assisting them to develop a more adaptive, resilient view of their lives. We have called this putting on rose-tinted glasses. Other, slightly less extreme examples of the idea include putting a positive spin on things. Still others use a recovery or compassionate case formulation model (Grant, Mills, Mulhern, & Short, 2004). In a more academic language these can be viewed as developing 'narratives' of resilience (Ungar, 2004).

In our development work, participants found the idea of rose-tinted glasses to be a useful one. The term itself reminds us it has limits, as it connotes the constructed nature of the reality we are talking about. Looking at something through glasses leaves the viewer one step removed. Using the term rose tinted conveys clearly that there may be something a

Box 6.3 Techniques and advice for helping children solve problems

The first step in helping young people to solve problems is to engage them with another person in the task. Here Accepting comes into the frame. If you fail to engage them, acknowledge this and, rather than blaming the client, do something for them to get the help they need. Get somebody else on the case rather than making the young person move on from the service.

Watch that you do not become enmeshed with the child or young person in a conscious or unconscious effort to spare them pain, difficulty and the uncomfortable feelings of doubt and uncertainty. Enmeshment can make you very unsure about what is 'yours' and what is 'theirs', a transference point that workers can explore in supervision. It can make adults too quick to present ready made solutions for children so that they don't get an opportunity to work out what they need to do themselves.

Before they can think about solving problems children and young people need help in generating possible solutions, i.e. in developing a repertoire of solutions. Many of the children we work with find it hard to imagine any alternative solutions to the one that they applied in a given situation. Hence Jason may not see any alternative to his act of hitting the police officer who cautioned him for stealing a chocolate bar from WH Smith. For those who tend to think in very concrete terms, it can be helpful to use a series of what we call 'scaffolding prompts' to help them consider alternatives. This can be done verbally, pictorially or through writing. Encourage the young person to generate ideas (possibly using stick cartoon people and speech bubbles). A helpful way of engaging sceptical young people is to ask them to consider how different individuals might have solved the difficulty they faced. The worker need put no judgement on possible solutions at this point. Rather, the young person can be encouraged to generate the type of solution that, for example, their worst enemy might conjure up, their best friend, their last teacher, etc. The point of this exercise is that it generates a repertoire of different responses and gives young people a concrete aide memoir of the way in which different people can respond in different ways and generate potential solutions.

Once a repertoire of responses has been assembled in relation to a given issue, children and young people can be asked to rank the possible alternatives in terms of how well they are likely to help in causing less stress for the young person.

Some young people will be responsive to games and role play that help them to generate different solutions to problems.

little artificial going on. Hence it faces the fact that for some people putting on rose-tinted glasses will actually be an act of denial. Young people in our development work warned us of this, since they might deny how emotionally painful an experience was to such a degree that they became eaten up by grief without knowing it, or they might delude themselves into thinking that dangerous, antisocial behaviour was good for them. As the young people rightly pointed out, the intervention needs to be used wisely. In Jason's case this is especially pertinent since his grasp on reality has been questioned many times. Reinforcing that would be very unhelpful.

But most of us would understand that there is a difference between bringing Jason down from flights of fantasy, and Accepting his need to construct his gay prostitute identity, at least in part, as something worth having. Even if he were to move away from this identity and life choice, he could accept it as something he has learned from.

In our experience, children and young people rarely need us to point out in graphic detail the error of their ways. Time and time again we have worked with young people who appear superficially confident, but who, within the context of a trusting therapeutic relationship, eventually reveal themselves to have extraordinary low self-esteem. They also display feelings of strong self-deprecation. This is the consequence of their take on what they have done, who they think they are, and what others have done to them. Dwelling with children and young people for too long in this realm can exacerbate or precipitate depressive symptoms. Often we do this without even realising it through the negative and pathologising reports we write on them. The accumulation of these in children's files from different members of their teams is gratuitously denigrating. Rather, it is so important that we look for and emulate ways of describing behaviour, presentation and events in a way that is not demeaning and/or pathological. This idea is key.

Of course a careful balance must be achieved. Some young people who engage in self-harming or criminal activities adopt a stance of normalising their experiences and complete endorsement of it by a therapist will merely reinforce the negative behaviour. As we have considered before, the Rochester Child Resilience Project, which explored resilience amongst poor urban children, found that positive future expectations and perceptions of personal competence were helpful only among participants when those perceptions were realistic (Wyman et al., 1992; Wyman, Cowen, Work, Koyt-Meyers, Magnus & Fagen, 1999). It may then be the case that the 'rose-tinted glasses' technique is most useful in positively reframing *past* experience.

Despite these caveats, the concept of rose-tinted glasses can be used in active discussions with young people. The idea helps them to understand the different filters through which their life and their experiences can be understood. The 'rose-tinted' metaphor helps us hang on to the fact that there is something of a distortion occurring, but that this distortion has a function, and that it may be for the good.

Take Jason. We know that he will be feeling some despair towards himself. Yet he may not be in a position to trust someone else enough to talk about that. Technically speaking, that would be a job for interventions in the next chapter, Core Self. But, paradoxically, going through a process of putting on rose-tinted glasses with him will help free him up for the challenge. So, the message for working with Jason will be to start by generating resilient narratives.

The idea of looking at rape, abuse and neglect, abandonment, alcohol and drug abuse in a way that connotes a positive spin may well seem perverse to many people. And yet we know, first, that for children and young people's self-worth to develop, and for them to resist being overwhelmed by feelings of shame and inadequacy, more resilient narratives about their experiences need to be developed. Second, we know that any individual resilient narrative is only partial. The idea of rose-tinted glasses is only one way of framing what is happening. Wider social and cultural forces continue to construct other narratives for children and young people. Hence in Jason's case, an individual resilient therapist might undertake some useful work with him on exploring his life to date through a resilient frame. This would include understanding the function of prostitution and stealing in his life, through a compassionate case formulation.

For Jason, work in this area will surely start with his 'delinquent' activities—prostitution and stealing. The goal here will be to help Jason understand the function of these behaviours and identities in his life. The second goal will be to encourage him to develop other identity narratives that can co-exist with these. Eventually Jason may be encouraged to hold on to the skills inherent in these behaviours and identities, but to let go of their maladaptive application. Techniques for helping children and young people more generally are to be found in Box 6.4 opposite.

Foster their interests

In Chapter 7, Core Self, we will consider the importance of bringing out children's talents, that deeper part of themselves where real potential to be particularly good at something lies. In this chapter our aim is less ambitious. We seek to focus on children's interests, and never mind whether they represent particular talents for them. We have already seen in Basics how drawing out a child's particular interest through a social group or other activity, in which they are drawn into a circle of potential friends or adult supporters, is an effective resilient strategy.

However, developing their interests need not necessarily involve a group activity, although for some children and young people the potential for positive outcomes might be increased if this is instigated.

Box 6.4 Techniques for helping children and young people put on rose-tinted glasses

Ungar offers a helpful twist on the use of genograms and sociograms. He builds on a solution-focused approach to genograms (Kuehl, 1995; Ungar, 2004). The diagrams he creates with troubled children and young people are not just genealogies, but trace power relations, ideas, problems and solutions across generations. They can be used to chart individual and family strengths.

In 2005, in a training session run by the Post Adoption Centre, London, Holly van Gulden introduced one of us to a game that helps children and young people to see themselves as people with different parts, rather than one negative identity. We have used this successfully, with children and teenagers. Her game is based on an origami paper arrangement known as a cootie catcher in the USA. (www.momsminivan.com/article-cootie.html tells you how to make one.) The game helps a child or young person understand that any negative self-perceptions they might have should be understood as part of a whole self, which is more than this. Van Gulden encourages children to list what they see as their personality traits, talents, etc., and then transposes them onto the cootie catcher. The cootie catcher can then be worked with to put across the idea that different parts of ourselves as being shown at a particular time, but that that does not mean that other parts are not there.

In this chapter we want to emphasise the importance of fostering their interests as a method of coping with adversity that has been associated with resilience (Gilligan, 1999). Again, we do not know for sure what the precise mechanisms are here, but the following are likely candidates. First, fostering children's interests can enable them to succeed, and thereby improve their self-esteem. This, as we suggested earlier, is likely to help them to feel that they are in control of their lives, and steer them towards an internal locus of control. Second, developing children's interests gives them opportunities for fun and enjoyment, the therapeutic effects of which should never be underestimated. In some cases where interests are artistic, musical, or sports related their therapeutic effects have been claimed, although not much research has been done on their relative effectiveness. Third, children can gain valuable solace in certain activities and may find that they help them strengthen their ability to be by themselves and to be less reliant on others. Fourth, finding their interests widens their opportunities for exposure to other resilient mechanisms, thereby playing a part in setting up chains of positive reactions. For example, developing Jason's interest in cutting hair gives him some valuable satisfaction in the moment, particularly if in this particular case the interest turns out to be a talent! But it also leads him to future possibilities.

Calm her/himself down, self-soothe

Relative effectiveness studies of complementary therapies, massage and relaxation approaches are few and far between, particularly in relation to treating children's mental-health difficulties. However, in our experience we have certainly found that children and young people whose anxieties can escalate need strategies to calm themselves down at difficult moments. For this intervention to have an effect, children first need help in understanding what triggers anger or anxiety, and how this manifests itself in their bodies. There are many useful relaxation tapes, DVDs, books and worksheets available that can be used with people to collaboratively diagnose their difficulties and to then help them calm themselves down. A list of strategies and resources that children and young people we have worked with have found particularly useful are listed in Box 6.5. Of course, buying a tape, book or set of worksheets is, in our experience, often far easier than actually enlisting a child or young person in getting on and doing with you what it says on the tin. Some take to them very easily, and others are more complicated to engage.

Box 6.5 Techniques for helping children and young people to calm down

For children and young people who need help with anger the following quick techniques can be tried: punch bags, kick boxing, writing a letter to someone and then tearing it up, writing a diary, screaming and shouting in a room far away from other people, leaving the room, avoiding situations that they know will wind them up, using their mind to distract themselves and to go somewhere else in their head, having a bath with lots of bubbles, stroking themselves, talking to themselves in a calm voice.

Children who got very anxious suggested the following: relaxation tapes and breathing exercises, visualisations that take them through their worries and imagine themselves having mastery over the situation, planning cards that are a visual or written reminder of what they are doing at a given moment of the day, painting, drawing or cooking.

Plummer's workbooks contain a wealth of worksheets that focus on helping children and young people calm down when they become hyper-aroused (Plummer, 2001, 2005).

We have a number of messages from our experience of working with children and young people in constellated disadvantage. The first is not to give up too soon. For example, a young person might initially dismiss the idea of using relaxation tapes. Yet when the therapist produces one and puts it on in a session, the young person becomes absorbed in the process in spite of their initial reaction. The second is to try different things. A child may think that using exercise to calm them down is a good idea and yet have been extremely disdainful at writing a diary. We have found it helpful not to have too rigid an idea of what technique will work with which age group. What works for whom is really a very individual thing. And we have sometimes found ourselves successfully revisiting an idea that a young person has dismissed in the past. The beauty of the developmental process is that children are changing all the time.

A further approach that we use with some success is to introduce the idea of research with young people. It is worth telling them that the technique you are trying has been proven to work, or that it has yet to be definitely proven to work, and you would be interested in their opinion on the matter. And, finally, if at times it seems as though you really are not getting anywhere much at all, be comforted by complexity theory. Little things really can make a difference, and we might never exactly know what a person has made of our intervention.

Remember that tomorrow is another day

Again, this is one of the interventions where we do not have a wealth of direct empirical evidence to support our assertion that this is a resilient mechanism. However, much of relevance can be inferred from what researchers have demonstrated. There are two ways in which we might best understand this mechanism. First, it can be used to underline the useful ability to look into the future and to think about what might be beneficial. This can help avoid unnecessary stressors. Quinton and Rutter's (1988) work talks of the planning abilities of the resilient women in their sample of institutionally-reared mothers. The ability to plan infers a capacity to think beyond the moment, which in turn rests on the capacity to self-regulate, rather than simply to act on every impulse.

This intervention can also help children to move on from difficult experiences and to avoid the energy that is expended through being caught up in them. This ability can free children up to be open to positive chain reactions, rather than immersing themselves in a cycle of negativity. In Jason's case the intervention can be used in both ways. First, to help him gain some planning abilities over his life and to think ahead. The technique of asking him to talk aloud and to imagine days in his life, in specific detail, some time in the future can help develop this capacity. He could predict some very positive situations for himself, and fill in the detail on how these could be best achieved.

Second, remembering that tomorrow is another day will help Jason rid himself of the negative feelings he has about specific encounters that have gone badly.

Help child to lean on others when necessary

In Chapter 5 we wrote at some length about children's need for others in their life with whom they can bond and experience being part of a group. We need say very little more about this here. However, we have included this intervention in Coping because we want to make the point that some children may be so frightened and overwhelmed by the thought of leaning on others that they will need gentle encouragement to perform as if one day they could. For example, getting to the reasons why Jason does not rely on his friend Lee, when Lee is so available to him, are complex and may need the type of work indicative of that discussed in the following chapter. However, a start can be made that sees Jason experimenting with the very idea of relying on others. And Lee would be a good place to begin on this journey.

Conclusion

This chapter had modest ambitions (Box 6.6). Our aim was to show that children and young people can be helped to cope and that this involves guiding them to understand more about their interactions with the world and to develop more control. We reiterate that even small interventions can be potentially useful for longer-term outcomes. We took the lessons from resilience theory and applied them. Jason's story was used throughout to illustrate our ideas.

We have highlighted some of the difficulties we have had in trying to engage the very disadvantaged children and young people that we work with in the kinds of practices that come more readily to other clients. Persistence, continuity, the ability to try different techniques and approaches will certainly help. Trying things that children and young people might initially reject can be particularly taxing for practitioners. With this in mind the lessons from Chapter 2 need to be constantly revisited.

We make no claims in this chapter that we are effecting deep change in children and young people. This we leave to our next and final practice chapter. Chapter 7 is about working with children's Core Self and it is to this issue that we now turn.

Box 6.6 Concluding tips for Coping

1. Develop awareness of where, when and how the need to self-regulate occurs.

    Track back: Where does the behaviour come from? What are the triggers for it?

2. Think about:

    Circumstances (particular places, particular people, what's going on in the family, particular times of day).

    Internal triggers (e.g. anger built up inside, disappointment, frustration, feelings of inadequacy, failure, hunger, being tired, addictions, discomfort, trauma, expecting attacks, glass nearly empty approach to life, isolation).

3. What to do? What works?

    Remember that nobody knows exactly what will work in each situation. You are experimenting and in experimenting will become more of a resilient expert. The goal is to help the child take control of her/his behaviour.

    Make preparation: Plan strategies and make agreements.

    Don't give up after trying one thing. You need a combination of major optimism and the understanding that what you try might not work. The good news is that there are always other things to try. If at first you don't succeed, try, try again.

Chapter 7

Core Self

Thoughts that do often lie too deep for tears.

William Wordsworth

Introduction

Digging deep, and trying to achieve profound shifts in the Core Self of individuals is implicit in many schools of therapy. In some, for example psychoanalytic, cognitive and certain attachment therapies, they are explicit goals. Inherent in these approaches is that bringing about changes to children's core psychological functions will often have far-reaching protective functions and developmental gains for vulnerable children. Whether it is to develop 'reflective self-functioning' (Fonagy, Steele, Moran, Steele, & Higgitt, 1993), to address 'depressive cognitions' (Beck, Rush, Shaw, & Emery, 1979; Seligman, 1975), and/or to develop a pattern of 'secure attachment' (Ainsworth, Blehar, Waters, & Wall, 1978; Bowlby, 1969), there is a wealth of potential here for developing resilient programmes. Many of these approaches have formed the basis of resilience-promotion initiatives. Related but distinct is the research and resilience-promotion work founded on the concepts of self-esteem, developing self-efficacy, competence and confidence (Masten, Germezy, & Tellegen, 1988).

Often disadvantaged children do not have the experiences that will help them make developmental steps at the same time as many of their peers and they often experience situations in life that expose them to challenges for which they are not developmentally prepared. Their developmental pattern is one of delays, interruptions and setbacks connected to a lack of normative experiences. Talent and interest are obscured by the weight of unrelenting circumstance. Hope becomes sacrificed to the need just to survive. Therefore, givens such as biology and circumstance have a compounding and too often negative significance for disadvantaged children.

Nevertheless, children do have abilities, sensitivities, talents, even a genius perhaps for certain pursuits, which represent the promise of future social capital, or even happiness. When these resources appear to be absent, it is even more crucial that we unearth and use them to whatever advantage is possible. Sometimes just one of these elements can make all the difference. They can interact and combine to carve an even stronger impression on circumstances and create new possibilities, which could have a major impact on their long-term outcomes, in childhood, adolescence and into adult life.

Sally, as we have seen, did not have a primary school career. During those years she missed out on art, sport and educational trips. Also, outside school, she did not go to horse-riding, swimming or to friends' parties or only ever once to any of them before further attempts were abandoned. Despite the best intentions of those who cared for her during those early years, in terms of normal childhood experiences, the list is weighted heavily in the 'missing out' direction. This is the reality of deprivation and constellated disadvantage and it has led to Sally, when we take a snapshot of how she is doing at age fourteen, only just beginning to open up to what life can hold for her.

In this chapter, in particular, we look to building hope so that children can see their lives as having the potential to change and to progress. We want to help children to understand themselves, others and their own part in shaping their lives. We focus in on sensibilities and talents, real or potential, that may take a long time to bring about, but that can play a sustaining and abiding role in their lives. We need to remove blocks to them engaging in normal developmental progressions and to treat effectively any condition that undermines this process.

Whereas earlier in this book we have concentrated on shorter-term aims to build resilience or broader aims but external to the child, we are now stepping back to see what must be done with a longer-term perspective and at a deeper individual level. The focus here is on the internal life of children, the landscape of what we call their 'personal paradigm'. In Resilient Therapy, this is work on Core Self.

Whilst for other therapists Core Self work is their raison d'être, for the RT practitioner to use it requires something of a leap of faith. We, the authors, are all trained in therapeutic approaches that work at this level. However, we acknowledge their limitations for resilient work. First, like Basics, Core Self has only a tenuous connection to the formal resilience research and practice base. Second, many therapies that work at this level require clients to be what is known as psychologically minded. This risks excluding many of the people we work with. Third, such therapies are based on a strong therapeutic alliance model while, although we always endeavour to create this, we will work for children and families even where we have to start with the most tenuous beginnings. Fourth, and anticipating our discussion in the final chapter, therapy which is naïve to the dynamics of disadvantage risks reinforcing that disadvantage and pathologising those that should benefit. At this naïve level there is a danger of confusing 'revelations' and 'confessions' with therapeutic outcomes, forming a gratuitous archaeology of self.

What, then, is the 'core' in Core Self? It is, as we stated earlier, something of a pragmatic presentational device to call this Core Self. Working at depth sometimes means that mechanisms of change are more obscure and interwoven. Their action can seem mysterious. We may not, at this stage of development of therapy research, be able to elucidate them precisely or in such a way that is readily discernible from the effect of other compartments and interventions. This is no reason not to use them and, as we shall see, there are hints in the resilience research base of what they might be and how important they are.

In order to gain what benefits we can from Core-Self work, we will need to find our way through the undergrowth of children's thwarting circumstances and individual turmoil on a treasure hunt with very few clues. Indeed, a treasure hunt where there may not even be any treasure however hard you look. Before we proceed with this task, we need to get the measure of this undergrowth by spelling out the relationship between givens and individual processes.

Box 7.1 Core Self interventions

- Instil a sense of hope
- Teach the child to understand other people's feelings
- Help the child know her/himself
- Help the child take responsibility for her/himself
- Foster their talents
- There are tried and tested treatments for specific problems, use them

---

Core Self, givens and the individual

Recently, one area of increased resilience research in this area has been that of culture (Ungar, 2005a). Even within cultures and certainly across cultures there is an amazing diversity where differing capacities and methods of Coping act advantageously and yet in other cultural contexts are less prized. Indeed, we could see Core Self itself as an almost exclusively Western construct, stressing individualism, and a White middle-class Western one at that.

Values we might laud in a Western post-industrial context may not travel well, although we should not jump too quickly into a radical relativism. In terms of resilience, O'Dougherty Wright and Masten (2005: 24) pointed out that: '. . . the first wave of research revealed a striking degree of consistency in findings, implicating a common set of broad correlates of better adaptation among children at risk for diverse reasons'. Programmes of comparative research on cultural processes in resilience are only just getting under way (Ungar, 2005a) and other elements, such as strengthening ethnic identity, stand out as influential. Consequently, there may be much that we can import from the comparative study of resilience that turns a fresh light on what is possible in a Western context. Just therapy is a good example that we draw on in this book (Waldegrave, Tamasese, Tuhaka, & Campbell, 2003).

Of course, however well we define the locality and type of situation in which we are working, there are always subtler but often just as powerful influences operating through say community, family and institutions such as schools. The same point would apply to systems of help being provided through health and social-care organisations. These contextual factors can greatly influence whether what is done helps or further compounds a family or child's situation. Nowhere is this more marked than in situations of constellated disadvantage. Theoretical approaches underpinning systemic family therapy, for example, have argued that context may be the primary focus and guide for intervention (Barker, 1998).

Context is of vital importance for RT and deeply embedded in our Noble Truths. An analysis of the scenarios we work in forms a key aspect of our Noble Truth 'Accepting'. We apply 'Conserving' in order to preserve and enhance the effect of current positive influences as well as to underpin our interventions. Also, as part of Conserving, we aim to transform the negative influences on children and any hindrances to our efforts with them. We insist on 'Commitment' in practitioners involved with children if we are to achieve better outcomes. Many of the interventions RT employs, work through and with wider resources. 'Enlisting' resources as we go keeps our eyes firmly on building resilience. We bring in other practitioners and we engage them in coordinated joint endeavours knowing that they may be the key to change and, in constellated disadvantage, we can rarely, if ever, go it alone.

RT is necessarily contextually-sensitive work. However, what the resilience literature also tells us is that there are mechanisms at work that come from within the individual child and that attending to these can also significantly enhance children's life chances (Werner, 2005). We need to look at these in terms of how individual processes react with each other, and with the givens. Personal turmoil and complex compounding givens form a very thick undergrowth that we need to find our way through. Rutter's plea for us to look at holistic child–environment interactions reinforces the point (Rutter, 1990).

Outcomes vary, in a positive resilient or negative direction, as a result of the interactions of individual processes. For example, The Rochester Child Resilience Project (Wyman, 2003) has alerted us to how two processes interact—a sense of personal competence and a sense of realism. For children showing antisocial behaviour a sense of personal competence is protective the more it is linked to a sense of realism. Where there is a serious mismatch, then further developing a sense of personal competence may aggravate behaviour problems. The first move in building resilience might therefore be a reality check.

For the most part, we can not deploy one intervention and expect it to have a straightforward and clear effect on resilience. However, in Core Self, we take a big breath and relentlessly pursue individual processes that may have the capacity to do just that. They may represent crucial elements that provide turning points in children's lives (Quinton & Rutter, 1988). This may be through mechanisms of individually mediated 'desistance' (these are the forces that slow or reverse an expected pattern). Or perhaps through bringing quite new vectors into play. Whichever it is, in Core Self we look at how new meanings, the injection of hope and a personal paradigm shift can significantly alter the negative trajectory we might otherwise predict.

To be effective in Core-Self work we must always be vigilant to the fact that the very real givens and individual turmoil of constellated disadvantage obscure promise. We have to consider whether there are characteristics that have been thwarted until now and that we, as practitioners, need to uncover. We have already seen how resilience has been associated with such factors as higher intelligence and physical attractiveness. We have rather played down their importance in this book. This is because these are characteristics of children and their families that afford the least potential for change and building resilience. Nevertheless, if children do have such attributes, we can see how important they are to foster and how important it is to optimise their influence even if the most disadvantaged do not often possess them in high degree.

As we say, a little in this direction too can go a long way. There is a danger that we may fall foul of paralysis and collaborative inertia when faced with matter so dense and intertwined as we have presented in this section. This is where work on Core Self in the context of constellated disadvantage begins. Before we take a deep breath and launch into Core Self, there is one further level of complexity that we must appreciate: development.

Core Self and development

We are very keen to ground RT—a complexity driven, multidisciplinary paradigm—in a thoroughgoing appreciation of developmental science. This is currently a fertile area for new conceptualisations (Bronfenbrenner & Ceci, 1994; Lerner, 2005, 2006; Lerner, Freund, De Stephanis, & Habermas, 2001; Lerner, Lerner, & Almerigi, 2005). A consequence of this is always being mindful of a child's developmental stage. It will determine, for example, how much we see children as self-directing, responsible creators of their own worlds and to what degree they may indeed be victims of circumstances as a result of development alone. However, we should be cautious of too simple an acceptance of this general statement, especially where the givens have been so detrimental to developmental progress.

There are two points to be made here as far as our work on Core Self is concerned. The first is that it is a child's personal *development* more than their chronological age that we must always keep in mind. Note that we are using the word development, not developmental stage. We use a further term: personal developmental matrix. To take our argument one step on, a child's development manifests in the context of a number of different givens, triggers and potentials. This could be summarised as a dynamic multi-axial model with the child's developmental matrix at its nexus.

Understanding a child's personal developmental matrix is of paramount importance in Accepting where we are starting from. It is this that will to a great extent determine the parameters within which resilient interventions can be employed for disadvantaged children. This is especially the case in Core Self, which has so much to do with children's personal, individual process. The point is also important because disadvantaged children are particularly deceptive in terms of how one might expect them to present developmentally at a particular age.

This is not just a matter of intellectual development but also complicated patterns of social, emotional and behavioural development. They will have had fewer normative experiences. This is compounded by the expectations of others that they should, given their chronological age. In all likelihood they will have suffered neglect, denying them the stimulation necessary for optimum development, and they are also likely to have suffered traumatic boundary crossing between adults and children's worlds because of abuse. We have to take this into account not just in terms of whether they might show the symptoms and the effects of neglect and trauma, but also in terms of how these experiences have distorted their developmental matrix.

Sally's experience of sexual abuse is a case in point. When she first came into public care at the age of seven, Sally performed a mixture of highly immature behaviour allied to the most provocative and shocking repertoire of sexualised behaviours her foster carers had ever witnessed. This is a highly contradictory pattern of behaviour not least from a traditional developmental point of view. We are then tasked to unravel these components of her development and to work them together in a way that does not promote one aspect of her development to the detriment of another.

In situations like Sally's, our practice has made us increasingly aware that we should preferentially address mechanisms of neglect. We are pleased to say that a great deal of the sexualised behaviour then takes care of itself—well, at least until adolescence. This touches on another feature of what might be conventionally understood as an uneven developmental profile.

The growing awareness of the effect on the deeper strata of a child's character of early interactions—both physiological and psychological (Gerhardt, 2004)—means that we also see 'sleeper effects'. There are therefore certain times in a child's development when what may seem surface phenomena may have deep and long-term significance and a troubled nexus that we thought had been resolved may re-emerge. We can not necessarily access such buried worlds directly and we need to be flexible and creative in how we intervene to resolve these barriers to development. There are therefore not only limitations on what can be achieved but perhaps also surprises with regard to individual children's development to be taken into account.

The second point we want to make is that while we present one of our interventions as helping children to take more responsibility for themselves, their context can sometimes be so extreme and negative that it needs direct, even immediate, intervention. When the extent of the abuse Sally was suffering came to light and the continuing major risk to her in her birth home became obvious she had to be swiftly removed. In situations of high risk, when you have to take control, you need to take a lot of it. Not to do so could have severe and potentially devastating consequences for the child. This is the arena of 'must do's', clear situations of child protection, for example, and also of treating severe illness when it arises. Regarding severe illness, as we say in this chapter, if there are specific treatments, use them. We can not hope to work resiliently without addressing these problems.

We need to make just a few more points on these 'must do's'. With child protection, by saying that there is always something we can do with children and their families even in the most difficult of circumstances, we are not saying that circumstances are always good enough or that children are responsible for them. Clearly, extreme child protection scenarios are precisely where situations are far from good enough. 'Talking resilient' could be seen as increasing the risks. Indeed one of the criticisms of 'resilience' as a concept; has been that a by-product of focusing on what children can do for themselves can inadvertently put further responsibility and blame on to them for their own misfortunes.

This raises complex arguments for us all over when to intervene and in what way (Reder, Duncan, & Gray, 1993). An articulated appreciation of a child's developmental stage is vital to see how it links to their ability to protect themselves as well as to elicit and receive protection from the adults caring for them. There have been intervention programmes, attended by some success, on teaching vulnerable young children 'Protective Behaviours', for example, in a developmentally sensitive manner (West, 1989). These put the responsibility on the child, as far as it is possible and appropriate, to help themselves to deal with potential abuse. These are resilient mechanisms if we keep an individual child's developmental capacity firmly in mind.

A further 'must do' is that of treating children, as vigorously as we can, when they have clear physical and mental health disorders. We are aware that, unless treated, the children can not progress, The term 'catch up growth', describing the accelerated physical changes that occur when children are successfully treated for chronic physical conditions, has been more recently used in terms of neglected children's accelerated social and emotional development when moved to more nurturing patterns of care (Van IJzendoorn & Bakermans-Kranenburg, 2003). Of course, there are limits to how much catch up can occur and it is important that we understand the limitations to the outcomes we can expect even with the best of efforts (Rutter & The English and Romanian Adoptees [ERA] Study Team, 1998).

With these more general considerations in mind, we now turn to the main focus of this chapter—how do we influence those deeper currents at the bottom of the river? This submarine realm comprises a mix of individual as well as more general attributes that emerge and evolve over long periods of a child's development. The direction of the river also represents the effect of wider currents of child development. We have to imagine that there are treasures down there amongst the weeds, regardless of how murky and overgrown it may seem from above. Changes at such deep levels can lead to seismic shifts that do hit the surface and will make the world before and after look a very different place.

The dimensions of Core Self

Instil a sense of hope

For the Greeks it was Pandora who was the first woman on earth. Zeus ordered her creation and the pantheon endowed her with many talents: Aphrodite gave her beauty; Apollo music; Hermes persuasion; and so it went on. Her name means 'all-gifted'. When Prometheus stole fire from heaven, Zeus punished humanity by sending Pandora to Prometheus' brother. She took a box with her, which she was forbidden to open under any circumstance. Of course, Pandora opened the box. All the evil it contained escaped and spread over the earth. She tried to close the lid, but it was too late. All the contents had escaped except for one thing, right at the bottom. This was Hope.

This distillation of the Greek myth captures the essence of hope. It is what we have when everything else is taken away. Well, at least, if we want to progress. We have debated the inclusion of hope here as part of a resilient armoury and as many times as it is taken out it demands to reappear. It has made earlier appearances in aspects of Coping in, for example, fostering positive illusions. This we could see as a cameo role. We now place hope firmly in the Core Self compartment because it feeds not only into Coping, but also represents a quality fundamental to a wide range of research-based resilience constructs, for example, self-esteem and a sense of personal competence (Werner & Smith, 2001). In the world of adult therapy there is a vibrant movement associated with the concept of hope in the form of recovery approaches and positive psychology (Snyder & Lopez, 2006). We also see that hope is future-orientated. It supposes that life can be otherwise, rather than following the predicted pattern. It is therefore a potential source of desistance, interrupting ingrained negative trajectories and enabling us to transform what too often looks like predestined fate. We can also see in the myth of Pandora hope being all we have left when fate has been so overwhelmingly destructive.

Cognitive theorists have made us aware of the critical role played in mental health by hope (Beck, Rush, Shaw, & Emery, 1979). Despair, its alter ego, adds to our depression and appears to be a key component of suicidality (Hawton & Van Heeringen, 2000; Williams & Pollock, 1993). When we have hope, then we move on. Gaining hope is often seen as a turning point in an individual's life. Providing hope is part of the value of religious affiliations and a strong spiritual sense, which have also been closely associated with resilience (Garmezy & Rutter, 1983; Werner & Smith, 2001). It gives new meanings. Hope may be blind and it may be an illusion, but it still appears to be something we all need.

Sally's fostering was a big issue from the age of four onwards. This was when her first foster placement broke down. The question from then until she was fourteen was whether she would go to a children's home, something everyone in the team resisted. By the age of thirteen this issue had once again become acute. Sally was by turns desperately wishing for a foster placement that could last and fighting those hopes. Even she could see that the reality was likely to follow the now well-established pattern of honeymoons and then foster carers finding her just too much to handle.

She did despair and developed a number of compounding symptoms. So much so that she was considered for medication and we will follow that strand of her story later in this chapter. Sally, you will recall, was in therapy. She had an Art Therapist working with her for periods of time, over three years altogether but in bursts of three to six months at a time. During the second period of work, it was felt that Sally was becoming less responsive. At bottom was the uncertainty over ever finding a more permanent home. Sally was losing hope and with it many precious resources she had managed to build up despite her early years of adversity and turmoil.

To cut the story short, and it was a very long saga with many diverting moments, her therapist managed with Sally to hold onto the idea that she, Sally, would sooner or later settle in a placement. This was not naïve optimism, and we need to distinguish hope from that. Work did go on to look for placements, it had to, but also through the therapist working with what Sally herself could do to make a difference to any future placement. This was not easy work and perhaps the only reason that Sally tolerated her therapist exploring the issue at all was that she was sticking with Sally and had almost taken on a surrogate care role, albeit severely limited in time, scope and availability. We know that when children do not have a lot, what they do have has added significance. The therapist knew Sally long term. She had committed to Sally. This platform allowed the therapist to work in this way. It also provided Sally with some hope that she might make it to a placement that could succeed because of the work they were doing.

Hope affects the practitioners too. Burnout, low expectations and doing the minimum are very real daily accompaniments to working with such scenarios. You can understand why, with failure so likely and success so rare. The scale of the task and our sense of our own incompetence can get in the way let alone the myriad other blocks that can stop us from both seeing what would make a difference and getting stuck in.

It is our experience with practitioners, as well as families and children, that being convinced that there is always something you can do has a pronounced countervailing effect on the whole system. This conviction may need to be repeated a number of times or added authority may have to be employed for it to be heard. A range of interventions will already have been deployed prior to such moments bearing fruit, but the injection of hope does have a galvanising effect on chronically suboptimal situations where nothing productive has previously seemed possible.

In Sally's case hope did not work alone. Painstaking work had already gone into forming relationships and sustaining them. Perhaps Sally was developmentally ready at that time to look at the reality of her situation in a way that she had not been able to do previously. Sometimes we have to wait for the right moment and sometimes we have to wait until just that time when it seems that things can not get worse.

Revolutions occur when you can not go on in the same old way. Summarising the course of modern political revolutions, Dunn (1974) saw them occurring when there had been a period of rising expectations followed by a sudden downturn. There may be helpful lessons here for understanding the timing and preparation necessary for the salvaging effect of hope. Hope helped Sally at a crucial time when something very important to her appeared to be lost, but also when there were practitioners willing to stick with her despite all. Reviewing her history later, it is striking how we could draw a very clear line in her trajectory from this moment on compared to what had gone before.

Teach the child to understand other people's feelings

In 'Learning' we saw that programmes stressing the development of social and emotional literacy in children are highly rated (Masten, Hubbard, Gest,

Tellegen, Garmezy, & Ramirez, 1999). At one level this can be seen as didactic teaching to children of scenarios and responses they can apprehend and try out. At another it concerns the development of more fundamental capacities. Piaget (1977) and Kohlberg (1981) have worked on stages of moral development. Murphy and Gilligan (1980) reformulated these stages of moral development in terms of 'caring' and 'commitment'. Hoffman (1982) stressed the importance of developing empathy. All these ideas open up a broader and longer-term enterprise of promoting the capacity of children to be attuned to other people's feelings, to know themselves and to take self-responsibility.

To concentrate on the first of these interventions, understanding other people's feelings, one plea for more effort being applied in this direction has come from the work of Fonagy et al. on 'reflective self-functioning' (Fonagy, Steele, Steele, Higgitt, & Target, 1994). Their thesis is that achieving a secure attachment is so strongly correlated with resilience as to be almost synonymous with it:

> There is a . . . prima facie case that *resilient children are securely attached children* (our emphasis); i.e. that secure attachment is part of the mediating process where resilience is observed.
>
> (Fonagy et al., 1994: 235)

Central to this is the capacity to form mental representations of our own and others' feeling states. This is also highly correlated with the development of secure attachment patterns. It is what Fonagy calls the capacity for reflective self-functioning (RSF). Teaching and facilitating parents to develop RSF makes it significantly more likely that their children will develop a secure attachment in turn. Children at least as old as two years still remain able to adapt to new attachment interactions (Dozier, Chase Stovall, Albus, & Bates, 2001). Extrapolating from this work, could we not see the aims of such deep therapy as continuing to provide this nurturing influence even later in their lives?

We see three potential benefits of such deep therapy. First, the child is helped to a more secure pattern of attachment through the RSF efforts of the therapist/attachment figure. Second, the child is encouraged to develop capacities of RSF themselves in order to help them in terms of their personal resilience and, third, it serves as a preparation for them as adults parenting securely attached, resilient children in their turn.

There are a number of questions raised in this chain of thinking, some of which we have already debated in our chapter on 'Belonging'. We concluded that we could not be so categorical that secure attachment *is* resilience and that the outcome of this kind of deep individual therapy was not so clear cut. In the last chapter we will go on to question whether this kind of treatment is the best way to deliver the desired outcomes from a resilient point of view. Also, there are major practical issues in engaging children who are considered to have disorganised patterns of attachment in work of this nature.

As far as possible, from a resilient perspective, we try to use those already involved in Sally's life to intervene in this way. The therapist involved with Sally was the one that carried out this work, but only because there was no other stable figure in her life to do so at that time. Her social worker had only just got to know her and, we were told, would only be with her for three months in any case and Sally was just moving placements again. From our point of view this degree of instability and worker promiscuity was lamentable, but we accepted it. We had to. There are some implications here for organisations and how they choreograph their resources. This also needs attention if we are to achieve better outcomes. We will turn to this important issue in the next chapter. However, with Sally as our focus, lamenting must be transformed into getting on with the necessary work.

It is our experience that being able to carry out Core Self work is predicated on long-term embedded relationships if we are going to help children to develop such capacities as understanding others' feelings. Our work on Belonging urges us to work with and through those who have known the child best and longest in delivering this intervention. We have called this principle, hypothetically, the law of embedded therapy. Core Self mechanism (C) through long-term significant adult (A) leading to more successful engagement (E) means better outcomes (O):

$$C \times A \times E = O$$

Like all laws there will be the odd exception, but it is an important antidote to our tendency to base therapy in the clinic, make it short term and assume rather than make sure that engagement will work. For this reason we have elevated this law to a high status. It may well be true for all interventions, but particularly so in Core Self and Belonging. We can see from the above equation that if A is zero (and/or E is zero), then the outcome is zero too.

We must also hark back to what we know concerning Sally, that all the mentors and counsellors available in school, all the special programmes on emotional literacy that were delivered there, have passed Sally by. We can not rely on a purely educational frame for this work to be carried out, although we would of course use it if it were accessible and the resource materials made sense for her. A primary prevention programme would of course be more cost-effective, require less training for practitioners and could be delivered in relatively seamless conjunction with the child's formal education (Lerner, Lerner, & Almerigi, 2005; Reivich, Gillham, & Chaplin, 2005). But Sally is out of school. We are well into secondary prevention.

She does, however, have a therapist—it could take place there. On the other hand, when she is placed with foster carer Josie, the work goes ahead more progressively. Relationships, long term and sustained, are very important in this area of work in particular.

Well, Sally is still not yet with Josie, and the first half year with Josie was something of a trial in any case. As we said, Sally's therapist had to be the conduit for this work. The subject of the work was what was most to hand, what Sally might need to do so that a future placement had more chance of success, even if it was part of an undefined future she was preparing for. It took a great deal of linking ideas and experiences, obtaining the history of previous placements and reviewing and then reforming failed scenarios over a long time and with considerable going back and forth. Sometimes this work had to take a back seat. Sally needed reassurance and security over much more basic issues. She had difficulty taking any responsibility for what had happened. There were issues it brought up for her of her own abuse. Workers had repeatedly told her that she was not at all responsible for what happened. Now she was being told that she was responsible.

There were times, too, when the whole endeavour appeared to have run aground. At such moments, in order to get by, you have to fall back on to the methods we have outlined in our Coping compartment.

Working with 'understanding other people's feelings'; meant putting Sally in other people's shoes, fostering sensitivity to what they might be experiencing and understanding their behaviour on the basis of it. This requires an infrastructure of Sally having some sense of a consistent self. However, gradually she did seem to assimilate that she had a role in how things went and could perhaps change it. Looking back, her therapist has almost convinced herself that Sally's success with Josie was prepared in those halting, difficult sessions. Also, understanding this is why the therapist is still writing to Sally and why Sally calls her up from time to time now that she is seventeen.

Help the child know her/himself

Understanding others' feelings, knowing him/herself and taking responsibility for him/herself are related interventions in the sense that work on one is highly likely to have major implications for the other. Time and again capacities such as self-efficacy, self-awareness and self-regulation are highlighted in the research as characteristics of children that do well under difficult conditions (Werner, 2005). We know that the resilience research does not often represent the more complex case material we are presenting here, but we take from the research the hope that anything we can do to improve these abilities for children in constellated disadvantage may have considerable protective benefit.

Further, we extrapolate from the work of Dozier et al. (2001), mentioned above, that more secure attachment patterns may be achievable until quite late on into children's lives. They are not completely hard wired into children's constitutions and they vary with relationships. Also, as recent research has demonstrated, gene–environment interactions are complex in both directions (for a summary, see Rutter, Moffitt, & Caspi, 2006). What we can do, therefore, is more involved but also more open ended than we may have been led to expect. With Fonagy's notion of developing reflective self-functioning in parents and the work by Juffer and Dozier on how we can help to increase parental sensitivity to their children (Dozier, Chase Stovall, Albus, & Bates, 2001; Fonagy, Steele, Moran, Steele, & Higgitt, 1991; Juffer, Bakermans-Kranenburg, & Van IJzendoorn, 2005) we begin to see some ways in which we can help children, at an older age, to gain a better sense of who they are and how to act in a way that promotes positive relationships.

Of course we have a long tradition of life-story work to build on (Ryan & Walker, 2002). Traditionally this has been seen as an important link in fostering a stronger sense of identity and belonging for a child who has experienced disrupted patterns of care (Hart & Luckock, 2004). We could also see added benefits from focusing this work on resilient processes such as self-awareness. Interestingly, Juffer et al. compare the use of book learning methods with or without video feedback in developing maternal sensitivity (Juffer, Bakermans-Kranenburg, & Van IJzendoorn, 2005). While the parents involved in that study do not fit with those we have in mind, the authors report that those engaging in both forms of learning did best and that even using only book learning was superior to controls.

We think that showing people films of themselves is instructive. However, there may be added value in therapeutic techniques such as putting children in the role of director of their own film. RT supports the idea of giving people roles as directors of their own films with a strong sense of control and authorship. In particular, where children have histories of abuse, feelings of loss of control can be very prominent and it may have particular value there.

We could certainly have used this for Sally. It would also have been a useful and engaging way for us to offer her some focused feedback. We mentioned earlier the need for children to be realistic as far as assessing their capacities are concerned. Having children look at their own perform-ance enables comments to be made to address this in an objective, alongside way, rather than through direct confrontation. We have an added chance to work here on other interventions, for example highlighting achievements, which can be made an integral part of engaging in and completing this activity. The net effect is to give children a semblance of their lives in continuity and a part of a biography that could become a coherent auto-biographical self (Damasio, 2000).

Help the child take responsibility for her/himself

Self-management and self-regulation help reduce problem behaviours, build self-esteem and lead to better school achievements (Werner & Smith, 2001). We have distilled out of these connections a central component; children learning to take responsibility for themselves. We are talking not only of children's developing capacity for independence but also of their moral development.

Kohlberg developed a research-based model, devised in the 1970s, where he outlined a developmental progression of moral levels through which children processed (Kohlberg, 1981). Children were faced with dilemmas they could only solve over time by moving to a higher level. There were six in all, although he added a seventh some time later. The sixth level and above were not easily understood and perhaps Kohlberg did not explain them so clearly. Included in the model was the capacity for children to 'regress'. When moral dilemmas reached a certain crisis point, individuals might not necessarily transit smoothly to a higher level. There might be a moratorium or children could stick at halfway points and Kohlberg noted regressions under experimental conditions from the heights of level five, say, to two (Kohlberg, 1981). Box 7.2 summarises his approach.

Box 7.2 Kohlberg's classification

Level	Stage	Social orientation
Pre-conventional	1	Obedience and Punishment
	2	Individualism, Instrumentalism and Exchange
Conventional	3	'Good Boy/Girl'
	4	Law and Order
Post-conventional	5	Social Contract
	6	Principled Conscience

Kohlberg's ideas have been modified and reformulated by a number of later researchers (see Gilligan, 1982; Hoffman, 1982). They have been built upon in terms of the movement towards 'Positive Youth Development' (Catalano, Berglund, Ryan, Lanczak, & Hawkins, 2004; Damon, 2004), where there is an emphasis on presenting children with challenges rather than avoiding them. We outline Kohlberg's work in this chapter to illustrate the following: First, moral development while basically progressive, does not necessarily flow smoothly. Second, development is also prone, under certain pressures, to regression. Third, being able to progress morally means having enough of the right kinds of experiences to do so. Fourth, and last, as we have pointed out before, a child needs to be developmentally ready. Undoubtedly the capacities we are examining, understanding others' feelings, to know oneself and to be responsible for oneself, are developmentally sensitive.

As we have argued earlier in the chapter, children who have suffered more adversity show more discontinuous patterns of development and also, because of the pressure of circumstances, have, in Kohberg's terms, more reason to 'regress'. In addition they will too often have had the wrong kinds of experiences, i.e. experiences for which they are not yet developmentally ready. They may also have missed out on what Winnicott termed 'opportunities to contribute' (Winnicott, 1965a).These represent situations where children are enabled either by design or default to put their own stamp on events. Winnicott views being given such opportunities to contribute as the gaps children grow into in their moral development, where they have to fend for themselves, but not too much.

So, another reason emerges why taking responsibility is going to be especially problematic for children who grow up with such high levels of adversity. It is once again why we have to treat the most developmentally sensitive interventions in Core Self with some care. Yes, of course, we want to help children develop a sense of autonomy and control. However, overwhelming control can often be an all-consuming need for children who have experienced so little responsive and sensitive parenting as studies of children in care continue to show (Harker, Dobel-Ober, Berridge, & Sinclair, 2004a; Harker, Dobel-Ober, Akhurst, Berridge, & Sinclair, 2004b). This is not the kind of higher-order self-control we are presented with in the resilience literature. Children like Sally are more often at Kohlberg stage two, rather than moving from 3 to 4, let alone 5.

Didactic teaching, role plays, video and focused feedback provide useful techniques to help them take more responsibility for themselves, drawing on the day-to-day events of these children's lives. Once again the law of embedded therapy comes into play. Resilient practitioners will need to see this intervention as long-term work, not necessarily undertaken directly by themselves, and also subject to an array of developmental dislocations and complexities.

Let us pause a moment here to think more about the long-term nature of the work involved with the most disadvantaged children. They will be ready for large-scale developmental changes at times that do not necessarily fit with the norm and will challenge situations that rigorously expect them to be developmentally normative. What they may be working through are Kohlberg's interrupted moratoriums and longstanding regressive patterns. This intervention needs patient application over long periods of time. With consistent attention to the detail of children's lives it is likely to have a good outcome.

This gives us further justification for promoting the law of embedded therapy. Knowing over time allows us to see what they might be capable of and then get to work.

Then there are times when the pace of development can surprise us. Sally continued to have thoughts of living with an uncle when she was sixteen. She made urgent pleas for contact with him. Her workers despaired. They had held long-standing suspicions that he was a sexual risk to children. There was no hard and fast evidence. Sally could only see the positive side of rejoining the one family member that she knew might still be available to her. She wanted him invited to the meetings. She wanted the therapist to talk to him.

As a result of Sally's continued urging some contact was made. At age fourteen, Sally could more or less find her own way to his home in any case. Better the practitioners knew where she was than she did it without their knowledge. Also, Sally was beginning to settle with Josie. Sally might just confide in Josie if anything started to appear too risky. Still, there were worries, plenty of them, not least that Sally might not be able to appreciate the risk when she spotted it. The protective behaviours she had learnt might go out the window for the sake of keeping her family connection alive. Yes, we are taking risks here, but we present these as acceptable given that we were pursuing different aims within a coordinated strategic whole.

Then Sally tells us that she no longer wants to see her uncle, although she might telephone him from time to time. She points out that he does not make it to the meetings to which he is invited. Sally now holds herself and her needs in some esteem. This has allowed her to see clearly how her uncle struggles to make a good enough response. She recalled her last birthday party where he was so self-preoccupied that he hijacked the whole occasion. Sally was incensed and it led to her re-evaluating her plans in a major way. We could not have expected this although differing therapies offer some explanation of what's happening here, e.g. paradoxical injunctions or cognitive dissonance (Festinger, 1957; Palazolli, Boscolo, Cecchin, & Prata, 1980). To us, it seemed that something more had occurred and was a remarkable step forward in her development. As we say, the penny dropped. After this occurred, Sally now had more chance of being on a very different pathway.

Sometimes it is like that in Core Self work, the most significant changes for the better occur at what seem like the worst and riskiest of times. Sally became more aware of her own needs and began to forge what she wanted out of life. She aligned herself more closely to peers who were actively pursuing their plans for the future. She became significantly more discriminating as to who could help her in her life and she was more receptive to advice as to how to take care of herself.

Foster their talents

Thinking how talent might be distributed, do we say that some individuals have a lot of it and the rest diminishing amounts? Do we employ a cut off where we say that some have none at all? If so, then the children we describe in this book appear to fall disproportionately into the latter group. You might then think that we are wasting our time intervening like this for children like Sally. Foster her talents, when she has been rejected from schools, after-school activities, clubs and dance lessons so many times? Are we not just putting her back into the firing line? We should be doing something to stabilise her situation first, build her a secure base and then think of opportunities to try her new self out? Core Self work should, you might think, take place before we can expect any talents to emerge.

Well, yes and no. Yes, because Sally is in danger of exclusion whenever she tries out some new activity and the last thing we want to do is to reinforce this. Yes, because we don't know where to start or what opportunities to give her. Yes, too, because Sally is not stabilised, in her foster home, in school, in fact hardly anywhere in her life. The only sensible response appears to be the clinic and therapy. This was the reasoning behind Sally being offered art therapy. She then engaged in this for three years. This meant a year and a half travelling sometimes fifty miles by taxi during five out-of-town placements. On balance, everyone has considered it was helpful for her and that it did contribute to stabilising her life. It delivered some of the necessary help such as a supportive relationship.

But no, too. No, as Sally needs to get on with having normative experiences and a clinic takes us away from that. No, because Sally may well have a talent or even talents, and we need to be on the look out for them no matter how obscured and however deeply they have been buried. No, too, because many therapists, ensconced in their clinics, have not traditionally seen themselves as working with the outside world in this kind of way. Fostering talent holds out particular promise for children in disadvantage because it is dedicated to making the outside world work for them.

On the face of it, this may not seem easy. Perhaps it would be better to say, *begin* to foster their talents. How do we help Sally stick at horse-riding, say, when the first time she goes, the instructor calls up the foster carer to say that they can not have Sally back again? The foster carer calls the therapist and social worker. There is general agreement that it is another failed attempt to normalise Sally. It is another missed opportunity to get her going with something that will engage and interest her, give her outlets, fresh air, exercise, attachments and a sense of belonging to something that has a positive trajectory in the world. Well, we could have expected it and the whole experience reinforces the need to return to a clinic-based solution for Sally.

Well, hold on for just a second. Let us explore if there is any way we can get Sally back into horse-riding. What would it take for them to take her back? Does someone need to be with her to make it work, someone she knows and who can increase the likelihood that Sally will stick to task and not disrupt the whole scene? Might the therapist have to get up on the horse with her? Does Sally have to start by herself and build up to lessons with other children? How much would this cost? Will we provide the level of support needed? We raise all these questions because, looked at from this point of view, we do actually have some options. Could it be that horse-riding might not yet be totally written off?

The point here is that it is often the failure of *our* thinking, *our* capacity to stick to things and *our* problem-solving abilities that are the big question for children like Sally. We will consider some of the reasons that hold us back in our last chapter. These issues of what some would term counter-transference, others failures of imagination, do certainly contribute to the fact that we have not traditionally thought of therapy like this. As a notable exception we would point to the willingness of cognitive behaviour therapists to accompany their anxious clients through feared situations in the search for a better outcome (Grant, Mills, Mulhern, & Short, 2004). Of course, it is not at all easy work in Sally's circumstances and there are likely to be as many failures as successes in what we try out, however hard we try. Nonetheless, as we have noted continually throughout this book, a little success in such barren histories can go a very long way.

In the end, for Sally, horse-riding did not turn out to be the interest we were looking for and it did not represent her talent. However, despite it being a false start the lessons did not go so badly when the support was put in. She gained a certificate for going weekly for six months. None of the lessons was ever cancelled. She met a range of people who worked at the stables, who got to know her. The instructor felt proud of Sally and of herself because they had managed to retrieve what looked like a hopeless situation. Perhaps they could take on other children like Sally. They started to consider it as a special programme that they might offer in the future. Here we can see that Sally's positive chain reaction rubbed off on other children too.

The process also led to those around Sally thinking of what she would like to do next in something approaching a spirit of adventure rather than sheer desperation. As for Sally herself, she started to experience some choice in her life, some sense of competence and achievement and these were seeds that later, when she was placed with Josie at age thirteen, were reactivated in taking up cooking in a big way.

This work is often hardest in the early stages. That is why we have concentrated on establishing a foothold on the process at the beginning rather than when talent is firmly established. For some, conjuring up of opportunities may not have the desired effect but there are additional benefits from pursuing this in any case. For Sally there certainly were, but later.

Sally likes cooking and others like Sally's cooking too. Josie makes a big thing of this. When Sally is feeling down, and she often is, Josie will sit Sally down with her and they watch cooking programmes. They plan to try the recipes out. This involves Sally in travelling to the market and they pick out fresh vegetables. Sally tastes the fresh vegetables and she notices, as Josie persists, that these make her cooking taste better. She starts to pick over the vegetables in the market to find the most fresh. So it goes on and we can see how cooking, her talent, leads to other interventions being employed, aiming to comfort and to soothe, and the interventions of Belonging, Learning and Coping.

Cooking is really Sally's talent and she has it in some abundance. She receives a great deal of appreciation from others because of it. At age seventeen, it will probably be an area of her life that will lead her into further education, career opportunities and continue to give her solace when times are hard. However, it is not everything. Perhaps there are some disadvantaged children who have such over-riding talent that it does become everything, but this is not usual. Sally has and will continue to need a range of other resilient processes operating for her. Yet, if asked what keeps her going, first on Sally's list is her cooking.

We are at times in very real danger of retreating from exploring children's talents because of what seem to us to be insurmountable difficulties and a therapeutic mind set that relegates such activities to someone else's business or labels them unworthy of our consideration. In Belonging and Coping, too, we have reflected on the need for children to be helped into clubs and activities drawing on their interests at the time. Fostering talents builds on these interventions with a strong future direction. We need to be on the look out for talents and to imagine them when they have not yet emerged. When they do appear they can have a profound and long-term effect on the lives of children and help them to rise above the givens of their history. It can start a process of the world working for them. This is why we see it as valuable work, sometimes life-saving work, for children who are so devoid of the normal everyday opportunities most children and their families would take for granted.

There are tried and tested treatments for specific problems, use them

Children looked after by public authorities are at greatly increased risk for mental and physical health problems. One study puts looked-after children's rates of mental health disorders at over 60%, many times higher than they are in the general population (Department of Health, 2004). Physical health is likewise seen as a particularly vulnerable area (Polnay, Glaser, & Rao, 1996). Resilience studies indicate the importance of examining physical ill health as a potent risk factor in poor outcomes (Werner & Smith, 2001). It is therefore incumbent upon RT practitioners to employ specific treatments where appropriate and to employ them actively.

These may involve conditions with an inherited component, vulner-abilities acquired because of adversity or newly arising disorders. The point is that we need to be on the look out for them, recognise them and overcome the obstacles to their adequate and timely treatment. Not to do so represents a further disservice to disadvantaged children. Their multiple problems and the difficulty of treating them, should not act as a reason to neglect them even further. Agreed, there are obstacles here to be overcome, but we see it as a vital Core Self intervention.

If you have read this far in the book, you will know that we are not advocating treatment in isolation. It would not work in any case. We can see all the difficulties there will be to access this, professional barriers and child barriers, and it will call upon all of the resources available in the system to prepare for it, bring it about and support it through to its end. We urge the employment of this intervention, because so much of these children's progress depends upon giving them what is specific and necessary for them to catch up developmentally. Treating what holds them back releases them to make further steps, both now and in the future.

You will recall that, at age thirteen, Sally was losing hope. Her thera-peutic work seemed trapped in a perpetual need to comfort her but she would not be comforted. Her sleep patterns were disturbed and she repeat-edly cut herself. With her appetite wildly fluctuating, she talked persistently of killing herself. Months passed in this state. Even at her age, she fulfilled criteria for a formal diagnosis of depressive disorder and was considered for antidepressants alongside the therapy she was receiving. She did not want to take the medication. The team around her, despite the fluctuating per-sonnel, was of one mind in being reluctant to go down this path. However, in the end, and after a number of consultations with the psychiatrist, Sally tried the medication.

After all this, she took it so erratically that it was stopped. When asked why, she said that she did not want to be like her mother who had been almost continuously depressed, took medication 'forever' and who certainly had very little hope. The therapy had been going a year. The therapist used her relationship with Sally to persuade her to try medication again, but this time continuously. A great deal of effort was spent in going over why Sally might take medication and why not. The team's hope was that if she could take the tablets once daily for a month, they would help her. And, if they did, she would continue with them for a further four to six months and then stop. But she had to take them continuously, every day, during this time.

For Sally, there are few easy answers to her problems and she inhabits a contradictory world where offers of help carry threat and trusting others is what she desperately needs but can not do. Well, not unless she knew them really well and, even then, she felt in danger of being let down. Sally's experiences of trusting people had been so devastating that she had almost given up trying. For Sally, unlike Pandora, even hope had flown off too.

So, what happened? We could say that Sally did take the medication, she trusted it and it did help. A six month course made a big difference and she is on her way forward. However, it was not quite like that. She took the tablets for two months and thought she was pregnant and stopped. She did seem to be slightly better while on the medication. There was some engagement with her local tutorial unit, and she attended for the longest period she had since the age of eight. She lost what good effect the tablets had given her very quickly and was excluded. It transpired that she was not pregnant and she was persuaded to go back on the medication. Third time round, she managed four months of something approaching regular compliance.

So, a year went by with an almost continual negotiation over medication that might or might not have made a significant difference to her. We could have seen this as a waste of time and, from the point of view of just taking medication, a great deal of time was used up, of course. The psychiatrist involved had to count to ten a number of times coming out of busy clinic schedules to engage in yet another conversation over its potential value to her. He was taking a risk prescribing for her in the first place. She had self-harmed in the past. She was unreliable at best and downright reckless most of the time. She did not have a stable placement and no ongoing educational provision. Then, according to the evidence, there was controversy over the use of antidepressants in her age group.

This anthropological account of Sally's medication experiences suggests that with a single case study design and careful monitoring, we could have been more convinced that the medication worked for her. We thought on balance that the third trial of medication had been helpful. It was part of a recovery process that went on feeding into her being on a more positive trajectory over the next twelve months. Everyone had worked hard on this and, of course, what we were negotiating was hope a lot of the time. The hope that she could get better.

Conclusion

We can not go into all the complexities of working along Core Self lines with a child like Sally. This would fill a book itself, and more. Her life is richer, of course, than our schema can comprehend. However, we do have to get into at least enough detail of what Sally and her entourage experiences on a day-to-day basis to understand what is likely to happen when we intervene with disadvantaged children at this deeper level.

We have couched these interventions in terms of a developmental matrix rather than ideas of children needing to be 'psychologically minded' to take these steps forward. In particular, conceptualising Core Self work in terms of development means that we have to accept we will not see much change in these capacities except over months and years of painstaking effort. We also experience going backwards and then on again in relation to desired aims. We must embed such activity in long-term relationships and make sure that they work to build up the trust, support and engagement that is so necessary to Core Self. Sally, and those in similar situations, may not be developmentally ready and have little to respond with when we face her with normative expectations. Even if she can respond, there is a need for careful preparation, the planting of seeds as well as the relentless nurturing of them, since we know that they will not immediately germinate.

Somewhat in contradiction of this, we also have to conjure up an image of children such as Sally as if they had not had the particularly difficult experiences they have. We presume that there is potential there, however obscure. When they do show growth it may be just when we least expect it. The point is that we need to be alive to growth even if there is not the slightest indication that it is there.

Nevertheless, when growth does start, the effect can be life changing. One helpful technique that allows us to see more clearly what we are doing at this level is to take the retrospective view, following narrative sequences back into the past. Patterns of action run along and then stop. These junctures are rich. Something we would have expected did not occur and then a new line of development took off. These are the real turning points.

We have now completed our presentation of RT interventions and the Noble Truths that support them. Core Self cannot be isolated from other compartments in RT, nor from an appreciation of the Noble Truths. With this whirlwind of complexity, we have demonstrated just what a need for a well-directed choreography we have here. Yet, still other processes need to be included in order to get and to keep the RT show on the road. We turn now to organisations and other forms of collaborative practice to see what they can do for children living in constellated disadvantage to hinder or promote resilience.

Chapter 8

Making organisations work

He who gives up freedom for security will end up with neither.

Benjamin Franklin

Introduction

It is not often that you find organisations discussed in a book on therapy. Our experience is that practitioners do not concern themselves greatly with the organisations they work for unless they are bound for management positions. Often experienced practitioners move into management as a career progression. However, and with only rare exceptions, this will mean them moving out of practice. Too often, in our view, for practitioners management and the organisation seem a distant and impenetrable other.

In this chapter we are going to connect up with that other sphere. As we saw in Chapters 1 and 3, commentators are now beginning to explicitly link definitions of resilience with organisational and societal features (Prilleltensky & Prilleltensky, 2005). We have addressed some organisational issues in our previous chapters when they have impacted on the delivery of particular interventions. We are now going to turn this round and ask how can organisations work to facilitate RT? There are also implications of RT for current managerial practice, the status of practitioners and practice within organisations and also how organisations manage practitioner risk. In particular, we want to ensure that the considerable resources wrapped up within large health and welfare organisations work to best effect. We feel that RT has a lot to say on resources. We also want to explore additional ways of conceptualising work arrangements and to search for those that best capture the spirit and realities of delivering RT. Our aim is to construct a set of progressive collaborative systems that will help practitioners to make more progress in achieving RT goals.

RT is designed for complexity but is also itself a complex design. It aims to innovate as an ongoing programme of finding better solutions to building resilient practice. You will have noticed that Noble Truths, Compartments and interventions interact in creative permutations across time.

Employing interventions from Basics with an eye on fostering Belonging interventions and enlisting others to deliver other interventions alongside is de rigueur for an RT practitioner. Let us translate this into organisational terms. RT represents more than a stable and standard set of procedures. It is more than good team working, a clinical network, a care pathway or process of continuous improvement. We will need to look at all of these as possible steps on the way to RT organisational development. But RT takes us even further. We see it as a long-term programme of unstable activity, stable instability if you like, where there is improvisation, negotiation, choreographing and a constantly changing configuration of patterns of therapeutic work. This is what is needed for constellated disadvantage. While RT coheres through our central concept of resilience it is never a finished product. RT goes on innovating throughout.

Louis, for example, had been on and off in the spotlight of social workers since infancy. He occasionally came to the notice of agencies offering therapy in the traditional sense. However, if we took the long view, we would see that it was the family-centre worker who grew to be Louis' most significant practitioner as far as RT was concerned. She stuck with Louis and arranged for others to come in as necessary to deliver interventions that they were best placed to make work. She kept on thinking of more ways that she could foster a resilient Louis. She arranged for as much material help for Louis' family as could be achieved and she lobbied for more. She was involved in a constant search to enlist other practitioners who might be helpful. Not very many, as we have learned, and she often needed to go along to meet them with Louis to make sure that the relationship took. She provided further direct work herself and, throughout, she remained involved.

In even this brief summary of her relationship with Louis, we can see how she is crossing a number of boundaries that her organisation might place in the way. There is the long-term nature of the work, the willingness to shape her role to what is needed for Louis, and her accompanying him into new relationships to make sure they take. She took on new skills as and when she had to. She took 'Basics' very seriously. Her manager, who, interestingly, saw children and families herself alongside her management role, was permissive of this. However, she said that it was a nightmare both to manage and to evaluate the outcomes along the way.

RT practitioners, like Louis' family-centre worker, need organisations to respond positively to these challenges. They also need to go beyond organisational boundaries and forge links with those who can help children like Louis wherever they may be found. The more embedded these other helpers are in Louis' everyday life, of course, the better. Collaborative innovative systems that may fit better with working in this way have received more attention recently with the development of notions such as *communities of practice* (Wenger, McDermott, & Snyder, 2002), *networking*

(Ryberg & Larsen, 2006) and *knotworking* (Engeström, 2000). We will examine these in order to construct a system that resonates as well as possible with RT. We also want to use them to develop RT further.

This is only one chapter, however, and we will not do justice to all the inputs there are to current management theory, to new systems thinking in organisations or to the recent innovative forms of collaboration being proposed. This is a large area to even attempt to explore. To give some idea of the scope of this we can see that since the mid-1990s, at least, there has been a massive increase in the application of psychology, anthropology and sociological thinking to business and organisational theory. Influential examples of this include Senge's (1990) plea for systems thinking to be embraced by the leadership of modern organisations, psychoanalytic insights into unconscious processes operating in health and welfare organisations (Armstrong, Stroul, & Boothroyd, 2005; Cooper & Lousada, 2005), emotional intelligence (Goleman, 1999), complexity theory (Mittleton-Kelly, 1997; Plsek & Wilson, 2001) and the application of anthropological insights (Wright, 1994).

Correspondingly, ideas deriving from innovative practices in industry have transferred in the other direction. In the automotive sector, innovative practices such as W. Edwards Deming's work on Total Quality Management (TQM; Deming, 1982), 'Lean Thinking' (Womack & Jones, 1996) and Critical Path Theory developed by the Dupont corporation in the USA in the 1960s as well as the Theory of Constraints (Goldratt, 1996) have fed into respectively: Continuous improvement initiatives, the elimination of redundant processes and the care pathways approach. Knotworking, while now being applied to health care systems (Engestrom, 2000; Kangasoja, 2002; Reeves & Lewin, 2004) arose primarily in the Finnish telecommunications sector. Communities of Practice (Wenger, McDermott, & Snyder, 2002) have been taken up in partnerships between universities and community organisations in order to develop new technologies (Hart & Wolff, 2006).

RT is a new technology. It will demand new work arrangements by its very nature. It represents 'upbuilding' and has some very different things to say over how we use the resources available to us. Looked at in the light of RT, we will see that there are major obstacles to its realisation in the culture and behaviour of large-scale organisations. The tendency towards distancing and defensive practice, rejecting and excluding processes, all represent hindrances that RT practitioners need to see as legitimate targets for resilient transformation. We will suggest ways in which RT practitioners can respond. Organisations as we currently know them do play a critical role in the delivery of good outcomes for our most disadvantaged families and children. However, they do not represent all the work involved and many of them may need to change in quite radical ways if better outcomes are to be achieved. Therefore we have to ask whether other collaborative forms hold more promise and can successfully work with, across and challenge the limitations of current organisational practice to good effect. On the basis of seeing how organisations match up to RT and also how they might be helped to do so, we begin to map out a progressive strategy to address the systems of activity where RT can flourish.

The state of large-scale health and welfare organisations

In order to construct this resonant system, however, we must *critique* how organisations, particularly large-scale health and welfare organisations, operate in relationship to the priorities for RT. We ask for your cooperation with this for three main reasons.

First, organisations and how they might change is seldom a topic that practitioners themselves feel confident enough to address. They often see what they do as being impacted upon by the organisations for which they work. They are less aware of what they might be able to do and where to intervene with organisations to good effect. In short, workers have not been as trained, competent and confident to tackle the organisational dimension of practice as other aspects of their work. To many workers, organisational issues seem foreign territory and, as we shall see, the tendency to divorce management from practice in health and welfare organisations plays into this very forcefully.

Second, we are also aware that there is a political aspect to all our work. We will say more as to the avowed political thrust of RT in our last chapter. Organisations and the policies that drive them are often closely tied to a larger political agenda. And we are particularly interested in large-scale organisations as they hold considerable power and resources. This is why we concentrate on them in this chapter. Accumulating so much power, means that they are particularly prone to rhetoric, self-promotion and, at times, even self-delusion to an extent that seriously distorts the accounts that they provide of themselves.

Learmonth (2001), looking at how chief executives in helping organisations conceptualised themselves, found that they often pictured this as riding into a troubled situation as heroes and rescuers. Individuals in positions of influence can use structures of authority and control to satisfy their own psychological needs, whether it is for personal aggrandisement, fantasising themselves as rescuers or playing out other aspects of their own vulnerabilities, just as much as any of us, and perhaps even more so. In organisations this can have a profound effect on the culture. However prescriptive national policy may appear, it is open to wide interpretation. It is therefore very important to see through the public presentation of an organisation into how organisations, in relation to their users and employees, actually behave.

Indeed doing so connects us back to the sociological idea of practice that we introduced in Chapter 1.

This point is also emphasised by what we know from the resilience literature base. Building self-confidence, self-esteem and a sense of personal competence come to mind here. Research in these areas cautions how their beneficial effect for reducing antisocial behaviour is almost entirely dependent upon how near to an objective reality an individual's self-perception already lies (O'Dougherty Wright & Masten, 2005; Wyman, 2003). So, for example, an adolescent with inflated self-esteem who acts antisocially is likely to stay with or even amplify their behavioural patterns if their esteem is inflated further. We often see similar mechanisms at play in organisations. Therefore an early reality check is in order to know what needs transforming and how we can set about it.

Third, and lastly, by 'critique', we do not mean 'downbuilding', although the grandiosity of some organisations might lead us to think that this is one sphere that might even benefit from it. Nevertheless, RT does not support a deficit model of practice that dwells on all that is wrong and pathological. Critique can be understood in a more anthropological sense, as a key element in what is a field science of ethnographic data collecting and theorising. Practitioners accumulate important experience of the ups and downs of their organisations and networks. This is important data and needs articulating. It represents the tacit, implicit and often unsaid side of organisations. Sometimes this can appear to practitioners as the unsayable and unpresentable. When speaking to workers the downs tend to predominate. These sources of angst, whether they are focusing on management understanding, practitioner status, risk handling or the vexed issue of resources, are of significant interest to RT.

There is value, as Linstead (1997) has suggested, in developing a more thoroughgoing social anthropology of organisations. This not only allows us to critique them in the ethnographic sense used above (and including in our data the unsaid, tacit and implicit is a very important source of critique), but also to better understand their culture and how they actually behave. He also recommends it as a powerful input to enacting significant and sustained cultural change.

This stance fits well with our Noble Truths, for example 'Accepting', in which a systemic appreciation of practice in the sociological understanding of the term is promoted. As with other facets of working with constellated disadvantage, we can not be naïve in the face of some of the very real difficulties that organisations operating in this field present. Furthermore, we also need to see what there is currently within organisations that has an enduring beneficial effect, i.e. what it is that already contributes positively and needs to be conserved. Large-scale organisations by their nature tend to stick around longer and to have more defined tasks. We need these for Commitment. Finally, we must also look to where synergies develop. Are there points of connection for other collaborative forms, such as communities of practice and knotworking? Can we enlist them so that both they and organisations work to best effect?

As we have already discussed in Chapter 2, in our work groups exploring a resilient approach, practitioners working with disadvantage often voice very negative views when asked if they feel effective in their work. They show very low rates of positive self-assessment, feel distinctly negative due to the impact of the work on them and they feel exhausted by the burden of the cases they deal with. Maslach (1982) has characterised these three aspects as the cardinal symptoms of 'burnout', and our anecdotal research would indicate that, in the circumstances of constellated disadvantage, burnout rates are high. Other negative thoughts come from a feeling of incompetence, and a qualitative difference between practitioners and client groups. Exploring this further, one of the main concerns that practitioners raise is the constraint they work under; their lack of autonomy, their status and how their agency's structures, processes and culture place limits on what can be achieved.

Let us summarise what we see as the main features of large-scale organisations. When seen in comparison to the other collaborative forms that we will look at later in this chapter, they are stronger on bureaucracy, hierarchy, directives and policy and they are low on creativity and innovation. They tend to hold more risk, to have clearer lines of accountability and to have more resources than other collaborative forms. It may not seem that the resources are reaching the front line and indeed some have argued that the resources have been misplaced into narcissistic organisational processes and management needs rather than direct work to the benefit of service users. The organisation may protest the disparity between its funding and what it is expected to do. Overall, however, health, education and welfare spending is concentrated *in* organisations. More enduringly, they build up a knowledge and experience of their locale that is essential in terms of deploying those resources. We will pick up on these latter attributes further on when we explore what there is that we should build on. First we will look at some of the limitations of organisations that practitioners are pointing to. We critique organisations in terms of four interlocking themes: (1) management culture; (2) practitioner status; (3) the approach to risk; and (4) resources.

Management culture

Large-scale health and welfare organisations as well as some professional ones have tended to move towards a management culture where, increasingly since the mid-1990s, they have encouraged experienced high-performing staff out of front-line work. For example in social work and nursing, this has been seen as promotion and career progression even though there have been some compensating moves to enhance the pay and conditions of those that do stay on in practice. Alongside, front-line workers are viewed as being in need of increased managerial control and encouraged to see themselves as 'case managers' too; procurers of resources to address their client's needs rather than providing them directly. Turnover of front-line staff in some agencies is extremely high, with rates sometimes condoned as inevitable and even applauded as a way for staff to develop further.

We see the effect of these trends as fourfold. First, management is divorced from practice. Second, experience is taken out of direct practice. Third, there is a distancing of decision makers from the arenas affected by those decisions, namely the children and families themselves and, fourth, direct care to children and families is devalued.

While it can be argued that a managerial perspective gives helpful detachment and a broad sweep, it also loses detail and emotional information. We might then speculate on further disadvantages of this kind of managerialism if decision making is based on decontextualised knowledge. Also, if managers in these organisations become divorced from practice and are working with questionable knowledge, we do have to ask whether a great deal of so-called management time is in fact displaced activity. The more so when we consider an organisation's attitude to risk, as we do below.

There is a real challenge to RT practice here. We advocate engaging directly with constellated disadvantage and not distancing ourselves from it. All those involved need to be connected with constellated disadvantage enough to get to grips with delivering what will make a difference. While we urge that the most experienced workers deal with the most needy cases, we have a special need to connect up management with practice, as the story of Louis' family-centre worker and her manager illustrated. The fact that the manager could take the risks she did is because she understood from first hand the needs involved. The manager has a responsibility for resource. That resource, however, can only be realised to full effect with the sensitivity and responsiveness that goes with continuing first-hand experience. Distancing comes from distance in time too.

There are counter-arguments of course. For example, analytic therapies counsel a distance from the case in order to provide the necessary counterbalance to over-identification with client's problems and understanding countertransference reactions (Sandler, Dare, & Holder, 1992). The point is taken, and we value both supervision and group work aimed at recognising these influences and RT extends this into finding resilient solutions for children, families and workers. Our bone of contention is the increasing distance of managers from any first-hand experience of constellated disadvantage and over-identification on their part with the needs of the organisation rather than directly with the task at hand. Each of the authors of this book plays a practitioner manager role and has to work with the tension between front-line work and management practices that this necessarily entails. We argue that this is important experience and fertile ground for future research into countering distance and making resource decisions as sensitive as possible to field conditions.

Deming's work (1982) on the fourteen points towards a successful organisation also fits well here. His thinking has had a profound influence on improvement processes in manufacturing industries. In order to produce high-quality products, he urged that transformation is everyone's job and for managers to adopt the new philosophy; the implication being that improvement in services only comes about if managers adopt the same approach as the workforce. He also rejected inspection arguing that, since producing high quality was everyone's business, inspecting workers only made them feel less responsible for it.

In the same spirit, the move to managerialism in social work has become the target of the recently released Social Work Manifesto (Jones, Ferguson, Lavalette, & Penketh, 2006). This states: 'The main concern of too many social work managers today is the control of budgets rather than the welfare of service users, while worker–client relationships are increasingly characterised by control and supervision rather than care' (paragraph three).

From the perspective of RT, what we are really interested in is activity at the boundaries of these interfaces. This can be embodied in roles, for instance, practitioner managers whose experience can be particularly illuminating as to the tensions and contradictions between the needs of frontline practice and organisational imperatives. Activity theory (Leont'ev, 1978; Vygotsky, 1978) terms these *zones of proximal development*. Engström's definition of a zone of proximal development is the 'distance between the everyday actions of individuals and the historically new form of the societal activity that can be collectively generated' (Engeström, Brown, Cristopher, & Gregory, 1997: 174). They represent the creative impetus for resolving system difficulties, and opening up new space for growth. For example, one such system difficulty is that the needs of children and families in constellated disadvantage do not fit neatly with a uni-disciplinary, uni-agency outlook. They do not fit neatly with a care or critical pathway approach. They will need a plethora of interconnected pathways, all interacting well and customised to their needs. Those subject to and working in constellated disadvantage will be working at the margins of many mainstream processes for just this reason. Indeed, how we manage at those interfaces is probably the most critical factor in delivering the RT promise.

Practitioner status

The Social Work Manifesto referred to above refers to 'care' being pushed out and devalued. Allied to this there is an impact on practitioner status. Rhetorically a great deal of praise is given to front-line workers. However, the consequence of increased managerialism is often that the organisation rewards front-line workers relatively less, is less influenced by their views and can tend to view them as barriers in the way of modern and improved service delivery. We can see this in the 'resistance to change' debate in the UK, where professionals have been characterised as a major block to the implementation of new working practices (Plsek & Wilson, 2001). At such moments, the front-line staff can themselves become the problem for the organisation, rather than a resource for moving forward. Also, being identified with the poor and under-privileged can rub off on workers. Such 'guilt by association' is notable in workers starting to show the same kinds of negative self-assessment that the children and families do (Jones, Ferguson, Lavalette, & Penketh, 2006). The practitioner mirrors the clients' experience in developing a pattern of hostile dependency to their organisation.

The result is often high rates of staff turnover and problems with recruitment. Morale, as we have seen in our work, is almost uniformly low in statutory agencies working in these situations. There are some professions that are notable exceptions to the low-status rule and therefore worthy of some attention. Doctors, for example, are paid well, have retained fairly high status and their views are treated in the main as authoritative. They also engage in direct work with children and families and, the more expert they become, they still retain an expectation to practice at the front line. It could be argued that doctors do not become so involved in applying the kind of interventions that RT delivers, the care they offer is often brief and episodic, and that they have a primarily technical function mostly focused on physical health. While there is an element of truth here, it is also the case that they will be in touch with deprivation and disadvantage across the range of their work and subject to its difficulties for treatment including mental health. Frequently they will have long-term, albeit intermittent, relationships with the most needy families and have played a crucial role in intervening at crisis points. They, as much as any practitioner, would benefit from being recruited into RT practice, and their authority is sometimes very valuable for effective RT work. The danger is that if they are not engaged, then unhelpful interventions are promoted and valuable opportunities to work in a resilient mode are missed.

Many of the interventions that RT delivers are predicated on the use of appropriate authority and personal as well as structural power in getting things done. By elevating practice to its proper status, the front line is after all where the work is primarily transacted, then we will start to reflect what Pfeffer (1992) has urged as important; the move beyond recognising what needs to be done into ensuring it is.

The management of risk

Effective practice generally involves risk. Indeed RT could be seen as operating at the limits of established practice and therefore highly risk-taking. Also, we have spoken in Chapter 1 of 'inoculated resilience' and Sally's experience of being affected less by school exclusions and placement breakdowns as their numbers mounted up, which reinforces the same point. While we do whatever we can to reduce adversity, there is, as Nietzsche pointed out, truth in the statement: 'Whatever does not kill us makes us stronger' (Nietzche, 1992). Consequently the concept of resilience has a complex relationship to risk and RT inevitably shares in that relationship too.

In contrast, large-scale organisations are much more likely to err on the side of caution. There are reasons why this is so. In the UK, for example, the approach to risk with children involves policies largely informed by reviews of selected national cases that have raised widespread concern. The death of a child, Victoria Climbié, is a case in point and led to The Lamming Report (2003). This concluded by making over a hundred recommendations and formed the basis of a policy document 'Every Child Matters' (Department for Education and Skills, 2003), which now governs much of the thinking on children's services across England and Wales. It promotes the coming together of children's services with common aims and shared priorities. These are still being implemented at differing paces across the country and with varying degrees of integration taking place.

There are, however, a number of problems with such an approach. Munro, writing in 2005, noted that:

> The cumulative results of thirty years of child abuse inquiries have created the traditional solutions: psychological pressure to avoid mistakes, increasingly detailed procedures and guidelines, strengthened managerial control to ensure compliance, and steady erosion of the scope for individual professional judgement through the use of standardized protocols, assessment frameworks and decision-making aids.
>
> (Munro, 2005: 533)

This dynamic of policy making is one of the major influences in creating the limitations we have discussed above. It has additional effects. There are subtle but strong dynamics operating when risk is high. Staying in the arena of child protection, Reder and colleagues (Reder, Duncan, & Gray, 1993) have made us aware of the influential but more subtle psychological aspects to successfully managing risk. They highlight cases, for example, where workers, presumably not feeling empowered or confident in their roles, failed to see children who were at significant risk. Later the workers, when interviewed, said that they knew they should have insisted, but were swayed by the carer's powerful wish for the child not to be seen. It is the self-motivating capacities of autonomy, authority and taking responsibility that are being asked for here. The confidence to question and not be cowed can make all the difference.

Increasingly, then, we can see some of our best efforts to reduce risk as possibly increasing it. Munro (2005: 533) also speaks of the 'psychological pressure to avoid mistakes'. As we know from all walks of life, mistakes are human. Errors will happen. In industry the aim is to create workers who recognise this, are error sensitive and work hard to make sure this does not turn into defects in a final product (Womack & Jones, 1996). Taken this way and where blame is to be assigned in such high-profile cases, the net effect is of making practitioners risk averse and also possibly more risk producing than they, in a different organisational culture, might otherwise be. These dynamics are at the root of defensive practice and this is a point that all organisations would be prudent to heed.

In many ways we could compare an organisation's response to risk as prone to all the difficulties of any traumatised system. The immediate reaction is one of shock and, if this is not resolved, of either casting caution to the wind or of never stepping outside the front door again. Welfare agencies have been seen as being aware of risk but not translating this into effective policy and practice (Alaszewski & Manthorpe, 1998). Caught in the headlights, neither a reckless nor overcautious response takes us much further. These reactions need to be worked through in any process of recovery. Too often we see society and its organisational backbone as behaving in a shut-down manner. We institute wholesale policies based on an exceptional case. It must never happen here again. In child protection as in other areas of high risk, things do happen again despite our best attempts to prevent it. While it is important to do what we can to ameliorate that likelihood, the message that comes through tends to be a defensive one. When we need to be risk aware we become defensive and risk averse.

We do need to be risk aware and, in RT, we also need to be brave. Being brave is part of our Coping compartment and a vital one too. This means crossing boundaries and confronting defensive practice. We are doubtful whether many health and welfare organisations are yet ready for this let alone prepared to condone it. We are unsure to what extent they would empower us, their workers, with the necessary licence and autonomy to work resiliently. What would they say, for example, if we ask for commitments of workers for a child and family in constellated disadvantage for a minimum of a year as an organisational priority? The trend if anything appears to be in the opposite direction, moving away from empowerment towards increasing control and directive. We would not be asking for these commitments if we did not think they were achievable. However, our presentations particularly to local government management groups indicate that there are hearts and minds here that are yet far from won. Perhaps in some cases it would not go too far to say that there is a vested interest in maintaining an unconfident front line to justify redundant managerial roles.

Resources

This is a major issue. For RT we work with whatever we have. It is one of our central tenets and the cornerstone of making RT available for those who need it most. We therefore have quite a detailed and complex response to statements such as: 'If we had more resources then we could do more.' In constellated disadvantage children and families have very little. Yet, this is where we start and to complain that they should have more and that we should be starting from a different place is to miss the point. It is often a prelude to statements such as: 'Unless we have more resources we can not do anything.' We sense defensive practice here and displaced activities. In an RT frame we need to get on with what we can do.

Yet, of course, there is a resource issue. Do we have enough resources to do what is necessary and would more make a significant difference? By resources we mean extra resources invested into the situation and 'Basics' would argue that we lobby for this when we feel it would make a significant impact. Later in this section we question whether we have sufficient resources in overall terms. We argue that perhaps we do. However, before that, we need to act resiliently and look at how we are managing resource already; using ourselves creatively to get what is needed, and thinking about how RT can make it different.

Let us try to illustrate this through the story of Sally's art therapist. She metaphorically rolled up her sleeves in Chapter 7 and did what needed to be done. There was no one else to do the work on placement stability and especially to work with Sally to see what she could do herself to improve it. At that time Sally did not have her student social worker and the new social worker was only temporary. Sally had been excluded from school and was without settled educational provision. The therapist was aware of the urgency of employing Core Self interventions, notably developing self-awareness and understanding others' feelings. RT indicated in this instance that it would not be helpful for the therapist to spend her energy only on trying to muster better resources, although she could try to do that as well. She needed to get stuck in. Therefore we speak of a 'can do' mindset rather than resorting to 'it is not my role or responsibility'. For children like Sally, retreating from necessary tasks when there is no one else to carry them out is the road to further exclusion and disadvantage.

We have noticed that in certain health and welfare organisations there is an increasing tendency to establish standardised practices to control the use of resources. We can illustrate this through three icons of modern service delivery:

1 the use of thresholds;
2 providing a quantum of service;
3 provision being assessment driven.

First, *thresholds* for receiving services act as a barrier, a method of exclusion, and reinforce a 'done to' dynamic between service and user. Families experience services being withheld because, for example, their issues are deemed not severe enough. They may fall a long way below such a threshold. They may fall just below it. The family has identified themselves as having needs but they are denied a service. Sometimes their difficulties will become more intense. Possibly there is a crisis with child-protection issues intervening. Then they will achieve priority and receive a service. This happened with Louis' family when his older brother became more violent. Suddenly there was a plethora of services brought into the picture. There are a number of what we might term disturbances and troubles involved in this way of reacting. Examples are that the child/family is in a dependent, 'done to' and potentially excluded position in relationship to the organisation. Involvement is episodic and intermittent whereas the family's underlying problems are far from that. When services do come in, they tend to take over and drive the family into a range of other processes, which are primarily targeted at reducing risk.

Second, there is a tendency to supply a prescribed *quantum* of services, in terms of how much and for how long. This can be based on clear aims of intervention or it may be based on what is considered available. Either way, it tends to be an invariant prescription, The approach is strong on predictability but low on customisation. Flexibility is not an essential characteristic. Bespoke is not a governing principle. There is also an increasing tendency to go for short-term solutions rather than remain engaged with those in need for longer periods of time.

Third, and lastly, there is a stress on the fullest possible *assessments* prior to involvement of services in helping mode. This is harnessed to providing evidence that the case meets the threshold. It can often mean lengthy and multiple assessments each time a family accesses an agency. The fragmentation of service delivery into myriad agencies, which is becoming an increasing feature of children's services, would multiply this further. One can see the move towards integration and a common assessment framework as a way of offsetting some of these effects (Department of Health, 1999). Still, there must be concerns that this is more a matter of control and will engender a bureaucratic overload, placing more barriers in the way of disadvantaged families receiving help.

In place of these thresholds, quanta and assessments, RT sees the need to make services include not exclude, empower both families and workers and not place disadvantaged families in dependent positions. We want to engage with and not reject those who already have too great an experience of rejection. Services need to be customised, highly so. They need to be long term, probably intermittently long term, but long term nevertheless. RT eschews organisational promiscuity; by which we mean the tendency for families and children in constellated disadvantage to be faced with manifold workers, changing constantly and with differing aims. This includes mini-mising the number of assessing professionals. The families need the reverse. Children and their families will only be made the more resilient if they are helped into networks that sustain them and which they can lean on when necessary. They, in turn, need to experience predictions of good rela-tionships with others and practitioner help to connect them up with this. This represents the simple application of a range of RT interventions in the context of Noble Truths.

There are major implications here for how resources are managed. As we move from 'Accepting' to 'Conserving and Commitment', we ask if we are able to gain agreements of minimum standards. A further request is that new workers coming into long term-work with a family or looked-after child should stay with the work for at least a year. This is accepted practice in education and in some areas of the therapeutic world. Sally could have done with such a stipulation. Just this alone would significantly increase the progress she is likely to make. Louis' mother groans inwardly when she meets the new family worker and asks immediately, 'Well, how long you going to be around then?' How different it would be if we could give a commitment that is meaningful for their need. This leads us into 'Enlisting' those who can foster effective collaborations and not collude with organ-isational promiscuity. When we turn to the compartments and individual interventions, for example 'Belonging', continuity of involvement is abso-lutely fundamental.

Will practitioners have the necessary autonomy, authority and status to work with these Noble Truths and interventions to good effect? Systems that are predominantly concerned with policy, directive and controlling the detail of practitioners' work will inhibit this and can even kill it off. Overly hierarchical systems where practitioners do not feel able to act without the approval of superiors, who may be much more detached from the work, may miss what it is that needs to happen. Hence resources need to be freed from unnecessary constraint.

We see creativity and innovation as vital ingredients of the overall enterprise. Clearly the earlier-mentioned issues of having experienced, well supported and confident 'sharp-end' workers is important. Clearly, too, they need to earn their status and authority just as much as the organ-isation needs to have mechanisms for ensuring confidence in those to whom they are accountable. All this is well and good. The point, however, is that the wherewithal to act needs to be the priority. If we have such practitioners we should use them to their capacity and not ham-string them with bureaucratic checking and micro-management. This move is likely to free resources and reduce the need for oversight management. It also restruc-tures the management task so that it is less one of control and account-ability and more one of support to enhance the efficacy of workers at the 'sharp end'.

Here is what we might call the paradox of control: the more it is exercised, the more it is needed. At worst this can lead to totally self-defeating processes, infantilising practitioners who are then castigated for acting irresponsibly. If RT teaches us anything, it is that we must be bold and we must instil this into practitioners who will re-present it.

To instance this, our Noble Truth 'Commitment' to families does change a very important dynamic in the relationship between practitioners/the organisations employing them and users. The resources available in this dynamic become a matter of negotiation. By negotiation, we mean on the child and family's terms as well. Granted we need to be clear in our negotiations over what is possible, and available, and whether it will work for them. The last point is very important in the overall equation. We can not promise the earth nor should we. However, we do need to put the families and children, as far as developmentally appropriate, in control if we are to build a real partnerships with them (Hart & Thomas, 2000). We can not on the one hand say 'we want to make them responsible for themselves' and, on the other, place in them in an essentially dependent role in our relationship to them.

Many of the practitioners who have engaged in workshops with us have found this last point initially problematic. They are worried that RT practice would lead to children and families developing an over-dependency on them, and they as practitioners would be faced with overwhelming demand. Our response has been to encourage them to try the 'Commitment' approach next time, telling the family that they will be involved as long as they are needed. In the main, the experience then is that, by changing the dynamic, the families, carers, children and young people tell us more clearly what they believe they need and also when they do not need us any more. They co-determine what we focus on and, on the whole, they can judge when and if it is delivered.

Of course we are not passive partners in this enterprise and we may have to assert some very evident realities operating in the situation. The resource issue becomes a joint issue, constructed in time and as a function of the relationship. If we as practitioners agree that a resource we do not have at our direct disposal will make a significant difference we must work to obtain it. The resources brought to bear emerge as a customised representation of what is possible at the time and are aimed at optimising what can have a beneficial effect from our partnership. The bottom line is that if we work in an organisation that privileges continuity of relationships and encourages flexibility in roles and teams, as well as responsible risk taking, the chance is that the family's needs will be better met.

We are aware that this is not easy work and the Commitment approach may not have been included up to now in professional training and familiarisation with practice. We are proposing that it should. We are asking for a sophistication of practice and a willingness to go relational on the most fundamental issues of working with constellated disadvantage. Our own reactions to such situations however can get in the way of working with RT. We only have to consider the unconscious processes that are set up in situations of working with disadvantage to realise that we can stir up some very primitive responses indeed. If it is not our envy that undoes us, our reactions to distress and pain will surely trigger defensive reactions. While needing to recognise these difficulties, and we urge that countertransference issues do figure in RT practitioners' knowledge base; we do need an antidote. It is not enough to be aware of their effect. We must go further and act.

Organisations need to be held to account with a range of RT performance indicators. These would include the following indices:

- how many workers a family or child has experienced during the past year;
- the numbers of assessments carried out on families in constellated disadvantage, including whether or not this resulted in a resource being provided;
- how the resource was provided for; and
- what were the completed outcome measures based on RT intervention effects.

Measures of empowerment and sense of potency of front line workers could form higher-level performance indicators. This is alongside more simple indicators that record, for example, exclusions, placement instability and the overall level of the management burden in an organisation.

You may think this an un-resilient move; using such performance indicators and, on the basis of regular reporting on them, holding organisations to account. We must go back to our earlier point. Organisations need reality checks on the targets that matter or there is a significant risk of over-inflated claims, inappropriately high self-esteem as well as the displaced activities that go with this.

Of course, RT is not the only treatment approach that has been suggested for working with constellated disadvantage and the costs and resources involved need to be evaluated in terms of value for money. There is now a wide, competing range of treatments available and we shall look at the therapeutic aspects of these in more detail in our last chapter. Options range from what can occur in existing organisations, with the involvment of an undifferentiated mêlée of workers with unclear roles. This, as we saw in Chapter 4, can lead to duplication and overlap, on the one hand, and, on the other hand, to treatment programmes such as Treatment Foster Care (TFC) (Chamberlain, 1998). This is based on a large number of workers but with very tightly defined areas of expertise and responsibility. Then there is Multisystemic Therapy (MST) (Henggeler et al., 1999) where a lone worker may, with considerable verve and determination, carry the whole intervention.

With a strategic approach to constellated disadvantage, we can not be sure that any of these approaches will be the best one for the child and family in question until we have examined what will work for them. We are reluctant to sign up to one or the other because, with a strategic approach, a resilient approach, we may wish in the end to combine elements of all of them. We therefore argue for a flexible capacity that is tailored to the child and family's need and which can be fashioned on a bespoke basis. We also argue for making existing practitioner's roles more focused on what works resiliently and more able and ready to deliver it.

Costs have been estimated. With TFC, for example, this equates to £150k being invested per child worked with (Fonagy, Target, Cottrell, Phillips, & Kurtz, 2002). This can be compared to a current CAMHS worker with a fostered child and engaging in the team around the child at a cost of up to £1000. There is a massive variation in resources entailed by differing approaches. The argument with TFC and MST is that they save costs in the long run and are a good investment. They tend to work with children at risk of placement breakdown due to behavioural difficulties and offending. The costs to the legal, and later prison, system are massive of course. For such groups there might be an argument to be made.

For the wider group of children in constellated disadvantage, we argue that RT is 'investment to save' in the best sense. Embedding RT into practitioners' daily working lives has the potential to target resource more appropriately and to concentrate on those workable interventions that are most likely to be effective. It eschews organisational promiscuity, duplication, rigidity and/or confusion in the treatment system. It has added benefits in, for example, skilling up the workforce that we have already at relatively low cost in order to work smarter and better in a resilient frame for all the families they see. This reaches caseloads greatly in excess of those provided for in TFC and MST models.

We also have to consider redundancy in the system. This ranges from considerations of too many workers involved in any one case to an over investment in command and control hierarchies in organisational management. It is not simply a matter of the rise in non-essential occupations, although there is considerable debate in the UK at present time over the wisdom of such rapid expansion and reorganisation of, for example, the National Health Service (University of East Anglia, 2004; Walshe, Smith, Dixon, Edwards, Hunter, & Mays, 2004). The rise in middle managers, 'middlemen' or 'pen-pushers' as they are often less sympathetically termed, as well as the cost to the system of frequent reorganising have been seen as some of the major resource drains of our time. These are important debates and are reflected in a related set of redundant processes experienced at the front line. We should look at the cost of all those assessments, the wasted resource in rejecting users, the bureaucracy involved in administration of closing cases before we complain too much of lack of resource.

Lastly, we need to think more about an important intrinsic aspect of RT; that we empower, work with, for and focus on the needs and wishes of the most disadvantaged. It is crucial that we learn to bring the worlds of practitioners, children and families, and agencies together with the knowledge from research that indicates what can work. We could describe this as the emergence of a free economy, in the sense that the background knowledge is increasingly available to all (Henwood, Wyatt, & Hart, 2003). In principle access to the knowledge base is no longer a province of the privileged and professionally trained, although they would have a special responsibility to nurture its best aspects. The information concerning the allocation of resources is also becoming increasingly accessible and the issue of client/user/patient views as well as choice are also at the fore (Hart, Saunders, & Thomas, 2005; Henwood, Wyatt, & Hart, 2003). We could see this as another way in which children and families in constellated disadvantage are made more unequal, for it is they who are least likely to feel the benefits of these developments. However, we can also see that there may be benefits for them too, as accessing such sources of help is an explicit area of work for RT practitioners through the Noble Truth Enlisting, and the Basics and Learning interventions in particular.

This leads us back to the, perhaps provocative, statement we made above, that there could already be enough overall resource available to do what is needed. You may have been tantalised by this, or seen it as misguided and perhaps a bit shocking too. We need to explain ourselves. We do not want to give the impression that we are condoning situations where resources really are inadequate, resources are misdirected and the delivery of front-line fundamentals is seriously jeopardised. The argument above, as well as our plea for taking Basics as a vital component of therapeutic activity, should reassure you as to that. Nevertheless, from an RT perspective, resources do need to be thought through. This leads us to see that the resource issue is not so straightforward and dissolves into a number of what we would consider more productive debates. We can manage resource more effectively, we can reduce redundancy and we can do this by empowering and upskilling the workforce in resilient practice. Alongside we advocate working closely with practitioners who can make a difference but who are not professionals or workers in organisational terms. This is value for money. Furthermore, RT leads to us not just acting *as if* we are in a demand economy, but also gives us the hope that even for the most disadvantaged, with RT practice, such a goal is within sight.

Realising RT in systems of work activity

This chapter is nearly done. However, we still need to touch on the complicated debate we started with—how to understand collaboration in working with constellated disadvantage beyond organisational form.

Engeström concludes a review of activity theory with the view that 'the disappearance of stable timetables and centralized structures may become a threat to the identities of entire generations' (Engeström, 2000: 973). This is the challenge to organisations of highly innovative ways of working. If RT is a new technology and it thrives on innovation, then we have to look at emerging structures to see how it can best be promoted. Engeström builds on activity theory and links with Victor and Boynton's (1998) notion of *co-configuration* to characterise key elements in connecting customers to providers of services. However, an additional element of 'intelligent product' is included in the equation. The product is configured, or 'co-configured', towards increasing customisation in interaction with the customer.

Engeström (2000) describes the longitudinal process of 'tying, untying and retying together seemingly separate threads of activity' as *knotworking*. Further extensions to a knotworking approach have been seen in formulating how acute wards in hospitals work (Reeves & Lewin, 2004) and developing care agreements for patients with complex medical needs (Engeström, 2000). This does not equate to a team, service model or network. The activity enlists 'actors' as and when they are needed and not as a stable, defined entity working to deadlines. It is also more than a process of continuous improvement although it builds upon this idea. Where it goes further is in its capacity to deliver 'rapid improvisation and negotiation and constantly changing configurations of partners' (Engeström, 2000: 974).

Knotworking resonates with RT Noble Truths, particularly how it innovates and enlists partners in a context of relentlessly refining its services towards resilient outcomes. Those partners, of course, include the children and families in constellated disadvantage. Another added benefit of this way of conceptualising the work is how it helps us to notice the disturbances and troubles in a system as points for future development. Systems become disturbed, serve up contradictions or break down in a particular task. Children and families in constellated disadvantage are all too fully aware of this. Activity theory leads us to seeing the needs for 'reworking the objects and motives sustaining the activity conceptually and very concretely by way of improving and inventing new tools' (Kangasoja, 2002: second page). This is proactive and progressive resilient talk. For RT, new tools are new interventions, further refinements of our Noble Truths as well as initiatives to take us further into formulating optimal work patterning.

In the search to find fertile lands for RT development, we have also been impressed by the potential of cultivating *communities of practice* (Wenger, McDermott, & Snyder, 2002) to help link practitioners and facilitate the development of RT interventions. Our own work to date has benefited from the University–Community Partnerships or CUPP approach (Hart & Wolff, 2006), where there is strong partnering of academics and practitioners and even research-practitioners in a combined project. This has comprised a formal project team but with a fluctuating and expansive membership based on commonalities of practice in a larger community of interest. The tripartite coming together of health and welfare organisations on the one hand with parent groups on the other within the umbrella of an academic institution would have been hard to assemble without the hosting arrangements and resources that a university provides. The adherence to evidence-based and research-literate processes here is key and already highly valued. It can act as a powerful counterbalance to organisations operating as evidence-free zones.

Nevertheless, we are beholden to organisations and their resources for making these developments practically possible and signing up forms of collaboration such as knotworking and communities of practice. All well and good you may say to these new forms, but knots have to be tied somewhere and communities of practice are made up of organisations and not wholly separate from them. Organisations play an essential role and we need to make them work as efficiently, effectively and also as resiliently as we can.

Government policy in the UK has also been concerned to make organisations more responsive to the needs of the most disadvantaged through issuing a number of National Service Frameworks, for example for maternity and children's services (Department for Education and Skills & Department of Health, 2004). Such frameworks prescribe, often in great detail, what future services for these care groups should look like. Services are later measured against key targets as a way of justifying funding streams.

Writing of this from the point of view of complexity theory, Plsek and Wilson stated that the thinking in such frameworks 'fails to take advantage of the natural creativity embedded in the organisation and fails to allow for the inevitable unpredictability of events' (Plsek & Wilson, 2001: 747). They put forward the idea that we should be harnessing that creativity through 'minimum specifications'. Further, they go on to address the 'resistance to change' debate, pointing out that this is usually the result of a clash between competing 'attractors'. Attractors are what motivate people; the goals and aims they strive for. They go on to encourage us to understand them as they represent previous efforts to change in a positive direction. 'Good practice will spread more quickly within the health care system if leaders acknowledge and respect the patterns reflected in the past efforts of others to innovate' (Plsek & Wilson, 2001: 748). This will not be achieved through 'command and control leadership' (2001: 749).

We welcome the very helpful recognition of the negative effect of directive on innovation and also the identifying of attractors in implementing worthwhile changes. Nevertheless, it is our current view that large-scale health and welfare organisations do not represent the best vehicles for such creativity even at their very best. On the contrary, they tend to be a force for stability, accountability and consolidation at most. For those more compromised organisations there are some very real issues that need transformation if they are to host RT to any positive effect. While governmental prescription to organisations may need a lighter touch, we would urge that more heed be given to facilitating other collaborative forms alongside.

Large-scale organisations will nevertheless continue to host the majority of the available resources. When we are thinking of working with disadvantaged communities, it is very important that we work hard to influence organisations. Part of that influence is channelling resources with a Commitment dynamic operating between organisations and those they serve. We also must hone our methods of eliminating wasteful and redundant processes. Overall, the promise is that we can save resources and use those that we do have to better effect. There is a strong case for value for money in an RT approach. A substantial test of this claim remains to be carried out and the argument we present here is simply an early start in that direction.

However, organisations may not be readily influenced. This is a real challenge for us and RT practitioners wherever they work. We recognise, too, that many of the tenets of RT provoke strong reactions in managers within large-scale organisations. The management culture we have pictured here appears to have strong roots and managers have identified with what they perceive as its benefits rather than its untoward consequences.

There is, therefore, something of an edge to working resiliently and we need to embrace it. 'Be brave' as RT tells us and nowhere will we need this more than in making the work of organisations effective, 'lean', and resilient.

Conclusion

There is a lot here to sift and digest and our book only begins this process from an RT point of view. Our starting question, 'What can organisations do that helps?' has led us to indicate priorities for transformation along RT lines. These include using resources to best effect, which includes committing to the long term, realigning managerial resources to support and enhance front-line activity, and elevating practitioner status and autonomy. Where organisations hamper the straightforward application of RT principles, we need to be ready to challenge these and with good reason. But we also need to look elsewhere in order to foster support and interest, to develop our thinking, build on the evidence base, create projects and innovate. Although we have only touched on them here, knotworking and communities of practice appear fruitful ways forward in conceptualising this aspect of RT. They also promise a scholarly and relatively independent base from which to challenge organisational culture, structures and processes given the hostility that we have predicted to these changes.

Our challenge to organisations is to remain open and permissive to this work, and to release resources for the purpose of training and development and to embrace a resilient, evidence informed and evidence building approach in their existing practice. Organisations should not, however, be expected to deliver all aspects of the programme. Nonetheless, they do need to be party to developmental work going on at its boundaries and interfaces.

A further finding of RT is that we need to focus more on what is going on at the boundaries of organisations. This will involve boundary crossing and fostering hybrid roles. By itself this will serve an integrative function.

Integration and partnership are current buzz words. Our own Noble Truth Enlisting represents choreographed partnership, not random couplings. There are dangers in investing in large-scale organisational integration when customised, flexible, and responsive patterns of service delivery are needed. Too much directive, control and oversight and we will lose what is precious. On the other hand, innovating should not lead to unnecessary fragmentation in what is already a mixed economy of care.

In sum, we urge caution in rushing into organisational solutions in either direction for what in essence are issues requiring a step-by-step and discriminating, expansive approach. To this end we shall expand our sphere of interest and move on to the last chapter—to see how professional training and established schools of therapy can also feed into RT.

Chapter 9

Configuring RT for practitioners

There's nothing remarkable about it. All one has to do is hit the right keys at the right time and the instrument plays itself.

Johann Sebastian Bach

Introduction

If you are arriving with us at our last chapter we are assuming that you might be attracted to RT, or at least more than a little intrigued with what RT can offer. You, like us, see value in a search to make work in constellated disadvantage both possible and even rewarding. We hope you will have a clear idea of the compartments and interventions that comprise RT, as well as the Noble Truths that support them. You will have struggled, as we have, with how to make organisations work for RT, and perhaps you have some ideas not only about how you might develop your practice but also about making other forms of collaboration work for you too. In short, you may feel you are now up and ready to go. After all, it is *ordinary* magic as Masten says (2001: 79). Yet, like magic, it is remarkable too.

While, on the whole, we have received very positive feedback from practitioners at workshops, conferences and presentations, there have been other reactions when addressing some therapist practitioners. One of these is 'well, this just represents good practice anyway' and, when pressed, usually that means 'good *social work* practice'. Another group reacts by saying that many of the interventions seem fine and necessary, but is it their role to put them into operation. Yet others question whether this has anything to do with therapy at all. This has made us examine much more intensively the contribution of therapy, both historically and as it is currently practised.

Our aim, in line with the Noble Truths, is to develop RT on the basis of the good practice that already exists. There are now increasing numbers of scholarly reviews of therapies for work with families and children (see, for example, Fonagy, Target, Cottrell, Phillips, & Kurtz, 2002; Rutter & Taylor, 2002). What we learn is that although many practitioners use one mode of therapy there are others at the front line who use combined treatments, multimodal interventions, which are tailored to the multi-dimensional nature of the problems they work with. This is complicated to evaluate and research is needed. Allied to this is the need to have well-trained staff who can deliver therapies with integrity and a good evidence base in order to work effectively. Part of this is also well-supervised experience.

One of our compartments, Core Self, has an intervention that says if we have specific and well-tried treatments for a condition, then use them. Nothing in our presentation of RT should detract from our gratitude to, and reliance upon, the many therapeutic schools of thought, their trainings, methods of supervision, collective wisdom and research leading to proven effective treatments. While offering a new paradigm for therapeutic work in situations of constellated disadvantage, we are in many ways leaving the therapeutic world as before. However, it is also different.

In formulating a resilient approach to the problems of disadvantaged children, we have become acutely aware of the dynamics that exclude them from effective therapeutic involvement. Each of the children that we have presented in the course of this book will have had multiple experiences of being referred for help. Perhaps they have not been appropriately referred. Perhaps the family were not engaged. Perhaps the professionals had changed mid way and the family had withdrawn. It is a familiar road littered with repeated disappointments.

Louis, for example, was referred in total thirteen times, seven with his family of origin and the rest later as a looked-after child. Reviewing these we notice only one successful take. This was when Louis was eight years old. For some reason the referral had worked on that occasion and the family attended a local clinic setting as a family group with individually tailored programmes alongside. The work had gone on for nine months when the therapist told them that she was leaving. Of course, transitional arrangements were offered and then Louis and his mother met with the new team. However, the approach seemed to them very different, the appointment day changed and they missed the previous worker. The clinic did not seem the same. The receptionist had also left and there were different personnel on the day that they did come. The initial meeting was awkward and, although future dates were set up, Louis and his family did not go back.

Such examples are commonplace in our fictionalised case histories and they reflect reality. The family's need and the traditional world of professionals, especially therapists, often do not fit together well. This results in high rates of families in constellated disadvantage not attending appointments, turning down offers of referral and showing poor benefit when they do attend. They also report feeling demoralised by how they are treated and pathologised by how their problems are viewed. As Lynn Hoffman writes:

I sometimes think that 99% of the suffering that comes in through the door has to do with how devalued people feel by the labels that have been applied to them or the derogatory opinions they hold about themselves.

(Hoffman, 1993: 79)

This, our final chapter, turns to some of the reasons why we have arrived at this state of affairs, the challenges it poses and how RT can help us. Also, we will look at where RT fits into the current therapy scene and what we can take from that to develop RT further. We need to develop RT practitioners. You will recall that this is not just workers, but that we follow a sociological view on practice. Theoretically, we can *all* practise RT. Practically this is true too. We know this from our work with groups of practitioners including parents and carers. RT, we contend, is a new departure in this field and we will draw together the strands of how it innovates from all the chapters that have gone before. While we need to build on the work that others have already been engaged with, we also need to ensure that we have established a progressive therapy for constellated disadvantage, where the disappointments of therapy up to now can begin to be transformed into resilient working.

The challenge to care

Finding a clearly articulated way forward that works for constellated disadvantage is of particular need when we think how important it is to use the resources we have to maximum effect. In the UK over the past nine years we have seen the Labour Government invest significantly increased public funding aimed at projects such as neighbourhood renewal, the eradication of child poverty and health services generally. The promise is that by increasing capacity, we will target precisely these needs. The National Service Framework for Maternity and Children's Services (NSF) sets the blueprint for how we must work in this area (Department for Education and Skills & Department of Health, 2004). Its impetus was to eradicate health inequalities. Hence, one of its explicit aims was to focus directly on those with the highest dependency and those most at risk for mental health disorders. In the words of the NSF, 'we can not sit and wait for the most needy to come to our clinics. If our services are to have the necessary effect, we must go to them . . . failure to attend clinic-based appointments should not be seen as a lack of motivation or act as a trigger to close a case but as an indication of the need to review the nature of the service offered (Section 6.4).

Of course we are not pretending that working in these situations and with this group of families and children is at all easy. Working with children when their lives appear to be either persistently in limbo, or simply chronically suboptimal, presents its own very special challenges. RT accepts this but does so in a hopeful light rather than as the failing of an ideal that somehow precludes effective work. However, these difficulties are substantial and we have conceptualised them here in terms of the emotional, technical, practical and political challenges they represent.

Emotionally practitioners are taxed to engage in sustained, productive work when they feel that there is little hope of a clearly positive outcome. The work is often experienced as stressful and demoralising and workers may invoke professional defences, which leave clients feeling pathologised and blamed (Hart & Freeman, 2005; Menzies-Lyth, 1960). As we have already stated, working or living with disadvantaged children is often ascribed very low status. The least qualified and worst paid often find themselves assigned to the most complex children with little support. The desire to superficially process these children through organisations, to locate the problem in the child and family, rather than the workers, or to refer them on to other agencies and/or workers can be immediate and intense. So too is the need to ascribe responsibility for the child's future outcome to other agencies.

The growing fragmentation of the mixed economy of care in countries such as the UK compounds the negative effects of powerful occupational defences. It does nothing to help deal with Haynes' insights that, 'Professionals are sometimes less willing to act in creative and imaginative ways to deal with diversity because of the fear that they will be called to account for actions that don't "follow the book"' (Haynes, 2003: 19).

In the work that we have done to prepare for this book we have been struck by just how often practitioners, including therapists, can lose hope and feel lacking in self-esteem and self-efficacy. At one workshop we ran, in a room of approximately 45 workers, most said that they made no difference to children's lives when there was this much disadvantage. In other locations, family therapists, psychologists, etc., have been similarly dispirited. Ordinary magic is not just something that gets practised on, and with, children. If RT is to work and gain ground, then it needs to be effective for workers too. We constantly strive to be role models and practise on ourselves, as well as challenge each other. RT is designed as a reflexive programme of work. We are not just targeting it on children and families. The compartments and interventions as well as our Noble Truths are aimed to work through and through with the practitioners as well as collectives of practitioners, teams and agencies who also need to be explicitly configured in to the delivery of services.

We go further to see RT as itself needing to be resilient. No doubt it does get, and will be, challenged. Can it withstand this, and grow from the experience of harsh receptions? It remains to be formally and systematically tested over time, of course. Our experience to date is that it can weather and even progress through these challenges. Well, it would not be resilient if it failed. And when we say failed, we mean an expected, or worse than expected negative outcome. Furthermore, RT needs to remain self-aware and learn particularly from its own evidence base. Quinton and Rutter (1988) have alerted us to the importance of 'turning-points' in people's lives. Could we not see RT as part of a wider impetus precipitating a 'turning point' for therapeutic engagement with children and families in constellated disadvantage?

Technically decisions regarding types of intervention and/or potential diagnoses can be problematic when a child's situation seems so uncertain or so chronically depressing. Formulating the precise logic behind diagnosis, therapeutic engagement and strategies often needs careful thought. Therapeutic goals can be elusive. The empirical literature shows that despite all the talk of evidence-based practice, many of us work in a fairly ad hoc and eclectic way (White & Stancombe, 2003). Deep down, most of us know that, 'In reality, complex adaptive systems often require individuals to step out of a tightly prescribed role, to take on the skills required for a specific context' (Haynes, 2003: 67). Yet many therapists and other professionals treat children narrowly in accordance with their professional training. There are very real tensions between the discipline of a refined treatment approach and what can appear to be a mish mash of techniques none of which we can be sure have had any effect (Kazdin, 1996a). There are also research difficulties in evaluating treatments when the emphasis is on combinations and integration of interventions (Fonagy, Target, Cottrell, Phillips, & Kurtz, 2002).

Nevertheless, there are real risks in going for limited formulations when complexity is the rule. For psychiatrists, for example, the temptation and pressure to label children who display extreme behaviours according to classifications of mental disorder can be compelling. Yet it is often very difficult to work out whether there is a serious mental disorder present or their symptoms can be understood normatively, as a dramatic response to dramatic adversity (Grant, Mills, Mulhern, & Short, 2004). Given the potential long-term implications of labelling children at a young age, the treatment implications and the loss of focus on context that may ensue, diagnoses for extreme situations need to be applied with extreme caution.

We should, however, not retreat from this because it is so fraught and messy. As some argue (Masten, 2001; Wolin & Wolin, 1994), a developmental vocabulary of resilience can help practitioners avoid the exclusive search for pathology. Within a resilient frame we can start to conceptualise the positives. Parents, for example, often find diagnoses of strategic use in the pursuit of material resources. Children do have conditions requiring treatment from which they can benefit. Medication may be used to gain strategic advantage in a carefully tailored programme of resilient development. These positive aspects to thinking in terms of mental health disorders should be embraced. We need to employ them in context and as one amongst a range of interventions in a strategic, individualised programme that focuses on an 'upbuilding', rather than a deficit, model of child mental health and emotional well-being.

Practically resources often fall short of what might be required to adequately address the depth and extent of the problem areas identified. For example, caseloads in routine CAMHS are often large and not everybody can be offered the intensive and prolonged work called for. Also, getting children to and from formal clinic-based therapy in a way that is therapeutic can be time consuming and may involve close liaison with birth parents, foster carers, social workers, a range of related social support and even taxi firms directly. Sometimes, in the lives of children like Sally, there is nobody there to ensure that all this happens without this child being let down, and her mental health further compromised.

We have to address these problems head on and not think that they are someone else's role or beneath our attention. We must harness resources that hold promise wherever we can, the more everyday the type of resource the better. In Chapter 2, we introduced the principle hypothetically at least, of 'embedded therapy' and elevated this to a law when we looked at Core Self interventions in particular. 'Belonging' takes us further in the direction of embedding therapy in child and family daily practice, highlighting resources already in operation. We have challenged, in our chapter on making organisations work, the ways in which necessary resources are too often denied for the wrong reasons. Also, in our chapter on Core Self, we saw how it is often *our* limitations as practitioners that mean we do not pursue worthwhile avenues. The outcome example we used there, how Sally does eventually go horse-riding, was only made possible because we worked at it. This is essential work in RT, and we need to use RT as a framework within which therapeutic decisions are those that are most effective given the resources available.

Finally, *politically*, engaging with disadvantaged children in chronic crisis can be complex. As a group they do not have a loud, effective and sustained political voice. These children and their families are not always prioritised by services and they often have few advocates. Not all therapists and other practitioners work with an 'inequalities imagination' (Hall & Hart, 2004; Hart, Hall, & Henwood, 2003; Hart, Lockey, Henwood, Pankhurst, Hall, & Sommerville, 2001). For those that do, a thorough understanding of the effects of health inequalities is at the heart of their practice. The Just Therapy movement, started over ten years ago in New Zealand, has taken inequality as central to their work (Waldegrave, Tamasese, Tuhaka, & Campbell, 2003). Here culture, gender and socioeconomic status become fundamental considerations in how they formulate their understanding of a family or child's problems. This in turn generates a therapeutic approach aimed at addressing these broader processes.

However, knowing that systems fail children and that they are the victims of poverty, disablism and other inequalities can also engender confusion over what needs to happen therapeutically. Just Therapy engages a systems approach with community development. RT complements this by harnessing the broadest range of therapeutic approaches to our endeavour and putting them together with social and welfare initiatives in a coherent articulated whole. Then, in RT, this context of inequality and social exclusion is worked through as a specific focus so that the practitioner's work is not overwhelmed and eventually undermined by it.

Implicit in the above has been the range of interventions RT currently employs and the Noble Truths that underpin them. RT, through bringing together the evidence base for a range of single interventions, offers us a platform upon which we can not only meet these challenges, but also articulate what it is that works and how. It takes us further into what combinations we might need and when. Sequences, preconditions and synergies vie for attention as critical additional components in making therapy work.

Developmental therapeutics

So, what does current practice tell us can be helpful with constellated disadvantage and in what way are we likely to feel hindered? The focus of this book means that we can not engage in an exhaustive examination of all child and adolescent mental health treatment approaches. In any case, there are wide-ranging reviews already to hand (Fonagy, Target, Cottrell, Phillips, & Kurtz, 2002). However, we will take a brief historical overview and then concentrate on features of the current therapeutic landscape that have particular significance for RT and constellated disadvantage.

We can see the beginnings of formal therapy with the advent of the child guidance movement of the 1940s. This was based in psychoanalytic thinking and developed applications through the pioneering child analytic work of Melanie Klein (Klein, 1997) and the object relations school she inaugurated. The model was predominantly an individualising one, focusing on psychopathology in the child and promoting reparative mechanisms to address this through the therapist–child relationship. The later contributions of others, Winnicott (1965a, 1965b) in particular, broadened the reach of object relations theory to encompass a more objective parenting dimension.

In the 1960s there was a concerted effort to develop an empirical knowledge base for child and adolescent mental health, establishing it as a growing scientific discipline. The pioneering Isle of Wight studies (Graham & Rutter, 1973) were seminal in establishing the basic diagnostic categories of concern and the size of the problem involved. While this mapped the terrain, there was little direct therapeutic guidance in the studies. However, it did offer a scientific basis for therapeutics with children and adolescents, a trend that is now beginning to take hold in the impetus for an evidence-based approach. We can see the much more recent development of cognitive, behavioural, cognitive/behavioural and even dialectical cognitive behavioural models as strengthened and elaborated on this platform.

Also there is a timeline we need to pick up from the late 1970s, which took us into the realm of family therapy and systems theory application to children's difficulties (Bateson, 1978), schools emphasising strategic (Satir, 1967), structural (Minuchin, 1974) and counter-intuitive models (Palazolli, Boscolo, Cecchin, & Prata, 1980, 1983), revolutionising how CAMHS clinics worked. It became possible to work with and through families, using shorter-term and much more intermittent interventions, reducing the need for long-term individual treatment of children. We might liken this to the virtual liberation of many adult mental health sufferers resident in large asylums in the 1950s freed by the advent of new drugs, for example, to treat schizophrenia. The offshoots of family therapy schools continue to develop, through narrative (White & Epston, 1990), brief solution focused (De Shazer, 1991), and multi-systemic approaches (Henggeler, Rodick, Borduin, Hanson, Watson, & Urey, 1986), all of which have called into question the appropriateness and efficacy of linear models of individual functioning. The strengths approach, based predominantly in social work practice (Saleebey, 2006), can also be seen as relevant in this survey of modern approaches to treatment.

In any CAMHS as well as in a great deal of social work and even educational practice today you are likely to see some elements of these approaches coexisting and interweaving. Treatment modalities have blossomed since the 1940s. There have been more recent developments that take us some way into successful working in situations of constellated disadvantage, such as Treatment Foster Care and Multi-systemic Therapy. However, from the perspective of RT, a dedicated programme of therapeutic work for these children and families has as yet not been designed. This has been the spur for us to develop RT, to trial it in our everyday practice and to write this book.

The following strikes us time and again. If we think of any major school of psychological therapy, the families we have concentrated on in this book are very often seen as having problems that are too complex, too intractable, too intertwined. Their circumstances are lacking in the basic requirements for any successful therapy to be established. Attached to these dynamics is the habitual tendency to pathologise those that do not respond. If the treatment does not effect a change, then the difficulty is said to lie with the 'object' of treatment rather than the approach. Children and young people living in constellated disadvantage are then categorised as 'beyond treatment'. This manner of thinking takes us into a therapeutic cul-de-sac. It gives us no therapeutic guidance as to what happens next. In particular, it does not help us learn what should and should not be tried in the future, in what combination and over what time span. Furthermore, it disengages us and alienates the families and children from resources they may desperately need. It also confirms those we are working for in their excluded low status, which in turn reinforces the low status of those who stick with them.

As we have argued throughout this book, in our current approaches to deprivation and disadvantage there is a real risk that we make what we need to improve worse. It is perhaps no surprise, then, that many major schools of therapy and therapeutic services are remote, and even shy away from a direct approach to constellated disadvantage. The complexity of these situations does not fit the dominant paradigms of traditional therapeutic delivery, the approaches of which continue to alienate therapists from children and families. The tragedy of this alienation is to further exclude those most disadvantaged from the help they particularly need. Coming from a resilient approach, what leaps out at us is how resources designed for the most vulnerable convert, through the dominant paradigms, into instruments of further disadvantage.

Now that we have summarised the therapeutic approaches we are most likely to meet in child and adolescent mental health services, we will go on to look at those most relevant to RT.

Therapies, disadvantage and RT

Family therapists take a systemic perspective and inherent in any resilient approach is an appreciation that context is vital to our understanding of how to intervene. Family therapy has adapted to build on the strengths of family units through brief solution-focused methods (De Shazer, 1991). We also see family therapy as influential in opening practice up to a wider group of practitioners through its development of consultation processes (Dare, Goldberg, & Walinets, 1990). Family therapy has been flexible, innovative and shows a willingness to develop through its reflexive methodology. It has also engaged with disadvantage and deprivation, particularly from a feminist viewpoint (Hoffman, 1993), and in the development of a multi-systemic school (Henggeler et al., 2003; Henggeler, Schoenwald, Rowland, & Cunningham, 2002). We will return to examine MST.

The difficulty we have had with engaging these systemic approaches in constellated disadvantage is that family therapy, for the most part, ends up talking of disadvantage and its effects rather than presenting any practical means of tackling of it. In this sense, we have seen family therapists as prioritising illumination of narrative over transformation of real-life practice. Family therapy can also be criticised for its lack of a sound evidence base (Fonagy, Target, Cottrell, Phillips, & Kurtz, 2002). It has yet to coherently encompass a specific focus on many of the interventions in RT— tools that are key to developing resilience and achieving better than expected outcomes. RT in comparison seems much more down to earth.

Turning to cognitive behaviour therapy (CBT), this has acquired a pedigree in the world of therapeutic interventions, and it is cited as the treatment of choice for a range of particular symptoms or difficulties including anxiety, depressive disorders (Brent et al., 1997; Kendall, 1993; Ollendick & King, 1998), and obsessive-compulsive disorder (March, Franklin, Nelson, & Foa, 2001). It also plays a role in multimodal treatments for conditions such as ADHD (Abikoff, 1991; Hinshaw, Henker, & Whalen, 1984) and conduct disorder (Tate, Repupucci, & Mulvey, 1995). Government guidelines in the UK recommend CBT as the treatment of choice for adolescent depression (National Institute for Health and Clinical Excellence, 2005).

The literature on adults points to a major reason why CBT has acquired such kudos. It has been subjected to a serious programme of research that has confirmed that it does indeed work. The way in which it has been practised has made it particularly amenable to research. It is a neat package of delivery and for a variety of disorders is extremely good value.

CBT is most often delivered in a series of structured sessions, typically ten, fifteen or twenty. For some children and young people this mode of delivery is very beneficial. They turn up for sessions. Even if the children and young people are reluctant, their parents get them there. They do the homework prescribed by the therapist, symptoms reduce, and they overcome their difficulties. We have all had the experience of working with children and young people in this way, and have felt the glow of satisfaction of a job well done. For example, doing our bit to turn a school-refusing teenager back into a school-attending one, or of helping a young person with an eating disorder return to healthy eating. It is a good feeling, and we can see why practitioners might want to concentrate on these client groups, research their efforts, validate the outcomes and publish them. They then move on to find other amenable client groups to fit the frame for further research and evaluation.

Practitioners, parents and carers living or working with children and young people in the context of constellated disadvantage who are reading this book may well be feeling quite glum at this point. A conversation took place recently when one of us met a worker from a therapeutic team for looked-after children. He had recently acquired a postgraduate qualification in CBT. The therapist joked about how much the training had cost his authority and yet he had not found a serious application of this method to his work with fostered children. 'Give me a kid with a simple phobia, anxiety or even depression', he laughed, 'and I'll cure them.' Each of the children he was working with had much more complex difficulties borne of a combination of social, educational, biological and genetic complexity. Stallard also questions how applicable CBT is to children and adolescents because of the developmental dimension to their symptoms (Stallard, 2002). Roth, a clinical psychologist, asserts that CBT must be integrated with other services that clients are accessing: '. . . there are some individuals for whom brief CBT is unacceptable or inappropriate (for example clients who present with highly complex difficulties that require more extensive input)' (Roth, 2006: 12). His point reinforces our concerns about applying CBT as a panacea in constellated disadvantage. Even where there is only slight complexity, CBT is likely to show very much more modest effects (Hammen, Rudolph, Weisz, Burge, & Rao, 1999).

So, for the children and families that we are talking about in this book— young people like Jason—a straight course of CBT, even assuming that it is available in the locality, is unlikely to help. This is partly because even the most skilful CBT practitioner is unlikely to get Jason to turn up for therapy each week, and to do his CBT homework. It is also because Jason's problems are more complex and need a strategic multi-dimensional approach. Hence RT's CBT interventions need to be used alongside others, and creatively, in order to effect real and lasting change.

Practitioners and parents/carers also need to be flexible about where and how they might use the techniques. As Mills, Grant, Mulhern, and Short (2004) demonstrate, CBT can successfully be employed within an assertive outreach model so that therapists are flexible in how they engage people. Ways of working that have become embedded in the assertive outreach approach include small case loads, home visits, and incorporating therapeutic work into everyday tasks that clients need help with anyway, such as shopping, or undertaking the work in a social setting, for example at a café (Mills, Grant, Mulhern, & Short, 2004: 152).

When we explore psychoanalytic schools, we continue to be concerned at the lack of a theoretical understanding of the impact of context and complexity on the difficulties being addressed. In Chapter 7, Core Self, we considered the claim of Fonagy and colleagues that parents, carers and children must develop a capacity for 'reflective self-functioning' (Fonagy, Steele, Steele, Higgitt, & Target, 1994) if they are to have any hope of resilience development. Falling short of this extreme position, we have taken elements of this and developed them in a resilient frame in Core Self and Belonging.

Also we continue to have concerns at the lack of a solid evidence base for long-term *intensive* work. RT tells us that we can deliver the benefits in other ways, through the everyday activities and contacts children have in the form of embedded therapy. In Learning (Chapter 5), we commented on the wealth of educationally-based programmes, aimed at developing children's social and emotional literacy. These programmes overlap with many of the aims of individual therapy. They are possibly more cost-effective, require less training for practitioners, are less stigmatising, and more inclusive when they can be delivered in relatively seamless conjunction with a child's normative experiences.

Even for children who have fallen out of formal education, and the children we are concentrating on are the most likely to have done so, we have argued throughout this book that interventions are probably best applied through channels already working positively in a child's life according to the principle of embedded therapy. We look to their social workers, foster carers and whichever family members we can enlist to promote such a development. When we can not see any avenues of help, then we have to resort to therapy in the more formal sense. However, the thrust in RT would be to shape any intervention to what is already going on in their lives and to place it as firmly as possible in the context of a range of other supporting interventions, themselves conceptualised as the interventions and Noble Truths of RT.

We are also concerned to make the most effective use of resources, scarce as they are and particularly scarce often for the most disadvantaged, although recent developments in the UK such as dedicated mental health teams for children in local authority care have gone some way to addressing this (Department for Education and Skills & Department of Health, 2004). Where there are already considerable resources we would try to maximise their beneficial effect. We need to be convinced that the therapy would begin where the child and family are at and take account of, and work with, the changing circumstances of such children's lives.

When these considerations are taken together, RT remains cautious over the value of individual therapy to children in constellated disadvantage and often sees long-term *intensive* individual work as a vehicle of last resort for delivering the help they need. Sometimes it appears to be the only route available for a child's therapy in a given situation and, as it was for Sally, it must be supported as such. Claims are made as to the potential benefits for high-dependency children of being helped through long-term work (Hunter, 2001). While we would agree that long-term *involvement* is often essential for resilient work, we do not see an intensive individual therapy model as being the only, or even the optimal, way of providing this.

Intrinsic to RT is that we work in partnership with parents where we can. We do not separate out therapy for parents from the general approach we take for children, their families and practitioners. There is, however, a long tradition of parent skills training, generally to extremely good effect. It has been shown to be particularly helpful for younger children with behaviour problems (Brestan & Eyberg, 1998; Kazdin, 1996b; Ruma, Burke, & Thompson, 1996). There are a number of models available but they all require considerable parental commitment and the greater the commitment and the more intensive the work the better and more sustained are the outcomes (Serketich & Dumas, 1996; Shadish, Montgomery, Wilson, Wilson, Bright, & Okwumabua, 1993). Unfortunately, although they can supplement our work, we can not rely on these trainings as being suitable starting points for work in constellated disadvantage. Low socioeconomic status, parental mental health problems, marital and relationship difficulties and a child's comorbidity all appear as poor prognostic factors.

Lastly, in this brief survey of some of the schools of therapy familiar to CAMHS, there are the pharmacological treatments from a medical/ biological model (Hayman & Santosh, 2002). Again, there is much that is important for us to hold on to from this approach. We are keen that psychiatrists, paediatricians and general practitioners join in with RT. Our experience of working in constellated disadvantage is that medication can and does play a significant role in many of the resilient plans we create. There are times when it is needed in order to get us off first base when the situation is really dire. However, when discussing the technical challenges for RT we were struck by the degree to which deprivation can act as fertile ground for the mimicry of any form of mental-health disorder. The tendency to pathologise, diagnose and categorise the epiphenomena of distress and despair, while well-meaning and scientifically based, has the untoward effect of suggesting that particular treatments are all that is needed. Medication may be presented as a sufficient response, rather than part of a customised matrix of helping interventions.

We have considered many therapeutic schools so far in this chapter. In Chapter 8, we looked at how organisations can contribute positively but can also add to the disadvantaging effect. Research programmes also need to be examined from this point of view. This is an important issue and we can only briefly touch on it here. Let us outline their difficulties. Most restrict efficacy trials to formats that abstract one problem out of an array. They concentrate on this problem in its singular form, and see all other intervening variables as either someone else's issue, or irrelevant.

Here we can see that research itself adds to the disadvantage of the cases we have discussed. Sampling often excludes those with multiple difficulties and the situation is funnelled into the form of a mono-problem with a narrowing down of treatment modalities. The effect is that the treatment becomes a mono-therapy. While this obviously eases research dilemmas and enables studies to be well defined and to offer clear findings, from the point of view of building resilience we have to take a more challenging research path. This needs to be sensitive to, and embrace, the multimodal, strategic approach to building resilience.

So, let us contemplate the dominant paradigms of therapy, research and organisational service delivery from the point of view of constellated disadvantage. We can see how the combined effect of such trends in all three areas, therapies, organisations and research creates a broad, interlocking and mutually supporting network of further disadvantaging processes. UK Government initiatives have been set to increase the number of workers in this field considerably and to design new structures of service integration (Department for Education and Skills, 2003). These structures are aimed at processing and managing interdisciplinary and interagency relationships. New forms of working have been devised, such as the team around the child. Yet, despite all this activity, so many families and children will end up still not being engaged and remaining just as alienated. If we continue to privilege displaced and decontextualised activities of structural and organisational change, many families, children and practitioners will remain disengaged and alienated with all the despondency that goes alongside.

This book aims to address the cycle of failure and frustration. The precise mechanisms that work in constellated disadvantage need to be grasped and put to use. Organisations either take on board valuing the capacities in practitioners that will deliver these or the cycle will go on. Having read this far, it should come as de rigeur to state that the dynamics of disadvantage are powerful dynamics. They cohere, persist and determine families' lives across generations. They see government initiatives come and go. They watch professionals arrive and very often quickly disappear. This is tough work, remarkable work. We need to make it ordinary work too.

Making therapy resilient—Signs of hope

We are not alone in starting down this track. There are signs of others having come this way in response to the problems of difficulties in engagement, poor suitability of available treatments and poor outcomes. Recently a number of new therapies have been introduced. We can think of multisystemic therapy (MST) concentrated predominantly on working with families where there are adolescents showing persistent antisocial behaviour (Henggeler et al., 1999). Treatment foster care (TFC; Chamberlain, 1998) is aimed at increasing the progress and placement stability of look-after children with behavioural difficulties. We highlighted dialectical behaviour therapy (DBT; Linehan, Armstrong, Suarez, Allmon, & Heard, 1991) and Just Therapy (JT; Waldegrave, Tamasese, Tuhaka, & Campbell, 2003). There is also the strengths perspective (Saleebey, 2006), which is targeted at social work practice in particular.

MST combines elements of systemic and structural family therapy, CBT, parent training, behavioural methods and supportive therapy. There is also a component of case management carried out by the therapist, who tends to work alone but gather resources as needed. Caseloads are small; four to eight families at a time and the work with a family intense. Therapists are available twenty-four hours a day and seven days a week and they may stay on average three to five months with any particular case. Therapists are skilled; trained to doctorate level. MST has been well evaluated (Borduin, 1999) and positive results have been obtained in trials focused on reducing antisocial behaviour, offending, substance misuse and psychiatric symptoms (Henggeler et al., 1999, 2003; Schoenwald, Halliday-Boykins, & Henggeler, 2003).

However, even in these studies, when we read the small print, there is always a small group of clients (sometimes impressively small, as low as 2%) who still do not engage with the treatment, or who leave the programme soon after its initiation. The long-term effect of MST is often good, but some studies report more disappointing results (Henggeler, Schoenwald, Rowland, & Cunningham, 2002). Nevertheless, overall, it must be said that the effectiveness of the MST approach is well demonstrated. However, in many of these studies we often wonder what happens with those who do not engage. The families in the case studies that we outlined at the beginning of our chapter could easily fall amongst the non-engagers. Furthermore, and perhaps a far more important point, these intervention programmes remain few and far between, and are often subject to short-term funding. They are very expensive. In some cases trials have been abandoned when practicalities of treatment proved too difficult (Rowland et al., 2005). Furthermore, treatment is generally administered to clients with a clear set of quite similar difficulties—delinquency, emotional disturbance—and to clients who live with their families of origin. How MST is to be used with clients in foster care, those in and out of foster care and home, adoptive families and young people with multiple comorbidities is less obvious.

Of course we should (and, indeed, in this book we do) use the insights from these programmes to inform the work of those of us who are not part of such highly specialised, supported, discrete and extraordinarily well-funded therapy initiatives. However, this book is for use by practitioners working in any contexts, and where constellated disadvantage is a hallmark. Furthermore, the social ecology of these clients may or may not be resource rich.

Unlike MST therapists, most of us working in children's services do not have a detailed manual to hand telling us what to do next. Furthermore, we know from experience that reading and hearing about the rich resources that staff and clients enjoy in these demonstrator projects, does not always inspire regular workers with enthusiasm or a willingness to try to replicate them. Knowing that positive outcomes are possible when a full-time master's level practitioner has between four and eight families on their caseload, an experienced supervisor and a detailed handbook, is unlikely to surprise anybody. But it can leave practitioners with more typical resources and caseloads feeling worse about their own practice, working conditions and clients. Disaffection can set in and potentially useful lessons fall on deaf ears. This is one of the main reasons why we have designed RT for use by regular workers. We aspire to it being accessible, realistic and sustainable *anywhere* in constellated disadvantage.

In contrast to MST, treatment foster care (TFC) is organised around therapeutic techniques, all of which are congruent with social learning theory—the overarching theoretical framework within which the treatment is organised (Chamberlain, 1998). Unlike MST, TFC does concentrate on fostered children, specifically those who are subject to multiple placements. Again, behavioural problems are the focus, particularly aggressive and antisocial behaviour, which triggers placement instability. The programme is individualised and flexible and is delivered through an array of professionals with very well-defined roles. They are recruited into a specialised team with a manager. Like MST, as we noted in Chapter 8, it is costly and the professionals also represent a considerable past as well as a current additional investment in training and expertise. Recruiting such professionals, and also the foster carers, to TFC programmes may prove challenging and if the numbers of children processed are few this pushes the costs even higher. Nevertheless, results of trials indicate that it does positively address behavioural problems, placement breakdown and psychological adjustment more generally.

Dialectical behaviour therapy (DBT) was first used with women who repeatedly deliberately self-harmed and where there was a diagnosis of borderline personality disorder (Linehan, Armstrong, Suarez, Allmon, & Heard, 1991). The method has been taken up for adolescents in in-patient units. It is based on a development of CBT, replacing a rational model of cognitions with a dialectical world view. Principles of this include interrelatedness, polarity and continuous change and there are also elements of systemic and complexity theory inherent in the approach. Again, it requires a considerable additional training of already highly-trained therapists and thus it has only been used so far for adolescents in captive settings. One aspect that has been highlighted is the need for consultation meetings (Katz, Cox, Gunasekara, & Miller, 2004) to maintain treatment fidelity and staff motivation. DBT is both structured and creative, these aspects representing a further polarity in treatment. For this reason, and like MST, it is difficult to see what exactly might be working and in what combination.

Just Therapy, as we have mentioned, privileges matters of culture and gender. It tends to be a combination of family therapy and community work. It addresses injustices directly as intrinsic to therapeutic formulations and the work that follows. It also harnesses spiritual resources in a culture, elevating resolution and hope to become worked-with therapeutic tools and aims (Waldegrave, Tamasese, Tuhaka, & Campbell, 2003).

The strengths perspective prefigures many fundamental tenets of RT and there is a great deal we wish to build on here (Linehan, Armstrong, Suarez, Allmon, & Heard, 1991; Mullaly, 1997; Saleebey, 2006). However, there are very real differences from RT. The strengths approach is avowedly non-prescriptive and it is not tied to specific techniques. Strengths relies on optimism and a positive spin without attempting to specify the precise mechanisms by which good outcomes can be sustained. Nevertheless, the emphasis on mobilising resources, opening up opportunities, privileging accomplishments and eschewing deficit talk are all characteristics to be welcomed, emulated and admired. Strengths work has been particularly valuable in making us aware of our use of language, for example the impact on the most disadvantaged of talking failure about both mental disease and physical disability or portraying them as victims of overwhelming circumstance. For RT, though, hope is different from optimism. RT builds therapy on outcomes that are real, sustainable and reflexive. We cannot rely simply on inspiration and a wellspring of goodwill that may be in short supply, and which in constellated disadvantage is often not present at all.

We could add other schools and we have done so earlier in the book. The recently published Social Work Manifesto (Jones, Ferguson, Lavalette, & Penketh, 2006; *The Guardian*, 2006) comes to mind and this also promotes key elements in common with RT. These are indeed signs of hope, and they are all significant elements in resilient working. We believe that resilience, despite all its shortcomings and difficulties as a concept, offers our best chance to work with children such as Janice, Sally, Jason and Louis and their world in a realistic, uplifting and effective way.

For example, it has been our experience that talking 'resilience' has had a marked effect on our audiences and the members of workshops who have collaborated in the project. The more we have aligned ourselves to a resilient mode of working, the more we have become aware of the habitual pessimism that often engulfs practitioners working in constellated disadvantage. We have also witnessed the paralysis that it creates, which disables practitioners from productive engagement.

This initial reaction needs to be transformed. Our own practice indicates that, although not easy, it is possible with hard work, hope and attention to detail. This is not evangelical zeal, but practical, imaginable efforts that are effective, evidence based, and repeatable. It is why we have also spent some time elaborating what we see as essential prerequisites for RT, our Noble Truths. They provide a template of what we see as ethical involvement. They are not a set of well-meaning precepts, but active agents that continue to inform our work at all stages.

As we have indicated, status is important. It is important for the practitioners and even more important that we transfer status to the work we do with children and families. Any school of therapy that is working in this direction needs to be enlisted. Institutions, too, can help with this. Most particularly, we have been helped by the positive upbuilding effect of a university becoming involved in the intricacies of everyday practice. This is the nuts and bolts of regular therapeutic application, rather than a glamorous, but short-lived, efficacy project. It is important to interlink the detail in both directions. Everyday practice is enlivened by rigorous academic collaboration. The management of effective detail is absolutely key here and deserves its proper status as a function of work in both directions.

Many workers with clinic-based populations and even those in constellated disadvantage will draw on an eclectic therapeutic toolbox. This is quite resilient. Key here is the fact that any activity works for the most disadvantaged. RT goes one step further than therapeutic eclecticism by articulating an integrated coherent whole, with the capacity to be comprehensive, sustainable and generalisable. The more we work in a resilient mode, the more disciplined we become about discerning what mechanisms are at play.

Growing RT

Throughout this book, we have kept three foci in mind. The first is systematically thinking about our daily child and adolescent mental health work with reference to the concept of resilience and the large body of research that has sprung up around it. Hence, throughout the book we constantly wrestle with the relationship between theory, empirical research and practice. Second, the book strives always to make explicit what we mean by therapy, therapeutics and how we envisage resilient therapeutic mechanisms. Third, we ground our discussion in what actually happens in practice—in the day to day life of children, families and workers.

RT works with disadvantaged children and their families anywhere. This is the whole point of the resilient approach. Grounded as it is in real-life experience, we aim to keep ourselves connected to what must be attempted in real life, rather than in the laboratory. Holding in mind the meaning of the concept resilience helps us here too. We are reminded that resilience promotes the idea of people doing better than the contexts in which they live or work might seem to allow. This goes as much for practitioners as it does for children and families. Resilient therapists do not necessarily pack up their bags and go when the trial is abandoned or the client chooses not to engage. In this respect, RT is concerned with structural changes as well as changes in individual family or child functioning. RT starts out in the recognition of complexity and relativity but is a *progressive* programme of action. In philosophical and stylistic terms, we could say it represents a return from the post-modern to modernist world, but grounded in the knowledge of its own transition.

It also represents a multimodal therapeutic and social-welfare endeavour within a coherent frame of reference called RT. We build on what has gone before and any practitioners coming to RT need to conserve what they already know and can offer that works. We draw on other therapies. However, we do not wish to be overly constrained by them. By embedding current therapeutic approaches into RT's Noble Truths, they are subtly but definitely transformed. They are harnessed to be even more effective, particularly for previously hard-to-reach groups, in an 'upbuilding' spirit that includes and elevates. We also learn to use combinations of therapies with other related interventions. By placing all the interventions that work in RT we have included them *all* as therapy in the same way that the concept of an RT practitioner is widened to enlist *all* those working, paid or not, with constellated disadvantage.

There are very real educational tasks associated with bringing RT of age. The language it uses needs to be as accessible as possible. Its use with different constituencies needs to be actively researched, as we have learnt in preparing for this book. We are engaging practitioners where they are working already. Our methods are those of everyday practice, supervision, showing and telling, live supervision and group work. We also trial our interventions within the context of everyday practice with the most challenging of situations. Then there is group work to report on practice and refine what interventions we employ. These groups also need familiarity with the growing and developing research base. RT, then, enlists practitioners into the research effort in a thoroughgoing way.

RT does shake a few foundations by bringing a sociological dimension to our understanding of practice. We see this as a liberation of therapy, seamlessly joining therapy to the dimensions of good social-work practice. It also helps us to give practice its proper status and authority. It connects the work with organisations and other forms of collaboration. We see it as spawning a research and practice synergy, where academic endeavour is connected through and through with practice expertise. As a consequence of this approach, there are roles that we have become increasingly interested in that cross the boundaries of current practice and research and other cross-boundary roles as well. The roles and functions of practice manager and academic practitioner may both enhance RT and embody its values in a way that a purely theoretical or clinical argument would always struggle to do.

RT can be practically complex and intellectually challenging. This is matched by its capacity to galvanise. We aim to make those who use it at ease with being uncomfortable. Our experience to date has been that RT may not immediately suit everyone, although it is designed for universal appeal. For some, it may appear too innovative and broad. It also requires a shift in mind-set to see constellated disadvantage as a very real and possible focus for therapeutic work and success. Concepts such as inoculated resilience can also be complicated to follow. It requires us to move on and across the boundaries of accepted knowledge, transferring ideas from say immunology and epidemiology as well as sociology into what has previously seemed a more pristine and self-contained world of therapy. An RT expert is an expert of a different order.

So, yes, another book on therapy. Do we need another one you might still be asking. There is still a great deal to be done. This book is only a beginning. We could say more and much of what we do say is only a beginning. Some implications of RT at this stage of development are suggestive rather than definitive, generative rather than stitched up. We do need to put RT further into the world and see what comes back. We need to trial it not only in everyday practice but also in research and debate as rigorously as we can. We would like to make organisations aware of its concepts and findings and to look at how we can engage collaboratively in making RT work in the world.

RT should learn as it goes and be reflexive as to its own place in the world. It needs to find its appropriate status and authority and perhaps give rise to corresponding organisational forms. All these subjects are deserving of treatment in their own right. As part of a resilient movement, RT might be considered a turning point as we launch this into the worlds of health and social-care practice. You will have read this book and may be wondering what it might do for you, personally, in your work and for the families and children for whom this book is intended. We respond by urging you to try it out.

Finally, a word of caution. Resilience is a bit like a world seen through the looking glass. We have turned the spotlight on ourselves and our current limitations in addressing the needs of those living in circumstances of constellated disadvantage. This raises a conundrum: that which is so depressing, demoralising and stressful in situations of constellated disadvantage is actually, when fully appreciated, that which holds greatest promise in terms of the changes that can be made. As we have seen, in a strange but definite way resilience feeds on adversity. The limitations we impose on what can be done are often our own limitations. We can see that little changes can make a disproportionate difference. RT focuses on what we can do rather than what we can not do. While it challenges, when we transform a critical eye to appraising that challenge, it is intellectually stimulating, emotionally fulfilling and motivationally inspiring.

It has been a central aim of this book to transform any undue tendency towards pathologising. We began our work in Accepting constellated disadvantage as a fact in the everyday lives of some children and families. We have gone on to stress the critical importance of building up their skills, capacities and resources. By saying 'Accepting', we have not intended to condone the dynamics and inequalities that lead to such circumstances. We can not be naïve to the political dimension of working in disadvantaged contexts. Indeed, RT counteracts disadvantaging dynamics wherever they are found.

RESILIENT THERAPY SUMMARY CHART

Noble Truths:	Accepting		Conserving	Commitment	Enlisting
Compartments:	Basics	Belonging	Learning	Coping	Core Self
	Good enough housing	Tap into good influences	Make school life work as well as possible	Understanding boundaries and keeping within them	Instil a sense of hope
	Enough money to live	Find somewhere for the child to belong	Engage mentors for children	Being brave	Teach the child to understand other people's feelings
	Being safe	Responsibilities and obligations	Map out career/life plan	Solving problems	Help the child to know her/himself
	Access and transport	Help child make friends and mix with other children	Help the child to organise her/himself	Putting on rose-tinted glasses	Help the child take responsibility for her/himself
	Healthy diet	Focus on good times and places	Highlight achievements	Fostering their interests	Foster their talents
	Exercise and fresh air	Make sense of where a child has come from	Develop life skills	Calming him/herself down, self-soothe	There are tried and tested treatments for specific problems, use them
	Play and leisure opportunities	Get together people the child can count on		Tomorrow is another day	
	Being free from prejudice and discrimination	Predict a good experience of someone/something new		Lean on others when necessary	
		Help child understand his/her place in the world			
		Belonging is not just about people			

Interventions

References

Abikoff, H. (1991). Cognitive training in ADHD children: Less to it than meets the eye. *Journal of Learning Disabilities, 24*, 205–209.

Ainsworth, M. D. S., Blehar, M. C., Waters, E., & Wall, S. (1978). *Patterns of attachment: A psychological study of the strange situation.* Hillsdale, NJ: Lawrence Erlbaum Associates, Inc.

Alaszewski, C., & Manthorpe, J. (1998). Welfare agencies and risk: The missing link. *Health and Social Care in the Community, 6*(1), 4–15.

American Academy of Child and Adolescent Psychiatry. (2005). Practice parameter for the assessment and treatment of children and adolescents with reactive attachment disorder of infancy and early childhood. Washington, DC: American Academy of Child and Adolescent Psychiatry.

Anthony, E. J. (1987). Risk, vulnerability, and resilience: An overview. In E. J. Anthony & B. J. Cohler (Eds.), *The invulnerable child* (pp. 3–48). New York: Guildford Press.

Apfel, N., & Seitz, V. (1997). The firstborn sons of African American teenage mothers: Perspectives on risk and resilience. In S. Luthar, J. A. Burack, D. Ciccetti, & J. R. Weisz (Eds.), *Developmental psychopathology* (pp. 486–506). Cambridge, UK: Cambridge University Press.

Armstrong, M. I., Stroul, B. A., & Boothroyd, R. A. (2005). Intercepts of resilience and systems of care. In M. Ungar (Ed.), *Handbook for working with children and youth* (pp. 387–403). London: Sage.

Aspinwall, L., & Taylor, S. (1997). A stitch in time: Self-regulation and proactive coping. *Psychological Bulletin, 121*, 417–436.

Baldwin, A. L., Baldwin, C., & Cole, R. E. (1990). Stress-resistant families and stress-resistant children. In J. Rolf, D. Ciccetti, K. Nuechterlein, & S. Weintraub (Eds.), *Risk and protective factors in the development of psychopathology* (pp. 257–280). New York: Cambridge University Press.

Barker, P. (1998). *Basic family therapy* (4th ed.). Oxford, UK: Blackwell Science.

Bateson, G. (1978). *Steps to an ecology of mind: Collected essays on anthropology, psychiatry, evolution and epistemology.* Boulder, CO: Paladin Press.

Baumeister, R. F., & Leary, M. R. (1995). The need to belong: Desire for inter-personal attachments as a fundamental human motivation. *Psychological Bulletin, 117*, 497–529.

Beck, A. T., Rush, A. J., Shaw, B. E., & Emery, G. (1979). *Cognitive therapy of depression.* New York: Guildford Press.

Becker, K. D., Stuewig, J., Herrera, V. M., & McCloskey, L. A. (2004). A study of firesetting and animal cruelty in children: Family influences and adolescent outcomes. *Journal of the American Academy of Child & Adolescent Psychiatry, 43*(7), 905–912.

Belsky, J., & Cassidy, J. (1994). Attachment theory and evidence. In M. Rutter & D. Hay (Eds.), *Development through life: A handbook for clinicians* (pp. 373–402). Oxford, UK: Blackwells.

Benard, B. (2002). Turnaround people and places: Moving from risk to resilience. In D. Saleebey (Ed.), *The strengths perspective in social work practice* (3rd ed., pp. 213–227). Boston: Allyn Bacon.

Bifulco, A. (2002). Attachment style measurement: A clinical and epidemiological perspective. *Attachment and Human Development, 4*(2), 180–188.

Block, J., & Kremen, A. (1996). IQ and ego-resiliency: Conceptual and empirical connections and separateness. *Journal of Personality and Social Psychology, 70*(2), 349–361.

Borduin, C. M. (1999). Multisystemic treatment of criminality and violence in adolescents. *Journal of the American Academy of Child & Adolescent Psychiatry, 38*, 242–249.

Bostock, R. (2004). *Promoting resilience in fostered children and young people.* London: Social Care Institute for Excellence.

Bourdieu, P. (1996). On the family as a realized category. *Theory, Culture and Society, 13*(3), 19–26.

Bowlby, E. J. M. (1969). *Attachment and loss: Attachment.* New York: Basic Books.

Boyden, J., & Mann, G. (2005). Children's risk, resilience, and coping in extreme situations. In M. Ungar (Ed.), *Handbook for working with children and youth* (pp. 3–25). London: Sage.

Brent, D. A., Holder, D., Kolko, D., Birmaker, B., Baugher, M., Roth, C., et al. (1997). A clinical psychotherapy trial for adolescent depression comparing cognitive, family and supportive therapy. *Archives of General Psychiatry, 54*, 877–885.

Brestan, E. V., & Eyberg, S. M. (1998). Effective psychosocial treatments of conduct-disordered children and adolescents: 29 years, 82 studies, and 5,272 kids. *Journal of Clinical Child Psychology, 27*(2), 180–190.

Brodsky, A. E. (1996). Resilient single mothers in risky neighbourhoods: Negative psychological sense of community. *Journal of Community Psychology, 24*(4), 347–363.

Bronfenbrenner, U., & Ceci, S. J. (1994). Nature–nurture reconceptualized in developmental perspective: A bioecological model. *Psychological Review, 101*(4), 568–586.

Brooks, R., & Goldstein, S. (2001). *Raising resilient children: Fostering strength, hope and optimism in your child.* Chicago: Contemporary Books.

Brooks, R., & Goldstein, S. (2003). *Nurturing resilience in our children: Answers to the most important parenting questions.* Chicago: Contemporary Books.

Brown, D., Pedder, J., & Bateman, A. (2000). *Introduction to psychotherapy: An outline of psychodynamic principles and practice.* London: Routledge.

Buchmann, D. (2002). Measuring family background in international studies of education: Conceptual issues and methodological challenges. In A. C. Porter & A. Gamoran (Eds.), *Methodological advances in cross-national surveys of educational achievement* (pp. 150–197). Washington, DC: National Academy Press.

Buckner, J. C., Mezzacappa, E., & Beardslee, W. R. (2003). Characteristics of resilient youths living in poverty: The role of self-regulatory processes. *Development and Psychopathology, 15*, 139–162.

Burchardt, T. (2006). Changing weights and measures: Disability and child poverty. *Poverty, 123*, 6–9.

Byng-Hall, J. (2002). Relieving parentified children's burdens in families with insecure attachment patterns. *Family Process, 41*(3), 375–388.

Cadell, S., Karabanow, J., & Sanchez, M. (2001). Community, empowerment and resilience: Paths to wellness. *Canadian Journal of Community Mental Health, 20*(1), 21–35.

Capps, L., Sigman, M., & Mundy, P. (1994). Attachment security in children with autism. *Development and Psychopathology, 6*, 249–261.

Carter, B., & New, C. (2004). *Making realism work: Realist social theory and empirical research.* Abingdon, UK: Routledge.

Cass, N., Shove, E., & Urry, J. (2005). Social exclusion, mobility and access. *The Sociological Review, 53*(3), 539–555.

Catalano, R., Berglund, M. L., Ryan, J. A. M., Lanczak, H. S., & Hawkins, J. D. (2004). Positive youth development in the United States: Research findings on evaluations of positive youth development programs. *Annals of the American Academy of Political and Social Science, 591*(1), 98–124.

Chamberlain, P. (1998). Treatment foster care. *Juvenile Justice Bulletin: Office of Juvenile Justice and Delinquency Prevention, December,* 1–11.

Chen, W., & Taylor, E. (2005). Resilience and self-control impairment. In S. Goldstein & R. Brooks (Eds.), *Handbook of resilience in children* (pp. 257–278). New York: Kluwer Academic/Plenum.

Child Poverty Action Group. (2006). Poverty facts and figures. London: Child Poverty Action Group.

Ciaprara, G. V., Barbaranelli, C., Pastorelli, C., Bandura, A., & Zimbardo, P. G. (2000). Prosocial foundations of children's academic achievement. *Psychological Science, 11*, 302–306.

Cicchetti, D., & Rogosh, F. (1997). The role of self-organisation in the promotion of resilience in maltreated children. *Development and Psychopathology, 9*, 797–815.

Cilliers, P. (1998). *Complexity and postmodernism: Understanding complex systems.* London: Routledge.

Clarke, L. (1999). *Challenging ideas in psychiatric nursing.* London: Routledge.

Clay, V., & Silberberg, S. (2004). *The resilience identification resource kit.* Callagan, Australia: Family Action Centre, Faculty of Health, University of Newcastle.

Clifton, K. (2003a). Mobility strategies and food shopping for low-income families: A case study. *Journal of Planning Education and Research, 23*, 402–413.

Clifton, K. (2003b). Independent mobility among teenagers: An exploration of travel to after school activities. *Transportation Research Record, 1854*, 74–80.

Clifton, K., & Lucas, K. (2004). Examining the empirical evidence of transport inequality in the USA and UK. In K. Lucas (Ed.), *Running on empty* (pp. 15–36). Bristol, UK: Policy Press.

Cohen, J. A., Mannarino, A., & Knudsen, K. (2004). Treating childhood traumatic grief: A pilot study. *Journal of the American Academy of Child and Adolescent Psychiatry*, *43*(10), 1225–1233.

Conrad, M., & Hammen, C. (1993). Protective and resource factors in high- and low-risk children: A comparison of children with unipolar, medically ill, and normal mothers. *Development & Psychopathology*, *5*, 593–607.

Cooper, A., & Lousada, J. (2005). *Borderline welfare: Feeling and fear of feeling in modern welfare*. London: H. Karnac Books.

Cornille, T., & Woodard Meyers, T. (1999). Secondary traumatic stress among child protective service workers: Prevalence, severity and predictive factors. *Traumatology*, *15*(5), 423–432.

Costello, E. J., Foley, D. L., & Angold, A. (2006). 10-year research update review: The epidemiology of child and adolescent psychiatric disorders: II. Developmental epidemiology. *Journal of the American Academy of Child & Adolescent Psychiatry*, *45*(1), 8–25.

Cowen, E., Work, W., & Wyman, P. (1997). The Rochester Child Resilience Project (RCRP): Facts found, lessons learned, future directions divined. In S. Luthar, J. A. Burack, D. Ciccetti, & J. R. Weisz (Eds.), *Developmental psychopathology: Perspectives on adjustment, risk and disorder* (pp. 527–547). Cambridge, UK: Cambridge University Press.

Cowen, E. L., Wyman, P. A., Work, W. C., Kim, J. Y., Fagen, D. B., & Magnus, K. B. (1997). Follow-up study of young stress-affected and stress-resilient urban children. *Development and Psychopathology*, *9*, 565–577.

Croom, S., & Procter, S. (2005). The NewCan Practise Framework: Using risk and resilience to work at the interface between professional expertise and parental knowledge and experience in child and adolescent mental health. *Practice*, *17*(2), 113–126.

Cross, T. L. (1995). Understanding family resiliency from a relational worldview. In H. I. McCubbin, E. A. Thompson, & J. E. Fromer (Eds.), *Resiliency in ethnic minority families: Native and immigrant American families* (pp. 143–157). Thousand Oaks, CA: Sage.

Crowther, R., & Marshall, M. (2001). Helping people with severe mental health illness to obtain work: Systematic review. *British Medical Journal*, *322*(7280), 204–208.

Damasio, A. (2000). *The feeling of what happens: Body, emotion and the making of consciousness*. London: Vintage.

Damon, W. (2004). What is positive youth development? *Annals of the American Academy of Political and Social Science*, *591*(1), 13–24.

Daniel, B., & Wassell, S. (2002a). *The early years: Assessing and promoting resilience in vulnerable children 1*. London & Philadelphia: Jessica Kingsley.

Daniel, B., & Wassell, S. (2002b). *The school years: Assessing and promoting resilience in vulnerable children 2*. London & Philadelphia: Jessica Kingsley.

Daniel, B., & Wassell, S. (2004). *Adolescence: Assessing and promoting resilience in vulnerable children 3*. London & Philadelphia: Jessica Kingsley.

Dare, J., Goldberg, D., & Walinets, R. (1990). What is the question you need to answer? How consultation can prevent professional systems immobilizing families. *Journal of Family Therapy*, *12*(4), 355–369.

De Shazer, S. (1991). *Putting difference to work*. New York: Norton.

Deming, W. E. (1982). *Out of the crisis.* Cambridge, UK: Cambridge University Press.

DeNavas-Walt, C., Proctor, B. D., & Lee, C. H. (2005). *Current population reports: United States Census Bureau.* Washington, DC: United States Government Printing Office.

Department for Education and Employment. (1999). *Extending opportunity: A national framework for study support.* London: HMSO.

Department for Education and Skills. (2003). *Every child matters* (Green Paper). London: Stationery Office.

Department for Education and Skills and Department of Health. (2004). *National Service Framework for children, young people and maternity services.* London: Department for Education and Skills.

Department for Work and Pensions. (2006). *Annual households below average income* (Annual Report). London: Department for Work and Pensions.

Department of Health. (1999). *Framework for the assessment of children in need and their families.* London: Department of Health.

Department of Health. (2004). *The mental health and psychological well-being of children and young people: National Service Framework for children, young people and maternity services.* London: Department of Health.

Doll, B., Zucker, S., & Brehm, K. (2004). *Resilient classrooms: Creating healthy environments for learning.* New York: Guilford Press.

Dominelli, L. (1997). *Anti-racist social work: A challenge for white practitioners and educators.* Basingstoke, UK: Macmillan.

Douglas, M. (1980). *Purity and danger: An analysis of concepts of pollution and taboo.* London: Routledge & Kegan Paul.

Dozier, M., Chase Stovall, K., Albus, K. E., & Bates, B. (2001). Attachment for infants in foster care: The role of caregiver state of mind. *Child Development, 72*(5), 1467–1477.

Dozier, M., & Sepulveda, S. (2004). Foster mother state of mind and treatment use: Different challenges for different people. *Infant Mental Health Journal, 25*(4), 368–378.

Dufour, M. H., Nadeau, L., & Bertrand, K. (2000). Les facteurs de resilience chez les victimes d'abus sexuel: État de la question. *Child Abuse and Neglect, 24*(6), 781–797.

Dunn, J. (1974). *Modern revolutions.* Cambridge, UK: Cambridge University Press.

Dunn, J. (1993). *Young children's close relationships: Beyond attachment.* Newbury Park, CA: Sage.

Dwyer, K., Osher, D., & Warger, C. (1998). *Early warning, timely response: A guide to safe schools.* Washington, DC: US Department of Education.

Eachus, J., Chan, P., Pearson, N., Propper, C., & Davey Smith, G. (1999). An additional dimension to health inequalities: Disease severity and socioeconomic position. *Journal of Epidemiological Community Health, 53*(10), 603–611.

Egeland, B., Carlson, E., & Sroufe, L. A. (1993). Resilience as process. *Development and Psychopathology, 5,* 517–528.

Egeland, B., & Erikson, M. F. (1990). Rising above the past: Strategies for helping new mothers break the cycle of abuse and neglect. *Zero to Three, 11*(2), 29–35.

Elder, G. H. (1974). *Children of the Great Depression.* Chicago: University of Chicago Press.

Elder, G. H., Liker, J. K., & Jaworski, B. J. (1984). Hardship in lives: Historical influences from the 1930s to old age in postwar America. In K. McCluskey & H. Reese (Eds.), *Life-span developmental psychology: Historical and cohort effects* (pp. 161–201). New York: Academic Press.

Elias, M. J., Parker, S., & Rosenblatt, J. (2005). Building educational opportunity. In S. Goldstein & R. Brooks (Eds.), *Handbook of resilience in children* (pp. 315–336). New York: Kluwer Academic/Plenum.

Engeström, Y. (2000). Activity theory as a framework for analyzing and redesigning work. *Ergonomics, 43*(7), 960–974.

Engeström, Y., Brown, K., Cristopher, L. C., & Gregory, J. (1997). Co-ordination, co-operation and communication in the courts: Expansive transitions in legal work. In M. C. Cole, Y. Engeström, & O. Vasquez (Eds.), *Mind, culture and activity*. Cambridge, UK: Cambridge University Press.

Eraut, M. (1994). *Developing professional knowledge and competence*. Brighton, UK: Falmer Press.

Essen, J., Lambert, L., & Head, J. (1976). School attainment of children who have been in care. *Child Care Health and Development, 2*, 339–351.

Farber, E. A., & Egeland, B. (1987). Invulnerability among abused and neglected children. In E. J. Anthony & B. J. Cohler (Eds.), *The invulnerable child* (pp. 253–288). New York: Guildford.

Felner, R. D. (2005). Poverty in childhood and adolescence. In S. Goldstein & R. Brooks (Eds.), *Handbook of resilience in children* (pp. 125–147). New York: Kluwer Academic/Plenum Press.

Festinger, L. (1957). *A theory of cognitive dissonance*. Stanford, CA: Stanford University Press.

Fimister, G. (2001). An end in sight? Tackling child poverty in the UK. London: Child Poverty Action Group.

Fletcher-Campbell, F., & Archer, T. (2003). Achievement at Key Stage 4 of young people in care. *National Foundation for Educational Research Report 434*. Nottingham, UK: Department of Education and Skills.

Flower, C., McDonald, J., & Sumski, M. (2005). *Review of turnover in Milwaukee County: Private agency child welfare ongoing case management staff*. Milwaukee, WI: University of Milwaukee.

Fonagy, P. (2001). *Attachment theory and psychoanalysis*. New York: Other Press.

Fonagy, P., Steele, H., Moran, G., Steele, M., & Higgitt, A. C. (1991). The capacity for understanding mental states: The reflective self in parent and child and its significance for security of attachment. *Infant Mental Health Journal, 13*, 200–216.

Fonagy, P., Steele, H., & Steele, M. (1991). Maternal representations of attachment during pregnancy predict the organization of infant–mother attachment at one year of age. *Child Development, 62*, 891–905.

Fonagy, P., Steele, H., Steele, M., Higgitt, A., & Target, M. (1994). The theory and practice of resilience. The Emanuel Miller Memorial Lecture 1992. *Journal of Child Psychology and Psychiatry, 35*(2), 231–257.

Fonagy, P., Steele, M., Moran, G. S., Steele, H., & Higgitt, A. C. (1993). Measuring the ghost in the nursery: An empirical study of the relation between parents' mental representations of childhood experiences and their infants' security of attachment. *Journal of American Psychoanalytical Association, 41*, 957–989.

Fonagy, P., Target, M., Cottrell, D., Phillips, J., & Kurtz, Z. (2002). *What works for whom? A critical review of treatments for children and adolescents.* New York & London: Guildford Press.

Forsyth, A., & Furlong, A. (2000). *Socioeconomic disadvantage and access to higher education.* Bristol, UK: Policy Press.

Freedman, M. (1993). *The kindness of strangers.* San Francisco: Jossey-Bass.

Freud, A. (1966). *The ego and the mechanisms of defence.* New York: International Universities Press.

Fuller, A., Bellhouse, B., & Johnston, G. (2002). *The heart masters: A programme for the promotion of emotional intelligence and resilience for school children aged 12 to 14.* Bristol, UK: Lucky Duck.

Furedi, F. (2004). *Therapy culture: Cultivating vulnerability in an uncertain age.* London: Routledge.

Garbarino, J. (2005). Foreword. In M. Ungar (Ed.), *Handbook of working with children and youth: Pathways to resilience across cultures and contexts* (pp. xi–xiii). Thousand Oaks, CA: Sage.

Garmezy, N., & Rutter, M. (1983). *Stress, coping and development in children.* New York: McGraw-Hill.

George, C., Kaplan, N., & Main, M. (1985). *Adult attachment interview* (unpublished manuscript). Berkeley, CA: University of California.

Gerhardt, S. (2004). *Why love matters: How affection shapes a baby's brain.* London: Brunner-Routledge.

Ghate, D., & Hazel, N. (2002). *Parenting in poor environments: Stress, support and coping.* London: Jessica Kingsley.

Giangreco, M. F. (1997). Key lessons learned about inclusive education: Summary of the 1996 Schonell Memorial Lecture. *International Journal of Disability, 44*(3), 193–206.

Gilgun, J. F. (2006). Children and adolescents with problematic sexual behaviors: Lessons from research on resilience. In R. Longo & D. Prescott (Eds.), *Current perspectives on working with sexually aggressive youth and youth with sexual behavior problems* (pp. 383–394). Holyoke, MA: Neari Press.

Gilgun, J. F., Keskinen, S., Marti, D. J., & Rice, K. (1999). Clinical applications of the CASPARS Instruments: Boys who act out sexually. *Families in Society, 80*(6), 629–637.

Gilligan, C. (1982). *In a different voice: Psychological theory and women's development.* Cambridge, MA: Harvard University Press.

Gilligan, R. (1998). Beyond permanence? The importance of resilience in child placement practice and planning. *Adoption & Fostering, 21*(1), 12–20.

Gilligan, R. (1999). Enhancing the resilience of children and young people in public care by mentoring their talents and interests. *Child & Family Social Work, 4*(3), 187–196.

Gilligan, R. (2001). *Promoting resilience: A resource guide on working with children in the care system.* London: BAAF.

Goffman, E. (1968). *Asylums: Essays on the social situation of mental patients and other inmates.* Harmondsworth, UK: Penguin.

Goldratt, E. M. (1996). *Critical chain.* Great Barrington, MA: North River Press.

Goldstein, S., & Brooks, R. B. (2005). *Handbook of resilience in children.* New York: Kluwer Academic/Plenum.

Goleman, D. (1999). *Working with emotional intelligence*. London: Bloomsbury.

Gonzalez, R., & Padilla, A. M. (1997). The academic resilience of Mexican American high school students. *Hispanic Journal of Behavioral Sciences, 19*(3), 301–317.

Gordon, E. W., & Song, L. D. (1994). Variations in the experience of resilience. In M. C. Wang & E. W. Gordon (Eds.), *Educational resilience in inner city America* (pp. 27–43). Hillsdale, NJ: Lawrence Erlbaum Associates, Inc.

Graham, P., & Rutter, M. (1973). Psychiatric disorder in the young adolescent. *Proceedings of the Royal Society of Medicine, 66,* 1226–1229.

Grant, A., Mills, J., Mulhern, R., & Short, N. (2004). *Cognitive behavioural therapy in mental health care*. London: Sage.

Grossmann, K. E., Grossmann, K., & Keppler, A. (2003). Universal and culturally specific aspects of human behavior: The case of attachment. In W. Friedlmeier, P. Chakkarath, & B. Schwarz (Eds.), *Culture and human development: The importance of cross-cultural research to the social sciences* (pp. 75–98). Amsterdam: Swetz & Zeitlinger.

Haight, W. L. (1998). 'Gathering the spirit' at First Baptist Church: Spirituality as a protective factor in the lives of African American children. *Social Work, 43,* 213–222.

Haight, W. L., Kagle, J. D., & Black, J. E. (2003). Understanding and supporting parent–child relationships during foster care visits: Attachment theory and research. *Social Work, 48*(2), 195–207.

Hall, V., & Hart, A. (2004). The use of imagination in professional education to enable learning about disadvantaged clients. *Learning in Health and Social Care, 3*(4), 190–202.

Hammen, C., Rudolph, K., Weisz, J., Burge, D., & Rao, U. (1999). The context of depression in clinic-referred youth: Neglected areas in treatment. *Journal of the American Academy of Child & Adolescent Psychiatry, 38,* 64–71.

Harker, R., Dobel-Ober, D., Berridge, D., & Sinclair, R. (2004a). *Taking care of education: An evaluation of the education of looked after children* London: National Children's Bureau.

Harker, R. M., Dobel-Ober, D., Akhurst, S., Berridge, D., & Sinclair, R. (2004b). Who takes care of education 18 months on? A follow-up study of looked after children's perceptions of support for educational progress. *Child & Family Social Work, 9*(3), 273–284.

Hart, A. (1998). *Buying and selling power: Anthropological reflections on prostitution in Spain*. Boulder, CO: Westview HarperCollins.

Hart, A., & Freeman, M. (2005). Health 'care' interventions: Making health inequalities worse, not better? *Journal of Advanced Nursing, 49*(5), 502–512.

Hart, A., Hall, V., & Henwood, F. (2003). Helping health and social care professionals develop an 'inequalities imagination': A model for use in education and practice. *Journal of Advanced Nursing, 41*(5), 1–9.

Hart, A., Lockey, R., Henwood, F., Pankhurst, F., Hall, V., & Sommerville, F. (2001). *Addressing inequalities in health: New directions in midwifery education and practice*. London: English National Board for Nursing, Midwifery and Health Visiting.

Hart, A., & Luckock, B. (2004). *Developing adoption support and therapy: New approaches for practice*. London & Philadelphia: Jessica Kingsley.

Hart, A., Luckock, B., & Gerhardt, C. (2002). The Attachment Project in context: Developing therapeutic and social support services for adoptive and long-term foster families in Brighton and Hove, a research-based evaluation. Brighton, UK: Faculty of Health, University of Brighton.

Hart, A., Saunders, A., & Thomas, H. (2005). Attuning practice: Findings from a service user study of child and adolescent mental health services. *Epidemiologia e Psichiatria Sociale (EPS)*, *14*(1), 22–31.

Hart, A., & Thomas, H. (2000). Controversial attachments: The indirect treatment of fostered and adopted children via parent co-therapy. *Attachment & Human Development*, *2*(3), 306–327.

Hart, A., & Wolff, D. (2006). Developing communities of practice through community–university partnerships. *Planning, Practice and Research*, *21*(1), 121–138.

Hawkins, J. D., Farrington, D. P., & Catalan, R. F. (1998). Reducing violence through the schools. In D. S. Elliott, B. A. Hamburg, & K. R. Williams (Eds.), *Violence in American schools: A new perspective* (pp. 188–216). New York: Cambridge University Press.

Hawley, D., & DeHaan, L. (1996). Toward a definition of family resilience: Integrating life-span and family perspectives. *Family Process*, *35*(3), 283–298.

Hawton, K., & Van Heeringen, K. (2000). *The international handbook of suicide and attempted suicide*. Chichester, UK, & New York: Wiley.

Hayman, I., & Santosh, P. (2002). Pharmacological and other physical treatments. In M. Rutter & E. Taylor (Eds.), *Child and adolescent psychiatry* (4th ed., pp. 998–1019). Oxford, UK: Blackwell Scientific.

Haynes, P. (2003). *Managing complexity in the public services*. Milton Keynes, UK: Open University Press.

Heath, A., Colton, M., & Aldgate, J. (1994). Failure to escape: A longitudinal study of foster children's educational attainment. *British Journal of Social Work*, *24*(3), 241–260.

Hechtman, L. (1991). Resilience and vulnerability in long term outcomes of attention deficit hyeractivity disorder. *Canadian Journal of Psychiatry*, *36*(6), 415–421.

Hemmings, A. (2000). The hidden corridor curriculum. *The High School Journal*, *83*(2), 1–10.

Henggeler, S. W., Clingempeel, W. G., Brondino, M. J., & Pickrel, S. G. (2002). Four-year follow-up of multisystemic therapy with substance abusing and substance-dependent juvenile offenders. *Journal of the American Academy of Child & Adolescent Psychiatry*, *41*(7), 868–875.

Henggeler, S. W., Rodick, J. D., Borduin, C. M., Hanson, C. L., Watson, S. M., & Urey, J. R. (1986). Multisystemic treatment of juvenile offenders: Effects on adolescent behaviour and family interaction. *Developmental Psychology*, *22*, 132–141.

Henggeler, S. W., Rowland, M. D., Halliday-Boykins, C., Sheidow, A. J., Ward, D. M., Randall, J., et al. (2003). One-year follow-up of multisystemic therapy as an alternative to the hospitalization of youths in psychiatric crisis. *Journal of the American Academy of Child and Adolescent Psychiatry*, *42*(5), 543–552.

Henggeler, S. W., Rowland, M. D., Randall, J., Ward, D. M., Pickrel, S. G., Cunningham, P. B., et al. (1999). Home-based multisystemic therapy as an alternative to the hospitalization of youths in psychiatric crisis: Clinical outcomes. *Journal of the American Academy of Child and Adolescent Psychiatry, 38*(11), 1331–1339.

Henggeler, S. W., Schoenwald, S. K., Rowland, M. D., & Cunningham, P. B. (2002). *Serious emotional disturbance in children and adolescents: Multi-systemic therapy*. New York: Guildford Press.

Henwood, F., Wyatt, S., & Hart, A. (2003). Ignorance is bliss sometimes: Constraints on the emergence of the 'informed patient' in the changing landscapes of health information. *Sociology of Health and Illness, 25*(6), 589–607.

Hesse, E. (1999). The Adult Attachment interview: Historical and current perspectives. In J. Cassidy & P. Shaver (Eds.), *Handbook of attachment* (pp. 395–433). New York: Guildford Press.

Hetherington, E. M. (1989). Coping with family transitions: Winners, losers, and survivors. *Child Development, 60*, 1–14.

Hetherington, E. M., & Kelley, J. (2002). *For better or for worse: Divorce reconsidered*. New York: W. W. Norton.

Hill, J., Fonagy, P., Safier, E., & Sargent, J. (2003). The ecology of attachment in the family. *Family Process, 42*(2), 205–221.

Himelein, M. J., & McElrath, J. A. V. (1996). Resilient child sexual abuse survivors: Cognitive coping and illusion. *Child Abuse and Neglect, 20*(8), 747–758.

Hinshaw, S. P., Henker, B., & Whalen, C. K. (1984). Cognitive-behavioural and pharmacologic interventions for hyperactive boys: Comparative and combined effects. *Journal of Consulting and Clinical Psychology, 52*, 739–749.

Hodge, D. R. (2005a). Developing a spiritual assessment toolbox: A discussion of the strengths and limitations of five different assessment methods. *Health and Social Work, 30*, 314–323.

Hodge, D. R. (2005b). Social work and the house of Islam: Orienting practitioners to the beliefs and values of Muslims in the United States. *Social Work, 50*, 162–173.

Hoffman, L. (1993). *Exchanging voices: A collaborative approach to family therapy*. London: Karnac.

Hoffman, M. (1982). Affect and moral development. In D. Cicchetti & P. Hesse (Eds.), *New directions in child development: Emotional development* (pp. 83–103). San Francisco: Jossey-Bass.

Howe, D. (1995). *Attachment theory for social work practice*. Basingstoke, UK: Palgrave.

Howe, D. (2005). *Child abuse and neglect: Attachment, development and intervention*. Basingstoke, UK: Palgrave Macmillan.

Howe, D., & Fearnley, S. (1999). Disorders of attachment and attachment therapy. *Adoption & Fostering, 23*(2), 19–30.

Howlin, P. (2002). Special educational treatment. In M. Rutter & E. Taylor (Eds.), *Child and adolescent psychiatry* (4th ed., pp. 1128–1147). Oxford, UK: Blackwell.

Hughes-Freeland, F., & Crain, M. M. (1998). *Recasting ritual: Performance, media, identity*. London: Routledge.

Hunter, D., & Killoran, A. (2004). *Tackling health inequalities: Turning policy into practice?* London: Health Development Agency.

Hunter, M. (2001). *Psychotherapy with young people in care: Lost and found*. London: Brunner-Routledge.

James, A., Jencks, C., & Prout, A. (1998). *Theorising childhood*. Cambridge, UK: Polity.

Jang, L.-J. (2005). *The 921 earthquake: A study of the effects of Taiwanese cultural factors on resilience*. Doctoral thesis. Denver, CO: University of Denver, Graduate School of Social Work.

Jones, C., Ferguson, I., Lavalette, M., & Penketh, L. (2006). *Social work manifesto*. (Available at: http://www.liv.ac.uk/sspsw/Social_Work_Manifesto.html – accessed 27 April 2006)

Jordan, A. (1994). *Skills in collaborative classroom consultation*. London: Routledge.

Jordan, J. V. (2005). Relational resilience in girls. In S. Goldstein & R. Brooks (Eds.), *Handbook of resilience in children* (pp. 79–90). New York: Kluwer Academic/Plenum.

Juffer, F., Bakermans-Kranenburg, M. J., & Van IJzendoorn, M. H. (2005). The importance of parenting in the development of disorganized attachment: Evidence from a preventive intervention study in adoptive families. *Journal of Child Psychology and Psychiatry*, 46(3), 263–274.

Jurkovic, G. (1997). *Lost childhoods: The plight of the parentified child*. New York: Brunner-Routledge.

Kangasoja, J. (2002). *Complex design problems: An impetus for learning and knotworking*. Helsinki, Finland: University of Helsinki, Centre for Activity Theory and Developmental Work. (Available at: http://www.edu.helsinki.fi/activity/publications/files/47/ICLS2002_Kangasoja.pdf – accessed 25 May 2006)

Karoly, P. (1993). Mechanisms of self-regulation: A systems view. *Annual Review of Psychology*, 44, 23–52.

Katz, L. Y., Cox, B. J., Gunasekara, S., & Miller, A. L. (2004). Feasibility of dialectical behavior therapy for suicidal adolescent inpatients. *Journal of the American Academy of Child and Adolescent Psychiatry*, 43(3), 276–282.

Kazdin, A. E. (1996a). Combined and multimodal treatments in child and adolescent psychotherapy: Issues, challenges and research directions. *Clinical Psychology: Science and Practice*, 3, 69–100.

Kazdin, A. E. (1996b). Problem solving and parent management in treating aggressive and antisocial behavior. In E. D. Hibbs & P. S. Jensen (Eds.), *Psychosocial treatments for child and adolescent disorders: Empirically based strategies for clinical practice* (pp. 377–408). Washington, DC: American Psychological Association.

Keddie, A. (2003). Little boys: Tomorrow's macho lads. *Discourse*, 24(3), 289–306.

Kendall, P. C. (1993). Cognitive-behavioural therapies with youth: Guiding theory, current status and emerging developments. *Journal of Consulting and Clinical Psychology*, 61, 235–247.

Kendall, P. C., Stark, K. D., & Adam, T. (1990). Cognitive deficit or cognitive distortion in childhood depression. *Journal of Abnormal Child Psychology*, 18(3), 255–270.

Kensit, D. A. (2000). Rogerian theory: A critique of the effectiveness of pure client-centred therapy. *Counselling Psychology Quarterly*, 13(4), 345–349.

Kerr, M., Stattin, H., & Pakalniskienne (2005). What *do* parents do when faced with adolescent problem behaviour? *Trust for the Study of Adolescence's international conference of parenting*. University of Sussex, Brighton, UK.

Klein, J. (2004). Interdisciplinarity and complexity: An evolving relationship. *Emergence, Complexity and Organisations, 6*(1–2), 2–10.

Klein, M. (1975). *Envy and gratitude.* London: Hogarth Press.

Klein, M. (1997). *The psycho-analysis of children.* London: Vintage.

Kleinman, M. (2000). Include me out? The new politics of place and poverty. *Policy Studies, 21*(1), 49–61.

Kohlberg, L. (1981). *The philosophy of moral development: Moral stages and the idea of justice.* San Francisco & London: Harper Row.

Kristeva, J. (1982). *Powers of horror: An essay on abjection.* New York: Columbia University Press.

Kuehl, B. P. (1995). The solution-oriented genogram: A collaborative approach. *Journal of Marital and Family Therapy, 21*(3), 239–250.

Lacher, D., Nichols, T., & May, J. C. (2005). *Connecting with kids through stories: Using narratives to facilitate attachment in adopted children.* London: Jessica Kingsley.

Lamming, Lord (Chair). (2003). *The Victoria Climbié Inquiry* (CM 5730). London: HMSO.

Latane, B., & Darley, J. (1968). Bystander intervention in emergencies: Diffusion of responsibility. *Journal of Personality and Social Psychology, 8,* 377–383.

Latane, B., & Darley, J. (1970). *The unresponsive bystander: Why doesn't he help?* Englewood Cliffs, NJ: Prentice Hall.

Layard, R. (2005). *Happiness: Lessons from a new science.* London: Allen Lane.

Lazarus, R. S., & Launier, R. (1978). Stress-related transactions between person and environment. In L. A. Pervin & M. Lewis (Eds.), *Perspectives in interactional psychology* (pp. 287–327). New York: Plenum Press.

Learmonth, M. (2001). NHS Trust chief executives as heroes? *Health Care Analysis, 9*(4), 417–436.

Leont'ev, E. N. (1978). *Activity, consciousness and personality.* Englewood Cliffs, NJ: Prentice-Hall.

Lerner, R. M. (2005). *Promoting positive youth development: Theoretical and empirical bases* (Chapter prepared for National Research Council/Institute of Medicine). Washington, DC: National Academy of Sciences.

Lerner, R. M. (2006). Editor's introduction. In R. M. Lerner (Ed.), *Handbook of child psychology. Vol. 1: Theoretical models of human development.* Hoboken, NJ: Wiley.

Lerner, R. M., Freund, A. M., De Stephanis, I., & Habermas, T. (2001). Understanding developmental regulation in adolescence: The use of the selection, optimization, and compensation model. *Human Development, 44,* 29–50.

Lerner, R. M., Lerner, J. V., & Almerigi, J. B. (2005). Positive youth development, participation in community youth development programs, and community contributions of fifth-grade adolescents: Findings from the first wave of the 4-H study of positive youth development. *Journal of Early Adolescence, 25,* 17–71.

Lieberman, A. F. (2004). Traumatic stress and quality of attachment: Reality and internalization in disorders of infant mental health. *Infant Mental Health Journal, 25*(4), 336–351.

Linehan, M. M., Armstrong, H. E., Suarez, A., Allmon, D., & Heard, H. L. (1991). Cognitive-behavioural treatment for chronically parasuicidal borderline patients. *Archives of General Psychiatry, 48*(12), 1060–1064.

Linstead, S. (1997). The social anthropology of management. *British Journal of Management, 8,* 85–98.

Loeber, R., & Stouthamer-Loeber, M. (1986). Family factors as correlates and predictors of juvenile conduct problems and delinquency. In M. Tonry & N. Morris (Eds.), *Crime and justice: An annual review of research* (Vol. 7, pp. 129–150). Chicago: University of Chicago Press.

Lomas, P. (1981). *The case for a personal psychotherapy.* Oxford, UK: Oxford University Press.

Lubeck, S., & Garrett, P. (1990). The social construction of the 'at risk child'. *British Journal of Sociology of Education, 11*(3), 327–340.

Lucas, K. (2004). Running on empty: Transport, social exclusion and environmental justice. Bristol, UK: Policy.

Luckock, B., & Hart, A. (2005). Adoptive family life and adoption support: Policy ambivalence and the development of effective services. *Child & Family Social Work, 10,* 125–134.

Luckock, B., Lefevre, M., Orr, D., Jones, M., Marchant, R., & Tanner, K. (2006). *Knowledge review on teaching, learning and assessing communication skills with children and young people in social work.* London: Social Care Institute for Excellence.

Luthar, S. (1995). Social competence in the school setting: Prospective cross-domain associations among inner-city teens. *Child Development, 66,* 416–429.

Luthar, S., & Suchman, N. (2000). Relational Psychotherapy Mothers' Group: A developmentally informed intervention for at-risk mothers. *Development and Psychopathology, 12,* 235–253.

Luthar, S. S. (1991). Vulnerability and resilience: A study of high-risk adolescents. *Child Development, 62*(3), 600–616.

Luthar, S. S., Cicchetti, D., & Becker, B. (2000). The construct of resilience: A critical evaluation and guidelines for future work. *Child Development, 71*(3), 543–562.

Luthar, S. S., & Zigler, E. (1991). Vulnerability and competence: A review of research on resilience in childhood. *American Journal of Orthopsychiatry, 61,* 6–22.

Mallon, G. P. (1992). Utilization of animals as therapeutic adjuncts with children and youth: A review of the literature. *Child and Youth Care Forum, 21*(1), 53–67.

March, J. S., Franklin, M., Nelson, A., & Foa, E. (2001). Cognitive-behavioral psychotherapy for paediatric obsessive-compulsive disorder. *Journal of Clinical Child Psychology, 30,* 8–18.

Marvin, R., Cooper, G., Hoffman, K., & Powell, B. (2002). The Circle of Security Project: Attachment based intervention with caregiver–pre-school child dyads. *Attachment and Human Development, 4*(1), 107–124.

Maslach, C. (1982). *Burnout: The cost of caring.* Englewood Cliffs, NJ: Prentice-Hall.

Maslow, A. (1943). A theory of human motivation. *Psychological Review, 50,* 370–396.

Masson, J. M. (2003). *Final analysis: The making and unmaking of a psychoanalyst.* London: Ballantine Books.

Masten, A., Germezy, N., & Tellegen, A. (1988). Competence and stress in school children: The moderating effects of individual and family qualities. *Journal of Child Psychology and Psychiatry*, *29*, 745–764.

Masten, A., Hubbard, J., Gest, S., Tellegen, A., Garmezy, N., & Ramirez, M. (1999). Competence in the context of adversity: Pathways to resilience and maladaption from childhood to late adolescence. *Development and Psychopathology*, *11*, 143–169.

Masten, A. S. (2001). Ordinary magic: Resilience processes in development. *American Psychologist*, *56*(3), 227–238.

Masten, A. S., Neemann, J., & Andenas, S. (1994). Life events and adjustment in adolescents: The significance of event independence, desirability, and chronicity. *Journal of Research on Adolescence*, *4*, 71–97.

McCann, J., James, A., Wilson, S., & Dunn, G. (1996). Prevalence of psychiatric disorders in young people in the care system. *British Medical Journal*, *313*, 1529–1530.

McCubbin, L. D. (2003). *Resilience among Native Hawaiian adolescents: Ethnic identity, psychological distress and wellbeing*. Doctoral Dissertation. Madison, WI: University of Wisconsin-Madison.

McCubbin, L. D., & McCubbin, H. I. (2005). Culture and ethnic identity in family resilience: Dynamic processes in trauma and transformation of indigenous people. In M. Ungar (Ed.), *Handbook for working with children and youth* (pp. 27–44). London: Sage.

Melzer, D., Jenkins, R., & Fryers, T. (2003). *Social inequalities and the distribution of the common mental disorders* (Maudsley Monograph). London: Psychology Press.

Menzies-Lyth, I. (1960). *The functioning of social systems as a defence against anxiety*. London: Tavistock Institute of Human Relations.

Miles, S. (2000). *Youth lifestyles in a changing world*. Buckingham, UK: Open University Press.

Mills, J., Grant, A., Mulhern, R., & Short, E. (2004). Working with people in assertive outreach. In R. Mulhern, J. Mills, A. Grant, & N. Short (Eds.), *Cognitive behavioural therapy in mental health care* (pp. 143–160). London: Sage.

Minuchin, S. (1974). *Families and family therapy*. London & New York: Routledge.

Mitchell, R., Dorling, D., & Shaw, M. (2000). *Inequalities in life and death: What if Britain were more equal?* Bristol, UK: Policy Press.

Mittleton-Kelly, E. (1997). *Organisations as co-evolving complex adaptive systems* (BPRC Paper No. 5). Coventry, UK: Business Process Resource Centre, University of Warwick.

Miyake, K., Chen, S., & Campos, J. J. (1985). Infant temperament, mother's mode of interaction and attachment in Japan: An interim report. *Monographs for the Society for Research in Child Development*, *50*(1–2), 276–297.

Modell, A. H. (1976). The holding environment and the therapeutic action of psychoanalysis. *Journal of the American Psychoanalytic Association*, *24*(2), 285–307.

Mullaly, B. (1997). *Structural social work: Ideology, theory and practice* (2nd ed.). Oxford, UK, & Toronto, Canada: Oxford University Press.

Munro, E. (2005). A systems approach to investigating child abuse deaths. *British Journal of Social Work*, *35*(4), 531–546.

Murali, V., & Oyebode, F. (2004). Poverty, social inequality and mental health. *Advances in Psychiatric Treatment, 10*, 216–224.

Murphy, J. M., & Gilligan, C. (1980). Moral development in late adolescence and adulthood: A critique and reconstruction of Kohlberg's theory. *Human Development, 23*(2), 77–104.

National Energy Action. (2005). National energy action policy and research. (Available at: http://www.nea.org.uk – accessed February 2007)

National Institute for Health and Clinical Excellence. (2005). Depression in children and young people: Identification and management in primary, community and secondary care. *Clinical Guideline 28*. London: National Institute for Health and Clinical Excellence. (Available at: http://www.nice.org.uk/CG028 – accessed 16 May 2006)

Nelkin, D. K. (2005). Freedom, responsibility and the challenge of situationism. *Midwest Studies in Philosophy, XXIX*, 181–206.

Newman, L. S., Duff, K. J., & Baumeister, R. F. (1997). A new look at defensive projection: Thought suppression, accessibility, and biased person perception. *Journal of Personality and Social Psychology, 72*(5), 980–1001.

Nietzche, F. (1992). *Basic writings of Nietzche*. London: Random House.

Noam, G. G., Warner, L. A., & Van Dyken, L. (2001). Beyond the rhetoric of zero tolerance: Long-term solutions for at-risk youth. *New Directions For Youth Development, 92*, 155–182.

O'Connor, T., & Zeanah, C. H. (2003). Attachment disorders: Assessment strategies and treatment approaches. *Attachment and Human Development, 5*(3), 223–244.

O'Dougherty Wright, M., & Masten, A. S. (2005). Resilience processes in development. In S. Goldstein & R. B. Brooks (Eds.), *Handbook of resilience in children* (pp. 17–37). New York: Kluwer Academic/Plenum.

Ollendick, T. H., & King, N. J. (1998). Empirically supported treatments for children with phobic and anxiety disorders. *Journal of Clinical Child and Adolescent Psychology, 27*, 156–167.

Østerlund, C., & Carlile, P. (2005). Relations in practice: Sorting through practice theories on knowledge sharing in complex organizations. *The Information Society, 21*, 91–107.

Palazolli, M. S., Boscolo, L., Cecchin, G., & Prata, G. (1980). Hypothesizing-circularity-neutrality: Three guidelines for the conductor of the session. *Family Process, 19*, 3–12.

Palazolli, M. S., Boscolo, L., Cecchin, G., & Prata, G. (1983). *Paradox and counterparadox: A new model in the therapy of the family in schizophrenic transaction*. London & New York: Jason Aronson.

Parker, E., Cowen, W., Work, P., & Wyman, P. (1990). Test correlates of stress resilience among urban school children. *The Journal of Primary Prevention, 11*(1), 19–35.

Parkes, A., & Kearns, A. (2004). *The multi-dimensional neighbourhood and health: A cross-sectional analysis of the Scottish Household Survey, 2001* (Centre for Neighbourhood Research Paper 19). Glasgow, UK: ESRC Centre for Neighbourhood Research.

Patterson, J., & Blum, R. (1996). Risk and resilience among children and youth with disabilities. *Archives of Pediatric and Adolescent Medicine, 150*(7), 692–698.

Pearson, J. L., Cohn, D. A., Cowan, P. A., & Cowan, C. P. (1994). Earned and continuous security in adult attachment: Relation to depressive symptomatology and parenting style. *Development & Psychopathology, 6*, 359–373.

Pfeffer, J. (1992). *Managing with power: Politics and influence in organisations.* Boston, MA: Harvard Business School Press.

Piaget, J. (1977). *The moral judgement of the child.* Harmondsworth, UK: Penguin Books.

Plsek, P. E., & Wilson, T. (2001). Complexity, leadership and management in healthcare organisations. *British Medical Journal, 323*, 746–749.

Plummer, D. (2001). *Helping children to build self-esteem: A photocopiable activities book.* London: Jessica Kingsley.

Plummer, D. (2005). *Helping adolescents and adults to build self-esteem: A photocopiable resource book.* London & Philadelphia: Jessica Kingsley.

Pollack, W. S. (2004). Male adolescent rites of passage: Positive visions of multiple developmental pathways. *Annals of the New York Academy of Sciences, 1036*, 141–150.

Polnay, L., Glaser, A., & Rao, V. (1996). Promoting the health of looked after children. *British Medical Journal, 320*, 661–662.

Pontell, H., & Klein, M. (2006). *Four decades of street gang research.* Upper Saddle River, NJ: Prentice Hall.

Poston, D. J., & Turnbull, A. P. (2004). Role of spirituality and religion in family quality of life for families of children with disabilities. *Education and Training in Developmental Disabilities, 39*(2), 95–108.

Preston, G. (2005). *At greatest risk.* London: Child Poverty Action Group.

Prilleltensky, I., & Prilleltensky, O. (2005). Beyond resilience: Blending wellness and liberation in the helping professions. In M. Ungar (Ed.), *Handbook of working with children and youth* (pp. 89–103). London: Sage.

Quinton, D., & Rutter, M. (1988). *Parenting breakdown: The making and breaking of inter-generational links.* Aldershot, UK: Avebury.

Radke-Yarrow, M., & Brown, E. (1993). Resilience and vulnerability in children of multiple-risk families. *Development and Psychopathology, 5*, 581–592.

Reder, P., & Duncan, S. (1999). *Lost innocents: A follow-up study of fatal child abuse.* London: Routledge.

Reder, P., Duncan, S., & Gray, M. (1993). *Beyond blame: Child abuse tragedies revisited.* London: Routledge.

Reeves, S., & Lewin, S. (2004). Interprofessional collaboration in the hospital: Strategies and meanings. *Journal of Health Services Research and Policy, 9*, 218–225.

Reivich, K., Gillham, J. E., & Chaplin, T. M. (2005). From helplessness to optimism. In S. Goldstein & R. Brooks (Eds.), *Handbook of resilience in children* (pp. 223–237). New York: Kluwer Academic/Plenum.

Resnick, M., Bearman, P., Blum, R., Bauman, H., Harris, K., & Jones, J. (1997). Protecting adolescents from harm: Findings from the National Longitudinal Study of Adolescent Health. *Journal of the American Medical Association, 278*(10), 823–832.

Resnick, M., Harris, L. J., & Blum, R. (1993). The impact of caring and connectedness on adolescent health and well-being. *Journal of Paediatrics and Child Health, 29*(1), S3–S9.

Ressler, E., Boothby, N., & Steinbock, D. (1988). *Unaccompanied children: Care and protection in wars, natural disasters, and refugee movements*. New York: Oxford University Press.

Richters, J., & Martinez, P. (1993). Violent communities, family choices, and children's chances: An algorithm for improving the odds. *Development and Psychopathology, 5*, 609–627.

Rogers, C. R. (1951). *Client-centred therapy: Its current practice, implications and therapy*. London: Constable.

Roisman, G. I., Padrón, E., Sroufe, L. A., & Egeland, B. (2002). Earned-secure attachment status in retrospect and prospect. *Child Development, 73*(4), 1204–1219.

Rolf, J., Masten, A., Cicchetti, D., Nuechterlein, K., & Weintraub, S. (1990). *Risk and protective factors in the development of psychopathology*. Cambridge, UK: Cambridge University Press.

Roth, T. (2006). Applying evidence-based practice in practice. *Healthcare Counselling and Psychotherapy Journal, April*, 9–12.

Rowland, M. D., Halliday-Boykins, C., Henggeler, S. W., Cunningham, P. B., Lee, T. G., Kruesi, M. J. P., et al. (2005). A randomized trial of multisystemic therapy with Hawaii's Felix class youths. *Journal of Emotional and Behavioral Disorders, 13*(1), 13–24.

Ruma, P. R., Burke, R. V., & Thompson, R. W. (1996). Group parent training: Is it effective for children of all ages? *Behaviour Therapy, 27*(2), 159–170.

Rutter, M. (1987). Psychosocial resilience and protective mechanisms. *American Journal of Orthopsychiatry, 57*(3), 316–331.

Rutter, M. (1990). Psychosocial resilience and protective mechanisms. In J. Rolf, S. Masten, D. Cicchetti, K. Nuechterlein, & S. Weintraub (Eds.), *Risk and protective factors in the development of psychopathology* (pp. 181–214). Cambridge, UK & New York: Cambridge University Press.

Rutter, M. (1993). Resilience: Some conceptual considerations. *Journal of Adolescent Health, 14*, 626–631.

Rutter, M. (1995a). Clinical implications of attachment concepts: Retrospect and prospect. *Journal of Child Psychology and Psychiatry, 36*(4), 549–571.

Rutter, M. (1995b). Psychosocial resilience and protective mechanisms. *Southern African Journal of Child and Adolescent Psychiatry, 7*, 75–88.

Rutter, M. (1999). Resilience concepts and findings: Implications for family therapy. *Journal of Family Therapy, 21*, 119–144.

Rutter, M., Maugham, B., Mortimore, P., Aliston, J., & Smith, A. (1979). *Fifteen thousand hours: Secondary schools and their effect on children* London: Open Books.

Rutter, M., Moffitt, T. E., & Caspi, A. (2006). Gene–environment interplay and psychopathology: Multiple varieties but real effects. *Journal of Child Psychology and Psychiatry, 47*(3), 226–261.

Rutter, M., & Quinton, D. (1984). Long-term follow-up of women institutionalized in childhood: Factors promoting good functioning in adult life. *British Journal of Developmental Psychology, 2*, 191–204.

Rutter, M., & Taylor, E. (2002). *Child and adolescent psychiatry (4th ed.)*. Oxford, UK: Blackwell Scientific.

Rutter, M., & The English and Romanian Adoptees (ERA) Study Team. (1998).

Developmental catch up and deficit following adoption after severe global, early privation. *Child Psychology & Psychiatry, 39,* 465–476.

Ryan, T., & Walker, R. (2002). *Life story work: A practical guide to helping children understand their past.* London: British Association for Adoption and Fostering.

Ryberg, T., & Larsen, M. C. (2006, April). Networked identities: Understanding different types of social organisation and movements between strong and weak ties in networked environments. Proceedings of the Fifth International Conference on Networked Learning, Lancaster University, UK.

Saleebey, D. (2006). *The strengths perspective in social work practice.* Boston: Pearson.

Sandler, J., Dare, C., & Holder, A. (1992). *The patient and the analyst.* London: Karnac.

Satir, V. (1967). *Conjoint family therapy.* Palo Alto, CA: Science & Behavior Books.

Schoenwald, S., Brown, T. L., & Henggeler, S. W. (2000). Inside multisystemic therapy: Therapist, supervisory and program practices. *Journal of Emotional and Behavioral Disorders, 8*(2), 113–144.

Schoenwald, S., Halliday-Boykins, C., & Henggeler, S. W. (2003). Client-level predictors of adherence to MST in community service settings. *Journal of the American Academy of Child and Adolescent Psychiatry, 42*(3), 345–359.

Schofield, G. (2003). *Part of the family: Pathways through foster care.* London: British Association for Adoption and Fostering.

Schofield, G., & Beek, M. (2005). Risk and resilience in long-term foster care. *British Journal of Social Work, 35*(8), 1283–1301.

Seden, J. (2002). Underpinning theories for the assessment of children's needs. In H. Ward & W. Rose (Eds.), *Approaches to needs assessment in children's services* (pp. 195–216). London & Philadelphia: Jessica Kingsley.

Segal, J. (1988). Teachers have enormous power in affecting a child's self-esteem. *The Brown University Child Behavior and Development Newsletter, 4,* 1–3.

Seligman, M. E. P. (1975). *Helplessness: On depression, development, and death.* San Francisco: Freeman.

Seligman, M. E. P. (1998). *Learned optimism: How to change your mind and your life.* New York: Free Press.

Senge, P. M. (1990). *The fifth discipline: The art and practice of the learning organization.* New York: Doubleday.

Sennett, R. (2003). *Respect in a world of inequality.* New York: W. W. Norton.

Serketich, W. J., & Dumas, J. E. (1996). The effectiveness of behavioral parent training to modify antisocial behavior in children: A meta-analysis. *Behavior Therapy, 27*(2), 171–186.

Sesma, A., Jr., Mannes, M., & Scales, P. C. (2005). Positive adaptation, resilience, and the developmental asset framework. In S. Goldstein & R. Brooks (Eds.), *Handbook of resilience in children* (pp. 281–296). New York: Kluwer Academic/Plenum.

Shadish, W. R., Montgomery, L. M., Wilson, P., Wilson, M. R., Bright, I., & Okwumabua, T. (1993). Effects of family and marital psychotherapies: A meta-analysis. *Journal of Consulting and Clinical Psychology, 61,* 992–1002.

Shucksmith, J., Philip, K., Spratt, J., & Watson, C. (2005). Investigating the links between mental health and behaviour in schools. A report to the Scottish

Executive Education Department Pupil Support and Inclusion Division. Aberdeen, UK: University of Aberdeen.

Smith, J., & Prior, M. (1995). Temperament and stress resilience in school age children: A within families study. *Journal of the American Academy of Child and Adolescent Psychiatry, 34*, 168–179.

Snyder, C. R., & Lopez, S. J. (2006). *Handbook of positive psychology.* Oxford, UK: Oxford University Press.

Social Exclusion Unit. (2002). *Making the connections: Transport and social exclusion.* London: Office of the Deputy Prime Minister.

Spencer, M. B., Dobbs, B., & Swanson, D. P. (1988). Afro-American adolescents: Adaptational processes and socioeconomic diversity in behavioral outcomes. *Journal of Adolescence, 11*, 117–137.

Stallard, P. (2002). Cognitive behaviour therapy with children and young people: A selective review of key issues. *Behavioural and Cognitive Psychotherapy, 30*, 297–309.

Stevens, J. W. (2005). Lessons learned from poor African American youth: Resilient strengths in coping with adverse environments. In M. Ungar (Ed.), *Handbook for working with children and youth* (pp. 45–56). London: Sage.

Stirling, M. (1992). How many pupils are excluded? *British Journal of Special Education, 14*(4), 14–18.

Stouthamer-Loeber, M., Loeber, R., Farrington, D. P., Quanwu, Z., van Kammen, W., & McGuin, E. (1993). The double edge of protective and risk factors for delinquency: Interrelations and developmental patterns. *Development and Psychopathology, 5*, 683–701.

Strong, P. M. (1979). *The ceremonial order of the clinic: Parents, doctors and medical bureaucracies.* London & Boston: Routledge & Kegan Paul.

Swanson, D. P., & Beale, M. B. (1991). Youth policy, poverty and African Americans: Implications for resilience. *Education and Urban Society, 24*(1), 148–161.

Tanyi, R. A. (2006). Spirituality and family nursing: Spiritual assessment and interventions for families. *Journal of Advanced Nursing, 53*, 287–294.

Tarter, R. E., & Vanyukov, M. (1999). Re-visiting the validity of the construct of resilience. In M. D. Glantz & J. L. Johnson (Eds.), *Resilience and development: Positive life adaptations* (pp. 85–100). New York: Kluwer Academic.

Tate, D. C., Repupucci, N. D., & Mulvey, E. P. (1995). Violent juvenile delinquents: Treatment effectiveness and implications for future action. *American Psychologist, 50*, 777–781.

Tayler, C., Farrell, A., & Tennent, L. (2003, May 1–4). *Children, communities and social capital: New ways of thinking about early childhood service provision.* Paper presented at Our Children the Future, Conference 3, Adelaide, Australia.

Taylor, C. (2006). *Young people in care and criminal behaviour.* London & Philadelphia: Jessica Kingsley.

Tew, J. (2005). *Social perspectives in mental health: Developing social models to understand and work with mental distress.* London: Jessica Kingsley.

The Guardian. (2006, March 22). *Forward thinking (Social work manifesto).* London. (Available at: http://society.guardian.co.uk/socialcare/news/0,,1735950,00.html – accessed February 2007)

Thomas, B., & Dorling, D. (2004). *Know your place: Housing wealth and inequality in Great Britain 1980–2003.* London: Policy Press.

Tiet, Q., Bird, H., Davies, M., Hoven, C., Cohen, P., Jensen, P. S., et al. (1998). Adverse life events and resilience. *Journal of American Academy of Child and Adolescent Psychiatry, 37,* 1191–1200.

Toynbee, P. (2003). *Hard Work: Life in low-pay Britain.* London: Bloomsbury.

Tschann, R., Kaiser, P., Chesney, M., & Alkon, A. (1996). Resilience and vulnerability among preschool children: Family functioning, temperament and behaviour problems. *Journal of the American Academy of Child and Adolescent Psychiatry, 35*(2), 184–192.

Ungar, M. (2004). *Nurturing hidden resilience in troubled youth.* Toronto, Canada: University of Toronto Press.

Ungar, M. (2005a). *Handbook of working with children and youth: Pathways to resilience across cultures and contexts.* London: Sage.

Ungar, M. (2005b). Resilience among children in child welfare, corrections, mental health and educational settings: Recommendations for service. *Child and Youth Care Forum, 34*(6), 445–463.

Ungar, M., Dumond, C., & McDonald, W. (2005). Risk, resilience and outdoor programmes for at-risk children. *Journal of Social Work, 5*(3), 319–338.

University of East Anglia. (2004). *Children's trusts: Developing integrated services for children in England* (University of East Anglia in association with National Children's Bureau, National evaluation of children's trusts interim report). Nottingham, UK: DfES Publications.

van de Weil, N., Matthys, W., Cohen-Kettenis, P. C., & van Engeland, H. (2002). Effective treatments of school-aged conduct disordered children: Recommendations for changing clinical and research practices. *European Child and Adolescent Psychiatry, 11,* 79–84.

Van IJzendoorn, M. H., & Bakermans-Kranenburg, M. J. (2003). Attachment disorders and disorganised attachment: Similar and different. *Attachment and Human Development, 5*(3), 313–320.

Van IJzendoorn, M. H., Juffer, F., & Duyvesteyn, M. G. C. (1995). Breaking the intergenerational cycle of insecure attachment: A review of the effects of attachment-based interventions on maternal sensitivity and infant security. *Journal of Child Psychology and Psychiatry, 36*(2), 225–248.

Victor, B. C., & Boynton, A. C. (1998). *Invented here: Maximising your organizational growth and profitability* Boston: Harvard Business School.

Vygotsky, L. S. (1978). *Mind in society: The development of higher psychological processes.* Cambridge, MA: Harvard University Press.

Waldegrave, C., Tamasese, K., Tuhaka, F., & Campbell, W. (2003). *Just Therapy: A journey. A collection of papers from the Just Therapy Team, New Zealand.* London: Dulwich Centre.

Walshe, K., Smith, J., Dixon, J., Edwards, N., Hunter, D. J., & Mays, N. (2004). Primary care trusts. *British Medical Journal, 329,* 871–872.

Weiss, B., Catron, T., & Harris, V. (1999). Traditional child psychotherapy did not reduce psychopathology compared with academic tutoring. *Evidence-Based Mental Health, 2*(3), 86.

Weiss, B., Catron, T., & Harris, V. (2000). A 2-year follow-up of the effectiveness of traditional child psychotherapy. *Journal of Consulting and Clinical Psychology*, *68*(6), 1094–1101.

Wenger, E., McDermott, R., & Snyder, W. M. (2002). *Cultivating communities of practice*. Boston: Harvard Business School Press.

Werner, E. (1986). Resilient offspring of alcoholics: A longitudinal study from birth to age 18. *Journal of Studies in Alcohol, 47*(1), 34–40.

Werner, E., & Smith, R. (1992). *Overcoming the odds: High risk children from birth to adulthood*. New York: Cornell University Press.

Werner, E., & Smith, R. S. (1982). *Vulnerable, but invincible: A longitudinal study of resilient children and youth*. New York: McGraw-Hill.

Werner, E. E. (1993). Risk, resilience, and recovery: Perspectives from the Kauai Longitudinal Study. *Development and Psychopathology, 5*, 503–515.

Werner, E. E. (2005). What can we learn about resilience from large-scale longitudinal studies? In S. Goldstein & R. Brooks (Eds.), *Handbook of resilience in children* (pp. 91–105). New York: Kluwer Academic/Plenum.

Werner, E. E., & Smith, R. S. (2001). *Journeys from childhood to midlife: Risk, resilience, and recovery*. New York: Cornell University Press.

West Stevens, J. (2005). Lessons learned from poor African American youth: Resilient strengths in coping with adverse environments. In M. Ungar (Ed.), *Handbook for working with children and youth* (pp. 45–56). London: Sage.

West, P. F. (1989). *The basic essentials: Protective behaviours, antivictimisation and empowerment process*. Adelaide, Australia: Essence Publications.

Weston, K. (1991). *Families we choose: Lesbians, gays, kinship*. New York & Oxford, UK: Columbia University Press.

White, M., & Epston, D. (1990). *Narrative means to therapeutic ends*. New York: Norton.

White, S., & Stancombe, J. (2003). *Clinical judgement in the health and welfare professions: Extending the evidence base*. Maidenhead, UK: Open University Press.

Wilkinson, R. G. (1997, February 22). Health inequalities: Relative or absolute material standards? *British Medical Journal, 314*, 591–595.

Williams, J. M. G., & Pollock, L. R. (1993). Factors mediating suicidal behaviour: Their utility in primary and secondary prevention. *Journal of Mental Health, 2*, 3–26.

Winnicott, D. W. (1965a). *The maturation processes and the holding environment: Studies in the theory of emotional development*. Madison, WI: International University Press.

Winnicott, D. W. (1965b). *Maturational processes and the facilitating environment*. London: Hogarth.

Winnicott, D. W. (1986). Delinquency as a sign of hope. In C. Winnicott, R. Shepherd, & M. Davis (Eds.), *Home is where we start from: Essays by a psychoanalyst D. W. Winnicott* (pp. 90–100). New York: Norton.

Winnicott, D. W. (2005). *Playing and reality*. London: Routledge Classics.

Wolin, S., & Wolin, S. (1994). *The resilient self: How survivors of troubled families rise above adversity*. New York: Random House.

Womack, J. P., & Jones, D. T. (1996). *Lean thinking: Banish waste and create wealth in your corporation*. New York: Simon & Schuster.

Wong, K.-Y., & Lee, T.-Y. (2005). Professional discourse of social workers working with at-risk people in Hong Kong: Risk or resilience? In M. Ungar (Ed.), *Handbook for working with children and youth* (pp. 313–327). London: Sage.

World Health Organization. (2003). *Global strategy on diet, physical activity and health*. Geneva, Switzerland: WHO.

Wright, S. (1994). *The anthropology of organisations*. London: Routledge.

Wyman, P., Cowen, E., Work, W., Koyt-Meyers, L., Magnus, K., & Fagen, D. (1999). Caregiving and developmental factors differentiating young at-risk urban children showing resilient versus stress-affected outcomes: A replication and extension. *Child Development, 70*(3), 645–659.

Wyman, P., Cowen, E., Work, W., Raoof, A., Gribble, P., Parker, G., & Wannon, M. (1992). Interviews with children who experienced major life stress: Family and child attributes that predict resilient outcomes. *Journal of the American Academy of Child and Adolescent Psychiatry, 31*, 904–910.

Wyman, P. A. (2003). Emerging perspectives on context specificity of children's adaptation and resilience: Evidence from a decade of research with urban children in adversity. In S. Luthar (Ed.), *Resilience and vulnerability: Adaptation in the context of childhood adversities* (pp. 293–317). New York: Cambridge University Press.

Yates, T. M., Egeland, B., & Sroufe, L. A. (2003). Rethinking resilience: A developmental process perspective. In S. Luthar (Ed.), *Resilience and vulnerability: Adaptation in the context of childhood adversities* (pp. 243–266). New York: Cambridge University Press.

Yngvesson, B., & Mahoney, M. (2000). 'As one should, ought and wants to be': Belonging and authenticity in identity narratives. *Theory, Culture and Society, 17*(6), 77–110.

Zohar, D., & Marshall, I. (2004). *Spiritual capital: Wealth we can live by*. London: Bloomsbury Publishing.

RESILIENT THERAPY: ORDINARY MAGIC

Basics - this potion conjures up the basic necessities needed for life

Good enough housing
Enough money to live
Being safe
Access and transport
Healthy diet
Exercise and fresh air
Playtime and leisure
Being free from prejudice and discrimination

Coping - these potions help children to get by in everyday life. Help child to:

Understand boundaries and keep within them
Be brave
Solve problems
Put on rose-tinted glasses
Foster their interests
Calm her/himself down, self-soothe
Remember that tomorrow is another day
Help child to lean on others when necessary

Belonging - we use the spells in this potion to help a child make good relationships with family and friends

Find somewhere for the child to belong
Tap into good influences
Keep relationships going
The more healthy relationships the better
Take what you can from any relationship where there is some hope
Get together people the child can count on
Belonging involves responsibilities and obligations too
Focus on good times and places
Make sense of where a child has come from
Predict a good experience of someone/something new
Help child make friends and mix with other children
Help child understand her/his place in the world

Learning - Learning not only includes school education, but also helping with their life skills, talents and interests

Make school life work as well as possible
Engage mentors for children
Map out career/life plan
Help the child to organise her/himself
Highlight achievements
Develop life skills

Core self - the potions here work very deeply to shape a child's character

Instil a sense of hope
Teach the child to understand other people's feelings
Help the child know her/himself
Help child take responsibility for her/himself
Foster their talents
There are tried and tested treatments for specific problems, use them

accepting   conserving
                      enlisting
commitment

RESILIENT THERAPY:
ORDINARY MAGIC

Angie Hart &/Derek Blincow©

Index

Page entries referring to boxes appear in **bold**.
Page entries for headings with subheadings refer to general aspects of that topic.